COMPLETE LIBRARY OF
ENTREPRENEURIAL WISDOM
Abridged Edition

Ginger Marks, CEO
DocUmeant Publishing & Designs

DocUmeant *Publishing*
244 5th Avenue
Suite G-200
NY, NY 10001
646-233-4366
www.DocUmeantPublishing.com

Published by

DocUmeant Publishing
244 5th Avenue, Suite G-200
NY, NY 10001

646.233.4366

Cover Design & Layout by DocUmeant Designs, www.DocUmeantDesigns.com

Library of Congress Cataloging-in-Publication Data

Marks, Ginger

   Complete Library of Entrepreneurial Wisdom: business, entrepreneurship, marketing, design, article series.

LCCN - 2016918884

First publishing date: 09/2013 Complete Edition

ISBN13: 9781937801786

INTRODUCTION

It has been eight years since I wrote my first article. Month-by-month, I have picked up my pen and gathered my thoughts about how I have grown over the last 30+ years as a woman and a business owner.

With all these articles sitting collecting dust, I have had a gentle nudge to find a use for them for quite some time. After being named Covington's Who's Who Executive of the Year, I decided it was high-time to share this knowledge in a complete works form. It was thus that this collection of my business articles, musings, and other works has finally been compiled into one nice neat package.

I have divided this collection of over 150 articles into categories to enable you to focus on the area of business growth that is most urgently calling to you. My hope is that you, the new—and also the seasoned entrepreneur—will read, learn, and therefore, bypass the hurdles that lay before you.

With the addition of an Index, keywords used throughout this collection may make your search even easier. Begin at the beginning or select a section or even just an article or topic that appeals to your current need. The choice to succeed or fail is yours and yours only to make. With a little advice from a seasoned veteran of business, who has seen both times of plenty and times of lack, perhaps the articles that follow will enable you to avoid the snags and snares that cause so many businesses to fail.

If you find the information worthwhile, I invite you to sign-up to receive my monthly Words of Wisdom ezine. Each month, as a publisher and designer, I offer information to help you succeed. A tip and a quote begin and end each ezine and your comments are warmly received and gain you a business link in the following month's issue. To register for this free newsletter and receive a couple of bonus items visit me here: http://documeant.net/#bonus.

To your continued entrepreneurial success,

Ginger Marks, CEO Calomar, LLC

CONTENTS

Marketing

Design

Article Series

Resources

Business

LET'S TALK TURKEY

When do you know it is the right time to bust loose from the 9 to 5 JOB? Do you have what it takes to really make a go of this opportunity we call a home-based business? What if you give up your job and things don't work out as you planned? These questions and more come to mind when you first begin to consider if owning your own business is right for you.

Right up front you need to look at the numbers. Read the details. A visit to the US Small Business Administration website reveals that 66% of start-up businesses are still operational after 2 years, while only 50% of those remaining will survive another 2 years. Furthermore after an additional 2 years only 40% of those remaining will continue to be serving the needs of the public. This means that after six years out of 100 businesses that opened their doors only about 13 will still be in business.

One thing I want to clarify here though is the fact that just because they are not in business after six years, those that are not operational could have closed for many other reasons than failure. On the contrary, this could mean that they were so successful that they wisely put together an "Exit Plan" and sold their thriving business or they may have moved or retired. Any number of reasons could account for this low number of viable businesses surviving for a mere six years.

Nevertheless, how do you keep from becoming just another statistic? Looking at the reasons start-up businesses fail will help you understand better what it will take for you to succeed.

Business owners who take the time to sit down and pen a business plan greatly increase their chances of survival. Why? The simple answer is that a business plan not only gives you direction but it details the way you will accomplish each phase of the business development. When you need additional funding what a financial institution is looking for is a clear statement of what you plan to offer and how you plan to take your idea from concept to delivery. Besides these reasons a well thought out business plan will help keep you on the track. It should be—and will be—your roadmap to success.

Insufficient funding is another reason businesses fail. With the business plan in place additional funding can be sought through investors and financial institutions. Consider applying for a small business loan through sources that are there to help you. Angel Investors is one source other than governmental assistance that you might apply to for support if you need additional backing. It is advisable to have at least two years of funding set aside in case things don't progress quite how you had planned.

As I often recommend, do your homework. Know your market and your competition. Is there even a market for your product or service? Decide who your target market is. Will you offer a product or service that should be geared to a local customer or will your business be better suited for the Internet community? Be sure that you have the proper education and experience to run a business. Lack in these areas can, and often does, lead to poor decision making which can cost you dearly in the end.

On the other side of the coin are the issues that lead to success. Do you have what it takes to be successful? Do you have that education? A proper education enables you to not only make good decisions but ensures you have the base knowledge to skillfully operate a business. Maturity is helpful here as well. With maturity comes the knowledge of how to handle difficulties with finesse. You may also have the resources in place to assist you in case of an unforeseen obstacle may rear its ugly head. Mature business owners, not necessarily the maturity of age, are able to focus on the goal and commitment to success. Actually talent can be a factor here as well. Do you have the natural talent and ability in place to achieve your goals?

Know when and how to expand your business, how to located suppliers and to spend within your budget. Many home based businesses are initially started for emotional reasons. Because many are started with no plan in place and very little start-up capital the home based business is at risk. However, due to the lower expenses many home based businesses are beating the odds and surviving past the expected norms.

So, know what you are in for, be prepared to take the necessary action to achieve your goal and commit to success and you will most likely beat the odds and join the ranks of the successful home based business owners.

CONSISTENCY IS THE KEY

Like most business owners your goal for your company and life is to create and enjoy a carefree lifestyle; one free of financial worry. In pursuit of this dream you have carefully considered the many types of business products and services until you found the one that feels right to you. You invest time and money in preparation for the day you announce to the world that you are in business. Embarking on this journey many new entrepreneurs incorrectly believe the old saying, "build it and they will come." Unfortunately, that is not always the case. Just because you stock your shelves and open the door doesn't guarantee success. It takes a consistent commitment to your business to guarantee your dream will be realized.

Oft times as new and seasoned business owners we grow complacent with our prosperity. You may work hard marketing your business for a time and then when "your hands are full" you may have a tendency to slack off. You may genuinely believe that if you actively continue to market your business you won't be able to meet your commitments. So you slow down the pace. This is exactly the wrong thing to do. If you sustain the marketing pace when things are at their peak you will create much more than just a mediocre level of success.

Two things will happen. First, you can eliminate the peaks and valleys of boom and recession. Second, you may have to enlist the advice and support of others. Now wouldn't that be a frightening thought? Sure your business growing out of control can be a problem, however if you look around, you will discover others who will gladly facilitate you when you need the extra help. A Virtual Assistants (VA) could be an idea choice. They will lend a hand for a very reasonable fee.

Newton's Law of Motion

Newton's Law of Motion states; an object at rest tends to stay at rest and an object in motion tends to stay in motion with the same speed and in the same direction, unless acted upon by an unbalanced force.

Hiring a VA is a sound business move. They can assist you with ongoing projects as well as filling your short-term needs. As with any professional, each VA has their area of expertise, so be sure to ask them if you don't know what theirs is. Realistically you could hire more than one VA. For example, I use one VA for all my audio conversion needs and another for research and gathering of documentation, while still another for writing and distributing all of my press release notices. If you don't already know a VA contact me and I will be happy to share the names of a few that I am familiar with; not only their name but their business ethics as well.

As you actively pursue your market, your reach expands; as your reach expands you reach new customers; and as you reach new customers your business grows. It is when you break this routine that you stagnate your business's growth.

Whether you build your business by networking or advertising or a combination of those two, consistency is the key that will unlock the door to your financial freedom and business success.

THE GOLDEN RULE OF BUSINESS OWNERSHIP

In the past thirty-plus years, as a business owner, I have learned many lessons. There are lessons on marketing, lessons on taxes, lessons on saving for emergencies, lessons on communication, and many others that have enabled me to become a successful business owner. However, there is one rule that I learned that has skyrocketed my business to the success that I have recently encountered. Yes, even while the rest of the world is complaining about being in a recession, my business income more than doubled!

The simple implementation of one action on my part has changed not only how I do business, but also how I live my life. That is learning that when you freely give of your time and talents to help others you receive more than you ever give.

When was the last time you helped someone? If you are like most business owners you probably spend more time helping yourself out than you even realize. Our days are consumed with promotion, marketing, family, and making a little money on the side—and usually in that order.

What made the difference for me was when, in 2005, I began developing and in early 2006 founding the WINning Sisters. This was, for me, a labor of love. With a small group of like-minded business owners commitment, we began taking new business owners by the hand and introducing, helping, and teaching them the ways of business ownership. Much like the Big Sisters of America, we befriend our Little Sisters and help them in whatever way they need to become comfortable in "the business of being in business."

When you freely give of your time and talents to help others you receive more than you ever give.

Sometimes that means to help them grow as people and other times it is more just introducing them to another source. Whatever the challenge, we are there to help, inform, and, sometime, just to hold their hand. We also share weekly from our knowledge with a Skype hosted chat that we named the WINning Sisters Networking 101. Usually the forum is open so that those with questions can find answers, but quite often, you will find that there are special guest speakers who freely give of their time to share from their area of expertise.

E.g., at a recent chat Charly Leetham shared from her stores of knowledge on the subject of S.E.O. (Search Engine Optimization) and another time Patrysha Korchinski shared for three weeks straight on the topic of Business Branding (available online through our archive).[1]

So, to be perfectly clear, the Golden Rule of Business Ownership is, "You can't out give God!" When you approach your business from the standpoint of, "What can I give," or "How can I help someone today," rather than focusing on receiving you will find others flock to you. In the process, you will see a substantial increase in your profit margin. Why? Because you can't out give GOD! Don't believe me? Give it a try. I guarantee you will be pleasantly surprised.

---

1   The WIN Network and WINning Sisters have closed, for the time being.

IS YOUR PRIDE A STUMBLING BLOCK TO YOUR SUCCESS?

The Bible clearly warns us that pride goes before a fall. I know some of you don't believe in God, but you must admit the Bible is full of sage advice. This piece is no exception.

There is clearly a difference in being a "Guru" and a "Know-It-All." Be careful not to cross that line; it can make the difference between amazing success and failure. For example, I used to hang out with some very smart people that always had a kind word and helpful advice. We could chat for hours about many different subjects. Sometimes helpful advice was shared but most times not. When we went to chats together everyone had equal time to converse. Then one day, something changed. They began to dominate all conversations and chats. I began to feel like it was their way or no way at all. Could they possibly be right about everything? When would the other chat room attendees get a word in edgewise? "We are on a mission to change the world," was their retort when anyone suggested their means were not the best or even the only way of accomplishing the intended goal.

Another example I recall is the time when another person I care about was critically lambasted for not agreeing with the speaker's concepts. Being rude to your audience is not the method to win friends and influence people. This sort of thing happens when the speaker forgets that they are the person most responsible for clearly relating their message.

A conversation is a two way street. It is when you get to the point that you begin to feel that if someone else doesn't understand you it is the fault of not listening to what you are saying and not that you couldn't have better stated your message. This is when you make the proverbial turn and you begin to lose credibility in the eyes of those watching from the sidelines as well as with those whom you are conversing.

Business communication coach and friend, Felicia Slattery, owner of Communication Transformation states, "When you are the speaker, it's your job to be sure your audience fully understands your message. After all, as a business person, your message is a reflection of you and your business. If you present your message clearly so your audience can follow you, then you're showing that audience you are knowledgeable, helpful, and professional. Allowing your audience to provide feedback and using that feedback as a way to make your presentation better is the hallmark of a competent communicator and good business person overall."

There is a fine line between humility and timidity too. A little too much in either direction and you end up failing at every turn. For example, hiding in a corner taking it all in or 'lurking' on a network chat board will add to the number of places you can say you have been in the daily course of business. However, don't expect to get any referrals. Unless you openly participate the other members won't even know you are there. And it goes without saying, if they don't know you are there you will not gain any benefit from attending.

Put on your party dress and shoes and get out there on the dance floor. Make friends first and the business will come. Then focus on your strengths but don't overdo it. Offer advice when asked in a spirit of love and kinship.

No matter what stance you take be certain of one thing; your reputation will precede you. Promoting your own importance leads to stumbling. But focusing on and meeting the essential needs of others gives us the healthy approach of the wise and successful entrepreneur.

BACK TO BUSINESS

It is that time of year again. The kids are getting back to school and it is time to pump it up a notch with our businesses. What is your idea of getting off the starting block? I was thinking about that the other day and thought that this might be a good place to begin my search.

Some of the things that come to mind are:

1. Advertising
2. Promotion
3. Sales
4. Events
5. Networking
6. Charity

All of these means it seems are just simply the tip of a mountain of ideas. Let's take the first one for example, advertising. You have online and offline. Then you have to consider what form of online or offline advertising suits you and your needs best. The worst thing you can do is throw good money in the wrong direction. You need to **decide first who your target market is and what motivates them to buy**. That is a topic for another conversation though.

Promotion sort of flows out of the advertising river into a whole new income stream of its own. If you want to promote your business you must first decide whether you want to do it in print or live interaction. Promotion can be done with article writing or simple advertising or sales flyers. You might consider joining a group like the one I ran into recently that stuffs their product packages with your promotional pieces. What a neat concept. You produce the promotional piece and they put it in the box with the item they are mailing out to their customers. It can be a business card, brochure or even a promotional or sale flyer. Print up 500 pieces and send it to the member that is requesting them and they insert it into their mailings. I would be happy to share this resource with you if you are interested.

How about those of us who enjoy the live interaction of an audience? There are multitudes of opportunities to promote your product or service doing seminars and chats. Just days ago I finished writing my first book titled, *Promotional Skills for the Next Generation*. I have it for sale in PDF version presently while I am awaiting my ISBN# to be able to sell it through vendors both in digital and print mediums. If you would like a copy email me and I will be happy to send you your pre-release first edition copy.[2]

---

2   Presentational Skills for the Next Generation, Third Edition, DocUmeant Publishing http://www.amazon.com/dp/0978883144.

What about **Press Releases & Public Relations?** They can be tied into your business promotion in a very powerful way. Consider hiring a professional who can not only pen the perfect press release but get it into the right hands. Don't attempt to do this on your own if you want real results. My PR Company of choice is EMSI, founded by Marsha Friedman. If you want her assistance, email me and I will be happy to put you in touch.

One thing we fall back on often is the use of **sales**. These can generate interest and sometimes are the catalyst to revenues from those potential customers who are sitting on the proverbial fence. I have recently begun offering **coupon book promotion** to my clients as this is a WIN, WIN, WIN! for everyone involved. Companies that would otherwise not let the associate promote their business can use these simple, non-threatening advertising options to their advantage. One thing that I have learned from this experience is that when offering a coupon you would do better to *offer a dollar amount off rather than a percentage*. Why? Well it seems that people don't perceive the value of percentage as quickly as they do an actual dollar amount.

As for **events** my recommendation is GET INVOLVED! If you can find the time, get involved in putting them together. Attending is one thing and will garner you *some* networking time, but when you are involved with the planning and promotion not only do you gain valuable experience but personal one-on-one with the movers and the shakers as well.

This leads us into the **networking** environment. As you already know networking is a huge factor in the success or failure of your business. Just do it! Online or off, in person or in the chat room. It really doesn't matter. This is a powerful tool. Use it wisely. Make friends and let the conversation flow naturally into business informational exchange. Don't begin with an ad! This is the quickest way to turn the other members off.

Have you considered **aligning with a charity**? This is something that can be beneficial to others while being a promotional tool for you at the same time. Take this opportunity to use the press release to promote your business. During the holidays is a perfect time to make these associations.

Whatever your comfort level is, the key is to get off the bench and begin taking the actions to allow your business to grow and flourish. Set a goal, reach for the stars! If you end up in the clouds you have gained, at the very least, experience.

BE A GOOD LISTENER

You may be wondering what listening has to do with successful entrepreneurship. The very term ownership implies responsibility. It is a position of authority and therefore demands you to give the directions that will shape your business' future. You are the go-to guy or gal. People look up to you and hang on your very words. Not the other way around, right? Well, yes and no.

While much of the time this can be true it is also imperative that you take the time to listen as well as talk. And, if you haven't taken the time to listen you may be causing irreparable damage to your growth.

1. **Listen to your employees.** Listen with an open ear to what your employees are saying. Are they happy and excited or just trying to make ends meet? Are they talking about what the business' customers are involved in, how they feel about your company or what they've expressed they would like or need? Listen up. You may just learn some very important information.

2. **Curb your ego.** It takes letting go of your human tendencies towards a run-away ego. Haughtiness can severely deprive you of valuable connections. You become insensitive and callus to others. You can become so egotistical that you miss the very thing you need to learn to grow your business.

3. **At the head of ego is vanity.** When you are fixed on yourself you can't relate well with others. Curb your ego and vanity and you may discover new avenues of income and ideas that you never even considered before.

4. **Listen attentively.** Rather than preparing your response while you only have a small part of the conversation, listen to the whole of what is being said. Then, take a moment to form your reply. This *reflective thinking* moment lets the person you are speaking with know that you are indeed carefully wedging your response and truly listening to all of what they are saying.

5. **Relate to them on their level.** When you join them where they are they will better understand you and what you are trying to relate to them. For example, if you were speaking to a young child you would want to use easily understood, elementary level language. On the other hand, if your audience is a group of doctors or PhDs your vocabulary, examples, and such would be much more specific and educational.

6. **Empathize.** Show you care by listening attentively and then begin your reply with words that tell them you understand their situation. This can be easily done by relating to them. Opening with a comment like, "While I have experienced similar challenges I have found that . . . worked well for me to counter the issue you are experiencing."

7. **Be patient.** This may be the most difficult of all the 'good listener' attributes. Even I find myself guilty at times of impatience. How often do you find yourself trying to rush your spouse of friend by finishing their sentence for them? If you stop this habit it will allow the other person to say something you may not have expected. Give them the time and space, not to mention the respect, to fully express their thoughts. You would want them to do the same for you, I am sure.

Listen with an ear to hear what they are *trying* to say. Not only will you gather information that will help you identify and solve problems, but you may even come up with a new product or service that will fill a need your customers are expressing and desire to solve.

BE CAREFUL WHAT YOU WISH FOR . . .

. . . especially for your small business

We all want to see our businesses grow and thrive. Some even hope that future generations will one day take the helm. But, without careful planning all your dreams of success could come crashing down around you.

If you hope to sell more and continue to do so, you must be prepared to deal with that growth. Too often we market ourselves right out of business. How and why would I conceive such a harsh statement? Easy, each sale creates a new customer; this creates a demand on our time. When you are fulfilling that demand your time to create invoices and marketing is limited. This leaves a crack in your business. Gone unprotected, over time, this gap can widen in to a chasm.

To ensure that no customer or invoice slips through that crack an auto responder is the perfect solution. No business can survive for long without one. You can automate the delivery of thank you notes, gift cards, a follow-up survey after the sales and even past due invoicing. You'd be surprised at how much your customer will appreciate these timely pieces. The best thing about the trusty auto responder is that all of these mundane tasks are done for you; which leaves you free to do what you love, build and grow your business.

While you are considering your options in this electronic age a 'real' card in the snail mail has a significant advantage over the digital alternative. Therefore, sometimes you may want to send a 'real' note rather than an email thank you. Yes, you should immediately follow-up with an electronic version. But, there is now a system in place that allows you to set-up a campaign, a specific card that can be programmed to send out to a single person or group on a specified date. Yes, a 'real' card. And what better way to follow-up with your customer than a real thank you note in the mail? This system is Send Out Cards®. No, I am not a rep, but I highly recommend it for all business owners. Email me and I'd be happy to point you in the right direction.

You also have to make sure you get paid. Invoices need to be created, revenue needs to be collected, and past due bills need to be followed up on. Therefore, another thing to consider while expanding your business' back office tasks is hiring a competent Virtual Assistant (VA). VAs have specific talents and abilities, so be sure you hire one that fits your need. Some are best at pulling a team together, while others merely answer your phone and deliver your messages. Some prefer marketing type work, like uploading articles and sending out press releases. Be sure to ask them their area of expertise before you sign on the dotted line.

While some VAs are able to send out invoices, a professional bookkeeper may be a better idea. If you are not yet ready to take that step consider using a system like FreshBooks, Infusionsoft or VerticleResponce* to help you automate your timekeeping and invoicing needs. While FreshBooks focus is billing automation the two latter mentioned offer auto responder tools as well as invoicing. So, identify your need first. Then you will know exactly what to look for and choose the right tool for your business.

Having all your systems in place will free you up to deliver high-quality products and services, which in turn creates satisfied customers that buy more and refer your business to their friends.

PLAN TO SUCCEED

Building a successful business is no easy task. It takes commitment and dedication. Once you decide on a product or service that resonates with you your next few steps will make all the difference in your success. Start with putting down on a piece of paper a business plan. It amazes me how many small and medium size business owners have not taken this one important step. Without a business plan in place you are headed down the road without a map.

A business plan doesn't have to be 500 pages long with every possible scenario explained in painstaking detail but it does need to be written down. The simple way to start is to tackle one section at a time. Sit down and give it some serious thought. Then with paper and pen in hand start out with writing your Mission Statement. This is a simple paragraph or two that states your heartfelt reason for wanting to share your product or service with others. For example my Mission Statement for a volunteer group I founded called the WINning Sisters of Ryze reads like this:

> **Our Mission:** We are a group of women dedicated to bringing the best of the networking world to our sisters so that they can network with efficiency and effectiveness. Our goal is to enable and empower each other with the knowledge of available resources and proper networking etiquette, aptly named Netiquette. We believe that when we warmly welcome each other and sacrificially touch each other's lives we will all benefit from the interaction and the relationships that we are able to build.
>
> We seek to accomplish our mission by offering a helping hand and a genuine, sisterly welcome to those around us who may need assistance in getting acclimated to this networking experience.
>
> To complete this task we have developed a program whereby members will identify and offer visitors a personally guided tour of Ryze, enlightening them of the available features and how tos to take advantage of this valuable resource. It is with this purpose in mind that we have created and now offer each of our sister Ryzers the opportunity to attend an initial orientation chat that will vary in its content. We are dedicating time and effort to ensure that our fellow networkers have a pleasant and welcoming experience during their stay at Ryze and beyond.

Next make a list of what it is you are physically going to provide. Knowing what your product is exactly will be helpful in helping you map out your plan of action for taking it to market. If you want to provide a service then you will need to develop your marketing and inventory much differently than if you are providing physical products. I am sure you can clearly see the reason this step is so crucial.

Once you have those pieces in place you will add how you plan to share your product or service. It is this knowledge that will give you the basic direction of how to take your business public. Consider here if you will need helpers to achieve your goals or if you plan on being a sole proprietor. Your Action Plan will need to state not only what you are going to do to make your business grow but if you have employees or partners or you're building a network knowing what the job description and responsibilities are for each person involved can, and often does, eliminate questions and frustration on down the line.

Another thing you might want to include is your policies. Although you might not want to think of it now knowing ahead of time what you or your staff should do when a customer complaint, return, or any of the numerous other situations that arise in the business setting will prove time well spent.

Now grab your pen and put your very own Business Plan together and use it to keep yourself focused on the goal. It should become a check point to ensure that you are getting done what you intended to as your business continues to thrive and grow. Realize that this will and should take some thought and effort. Most business plans involve not only thought but research and can take anywhere from several days to weeks to complete correctly depending on if you need to include specific details of the financial aspects of your business for investor or bank loans.

One final thought, know that your initial idea may change as time passes. Be willing to modify your business plan, if need be, to incorporate those changes. However, do not use those changes as an excuse to derail your effort. You should plan on revisiting your business plan at least yearly to reevaluate and redirect your efforts so that you continue to grow your business at the pace and in the way you foresee it growing.

10 STAGES OF SUCCESS

When you first decide to take up the mantle of business owner usually you are filled with excitement. In this stage we eagerly seek opportunities to tell everyone we come in contact with about our new business. We often begin by telling them about all the wonderful products/services we have to offer and then if they seem even remotely interested we might even tell them how they too could join our team. This is what we'll call the **Excitement Stage**.

However, as the excitement dies down we soon come to realize the importance of putting together a business and marketing plan. This is a simple stage to complete so don't fret. Most importantly this sets the groundwork for your plan of action that will ensure your business' success. To accomplish this **Planning Stage** all you need to do is sit down with a pen and paper and commit to writing what you want to accomplish and how you are going to go about getting it.

As an example let's say you want to have four new clients/customers each month for the next twelve months. Next you list the details of how you will accomplish this. Realize that in order to obtain four new clients each month you will need to share your business with at least four times that number of people. Remembering that old saying, "Some will, some won't, so what!" will help to get you past the nos that are sure to come.

Once you have a solid business and marketing plan in place, follow-through. Mary Kay offers this one extra piece of advice that all business owners need to embrace. That is the habit of repeating the saying, "Why not me and why not now? It's my turn and my time to succeed." Adopt this saying as your own.

Only your lack of action will stand in the way of your success. Venturing into unknown territory is the scariest part of new entrepreneurship, but once you take that first step you will find the second step comes that much easier. In order to implement your business plan you must take action. Therefore, **Initial Action** is the third stage. Whether that means you must pick up the phone, go out and physically talk to others, or even network online you must accept the fact that it is up to you and you alone to take the action to make your business succeed.

Now that the initial action has been taken your business is on the move. The next phase that we all go through is the **Question Stage**. What was I thinking? Did I do the right thing? Questioning your ability to make it work is a normal reaction at this point. This occurs when we begin to listen to others and lose sight of our dream and our goal. You make several phone calls and don't make any headway or have a conversation with someone that puts doubt in your mind and you begin to doubt your capability. If you refocus on the positives you have accomplished instead of the negativity that is plaguing your mind you will bounce back quickly from this stage.

Visualization is the next important stage. See yourself in that brand new car or home. Picture yourself on vacation in some exotic locale. When you take the time to give form and voice to your goals you implant the seed of that success in your very being. This is why so many companies realize the value of creating *dream boards*. Focus on the prize and not the bumps in the road. Keep moving, keep dreaming, and keep doing.

Coming to the **Realization** that this is harder than you originally thought it would be is next in line. Accept the fact that this is yet another phase you are going to go through. If it was easy everyone would be a successful business owner. This is not the case and you well know it, so recommit to your success and keep moving towards your prize.

Rationalization is denial of your goal. Don't let this one be your brick wall. This is the most difficult of all the stages you will go through, the **Disillusionment Stage**. After making a few phone calls or talking to a few people and not securing immediate success you begin to think to yourself, "I don't really need this." Or worse, "I don't really *deserve* this." Thinking maybe you are shirking your other duties can also put a damper on your success. Maybe this is where you are saying to yourself, "Perhaps I should put this on hold while my children are home from school this summer. I'll get back to my business in the fall." I can assure you if you let this thought take hold you will be signing your business success' death warrant. Stay focused, stay true, and continue to take the actions daily to ensure your success or you will never realize your true potential.

Follow through is Key!

What will happen is you will end up in the eighth phase one known as **Paralysis**. You do nothing, you accomplish nothing. You don't return phone calls, you go on no appointments. You don't even show up at functions that your company needs to grow. You stop networking both online and offline. Most of all, you begin to question if you have what it takes to achieve your goal in the first place. The only thing you can do to break free from this paralysis is to recommit.

Recommitment is the make or break it phase of any business. Realizing that you can, and are, going to make this work and rediscovering the excitement that you had in the beginning can, and will, help you to stay on the path to success. Commit to *take charge of your future*.

The final phase in the process of reaching your goal is that of **Achievement**. I promise you, when you make it past the recommitment stage and continue to focus on your business and believe in yourself and your business, you will amaze everyone around you with the success you will claim. Your family will reap the rewards of your efforts and you will have helped others along the same path. True success can be found in this one simple principal, in helping others achieve you will find yourself achieving the goals you were striving for. By accepting the fact that you, and others you will assist on the way, will experience these ten stages will make it easier to get through them. You are the one, and only one, who will determine whether you win or lose. As you continue on this journey adopt the adage with your whole being, *"if it is to be, it is up to me."* Never lose focus of your reason why and your success will be secure.

HICCUPS

Was that a hiccup I just heard? Yes, even the large corporations experience down times. Take for example the recent headline dated May 16, 2011, "PSN working after hiccups, says Sony." Did Sony quit; did they give up and go hide under a rock when they launched the new Online PlayStation? Not only did they have one hiccup, but two in a row!

On Saturday, Sony announced that after almost four weeks its entire portfolio of online games, game forums, and Web sites would go back online. After service resumed in the Americas, Europe, Australia, New Zealand, and the Middle East, however, heavy traffic on the network caused it to be inaccessible again. Sony said it had to "turn the service off for 30 minutes in order to clear the queue" of too many password resets submitted at once.

So, what can you do to keep your business on track when you too experience a dreaded case of hiccups? Don't give up the ship! There is always your waiting public, those customers and clients who faithfully cheer your return as did the Sony customers who, themselves, unknowingly caused the second hiccup. Keeping this fact in mind will help you continue to seek solutions.

To avoid some of the hiccups other business startups have experienced, who have gone before you, I will list a few things that you can and should do at the appropriate time.

1. To Inc. or not to Inc.?

When you first start your company your focus should be on getting off the ground. Once you have a stable business and you can afford to there will be plenty of time to consider whether you should become a corporation, LLC, or simply a DBA. Each has its own advantage so consult a competent attorney to help guide you. But do consider protecting yourself and your family when the time is right.[3]

2. Get to know your customers

Your customers are the best source of information. Do you know why they use your services? What are their wants and what are their needs? Did you know there is a difference? They will be happy to help you to find out what service you should be offering them. Ask them. Email, surveys, or even a phone call will do the trick.

3. Hire competent help

As your business begins to grow you need to learn to let go. Hire your competition. Often those whom you have come across in your business development path who have similar skills are

---

3   The company I recommend and use myself is BizFilings http://www.bizfilings.com/

thought to be the enemy. They are NOT! They are potential partners for you. Rather than stunting your business growth by trying to 'do it all yourself', consider outsourcing some of your workload for a small referral fee. On the other side, why not let your competition know you are available if their plate gets too full.

4. Be prepared

Know that in business you will experience lulls as well as challenges. Being ready with a backup plan in place will help ease these situations immensely. Sometimes, this means a monetary backup and sometimes a procedure. Either way, your plans should be set in place prior to the event. A good rule of thumb, on the financial side, is to have three months working capital set aside in case an unforeseen expenditure arises.

When I was in the medical field I often referred to the hospital or business procedure manual. This is something that every business owner should develop. If something unexpected happens to you what would happen to your 'baby'? So, at the very least, write a procedure manual if not a policy manual as well.

5. Ask and you will receive

Get payment upfront; at least a deposit. No matter what you buy online you always have to pay for it before it ships. So, what makes your business any different? Your customers are used to having to pay first. Therefore don't be afraid to ask for a retainer, deposit, or even full payment prior to providing them your product or service.

If your business offers services, consider developing an ongoing relationship with your customers. Set-up a contract for services on a reoccurring basis for a discount. That way, each month you can count on a steady income. This also lets your customers know your business is sustainable and professional.

6. Manage your relationships

Show your customers they are valuable to you. Always communicate in a polished, professional manner. Sure you can laugh with them, be friendly and open, but don't spill your challenges onto them, unless you are seeking their advice or help. And, never, ever, ever talk about another client or customer to them. This will cause them to wonder if you are talking about them behind their back.

When was the last time you simply said, "Thank you" to your customers? After your first business transaction is complete do you just go on to the next or do you take the time to send a note of thanks? In today's instant gratification society, we often forget that snail mail has more impact than does email. Consider sending a REAL card, rather than an email. Send-Out-Cards is the program I use to do this. I can easily maintain a database of customers and at a fraction of the cost for the card. In the time it takes to go shopping I can send out numerous types of cards at the click of my mouse button. If you don't have an account yet I can refer you to a representative that would be happy to give you a free trial run.

7. Tackle problems head-on

This is part of managing your relationships. However, it is also one of the most important things any business owner needs to do to continue to flourish. I remember a time when I had an issue with a customer who didn't like what they received from my design services. They had asked for work to be done a certain way, which took me extra trouble to create because it went against the norm. I had to spend time searching for a whole new program that would allow me to give them what they asked for. Learn that new program and design their product. Once they saw it in print they were very upset. I was supposed to know what they "meant" and this was not it.

Well, rather than argue and avoid this person, I offered to redo the work and refund their printing cost. They said that wasn't necessary, but I knew it was the right thing to do. So, we agreed that I would give them back half their printing cost and do the layout again for free. After all, the way they wanted it was the standard way of doing things and was a whole lot easier than what they originally received.

Now I have a valuable customer and they have not only been back for additional work, but they have become one of my best referral sources.

So, the next time you have an unhappy customer why not turn it around? Listen carefully and do the right thing. You too may develop this customer into one of your raving fans.

8. Know when to draw the line

Develop a work/life plan. Find a balance that you and your family can live within. Devote the time to develop your business without losing focus of your family's need for your time as well. When you forget you have a family not only does your family suffer, but you do as well. You need refreshing and your family needs to know you haven't forgotten they exist.

Be firm about your business time. Set a schedule and rules that fit your needs. Tell your family when you are on the phone to respect your conversation and you will respect theirs when they are on the phone as well. Running your business with a crying child in the background or a harping teen is no way to 'do business'. Set some ground rules and abide by them.

In closing I offer one last word of advice. Be ready for change. Nothing is ever constant. So, as your market changes, as it most certainly will, be ready and willing to change with it. As your business develops you may find you need to add or remove services. For example, I started DocUmeant years ago as a writing service. I now have three businesses with a focus on design and publishing.

Wherever your business takes you, listen to your customers, offer them the services they need, and enjoy the ride.

DISPUTE RESOLUTION: HOW TO GET POSITIVE RESULTS

There are times in every business when a customer has an issue with a product or service. It may be a minor issue but left unheeded it can quickly grow into a proverbial monster. And we all know one unhappy customer can do far more damage to your business reputation than you ever want to experience. Research indicates that it takes **ten positive comments to outweigh one negative**. So, when your time comes, as it indeed will, be prepared. Be sure your team is trained to handle any dispute in an effective and efficient manner.

Just today I had a customer contact me to question why they had not received a product they ordered. Rather than getting upset, I asked the customer a few questions to find out where the hiccup was located. Once I discovered the 'where' I easily found out the 'why'. This prompted me to place a phone call to my merchant services provider. After a very short time, I was able to find out exactly what the issue was and how to avoid further complication from the same issue in the future.

Would you like to know what that was? Well, it seems that when PayPal takes a payment from a credit card, they are 'by law' required to show proof of the charge. So, they do that rather than automatically forward the buyer to the download page like they do when it is a straight PayPal payment.

That receipt page has a very insignificant link that states to "click here to return to the buyer's website." This is not what your buyer wants to know. They want to know where to download their purchase. Since this was the cause of the confusion for the customer I inquired what could be done. The technician told me where and how to add advanced code to the button that would state whatever I desired. Well, in my case, I chose to write, "Click here to download your purchase." Now that makes things a whole lot clearer to the buyer and may just eliminate the problem in the future. Nevertheless, if I get another confused buyer, I'll ask one more question and resolve the issue that much faster.

As you can see from the above scenario, when buyers and sellers enter negotiations with mutual respect, they're more likely to come to a quick resolution. Here's what you can do to help make the process as smooth as possible.

Presume Good Faith

Begin the conversation with an open mind and give the buyer the benefit of the doubt. Listen to what the buyer has to say before jumping to conclusions, as many problems result from miscommunication or mistaken assumptions.

Be Constructive

From the start, make it clear to your customer that you believe the situation is resolvable. They'll usually reciprocate. Use a normal tone of voice when speaking and keep a level head. Loud or condescending tones will only aggravate the situation. This early show of mutual respect should make the rest of the conversation more productive.

Stay Focused

Stay focused on solutions while you're discussing the situation. If you're upset or annoyed, you might feel like giving the buyer a piece of your mind. That will probably just make it harder for you to come to an agreement.

Be Creative

Try to find solutions that allow both you and the buyer to come out on top. If you each offer to make a concession, it may be easier to put the matter to rest.

Think Long-Term

Considering the time it took my customer to answer my queries and help me resolve the issue I offered a discount on future services should they need any design work done. Keep this in mind the next time you have a customer contact you that needs your help. Not every battle is worth fighting. If you give the buyer a break today, it might even lead to more business opportunities tomorrow.

As a result of my careful handling and open communication the buyer sent me an email that stated, "Thanks, Ginger. I appreciate the great service!"

Preempt Disputes

One last thing you can do to help ease your buying customer's mind is to create a place on your website that clearly states your policies. When you know ahead of time that there could be delays in providing prompt service or deliveries, put a notice on your payment page that informs them of that fact. This may avoid a dispute from even being placed as they will see the message before they place their order. For example, if your message says, "All shipments out of Buffalo are currently delayed due to the blizzard," or "We will be closed December 24th through January 2nd," the buyer will understand the situation upfront thus eliminating any confusion.

DELEGATION: THE ART OF LETTING GO

After 30+ years as an entrepreneur the one thing that I find most difficult for the new business owners to learn is how to delegate. It seems to me that the personality trait that all business owners need is the one attribute that holds their businesses back from being a true success. That characteristic is the ability to get things done. They quickly take hold of the reigns and complete a task in an efficient time frame and manner. However, this is also to their detriment.

With the myriad of tasks—such as customer service, keeping track of inventory, production, marketing, or any other tasks that must be done to keeps the business thriving—there comes a time that delegation is the course of action the savvy business owner must learn to take if their business is to grow and thrive. The place to begin letting go is to learn to delegate those tasks that you don't like to do or are not qualified to do.

What follows may help you to see that delegation is not only practical but necessary to maintain your sanity.

1. Day-To-Day Drudgery

Take a look at your day-to-day tasks. Are there things that you could do blindfolded? I am talking about the mundane tasks. Things like taking calls, preparing mailings, filing, and such might be a good job for a VA (virtual assistant) or even your family member. If your mind is blank and you think all your tasks must be done by you, then I suggest you sit down at the beginning of the work day and for a week, write down every task. This "time audit" may just bring about an epiphany. If you're worried about costs, just remember how much of your valuable, revenue-generating time you'll be freeing up; your business can't grow when you're focused on busy work.

2. Embrace Your Limitations

Those tasks that require specials knowledge and skills are much more quickly delegated. Hiring out these jobs makes far more sense than wasting your valuable business-growth time on learning the skills necessary to perform at the accomplished professional's level of expertise.

In both these instances if you don't delegate the task you will end up wasting a lot of valuable time either procrastinating or in the learning process. Then also, in the latter case, you may not have the talent to accomplish the task. When you delegate these types of task to qualified individuals you save yourself both time and aggravation. Furthermore, you most assuredly will end up with a much better higher quality product than if you had spent hours and even days on the project yourself.

3. Learn To Let Go

This is the one dis-ease that most new entrepreneurs suffer from. I can hear the words ringing in my ear, "if I want something done right, I have to do it myself!" If you're the type of businessperson who believes this to be true, delegation is definitely going to be a challenge for you.

Take a deep breath and just let go. When you do finally delegate a task, realize it's now in other capable hands. Start off by letting go of some minor task and work your way up. As you gain confidence in working with others it will be easier to let go the next time.

4. Give Clear Instructions

As a designer I find that when I receive clear instructions on what my customer's vision is it is much easier to more quickly accomplish the perfect design. Imagine you got an order for an ad. That's all. They said not one word about color, size, or how and where it will be used. Where would you begin? It is the same with your helpers. The more succinct your instructions, the less hand-holding they will need, and therefore the more peace you will have in learning to delegate responsibility. Besides this benefit, the quality of work they provide will be exponentially increased at a much earlier stage in the process.

Delegation doesn't come naturally to small business owners. However, delegation is crucial if you want to develop a healthy, sustainable business and personal life.

AFTER YOUR ENTHUSIASM WANES

We've all be there. The project we are working on is practically done, we've nearly accomplished what we set out to do, and then the fear sets in. Or perhaps, you are completely done and as you sigh you realize that you have no exciting prospects or goals left to accomplish. This emotional upheaval is most evident in parenting, and is even given a name; Postpartum Depression. Like the birth mother or father, this depression can occur any time from the middle to after the blessed event.

As with birthing, this depression can affect you and your business. There will be times when you're sleep deprived and overwhelmed, you may have trouble handling even minor problems. You may be anxious about your ability to even run your business, thinking, *Is it really worth it?* You may even feel that you've lost control over your life. Any of these factors can contribute to business depression.

So, how do you keep going and pull yourself out of your doldrums? What can you do to stay on the path to success? Here are some ideas that may just help.

1. Change your mindset

Decide today that you won't quit. Say to yourself, "I'm not going to give up or give in to the naysayers!" As Winston Churchill once said, "Never, never, never give up." Go to your mirror and speak these words. Say them to yourself both out loud and in your mind every day, several times for thirty days.

Why do I say thirty days? NASA provides the answer. They did a test where they had the astronauts wear contact lenses that literally turned their world upside down. "Scientists discovered that each individual had developed new neural pathways, allowing them to operate more effectively within the new set of circumstances, and the window for this process, without exception, was 25 to 30 days."[4] The caveat here is you can't miss even one single day, it must continue without interruption for the entire time. So if you focus on changing the non-conscious brain, you will, by default, be working on eliminating your self-limiting beliefs and habits.

2. Counseling

If you can't make the adjustment yourself then perhaps counseling is the key for you. Don't feel like you can go it alone, if you have an addictive personality. Like the smoker who is trying

---

4   http://blog.christian-simpson.com/2012/02/what-nasa-can-tell-you-about-improving-your-life/

to quit, you may need that extra push to keep you motivated. It's good to talk things over. Counseling provides a non-threatening way to talk things out with a non-biased, third party. The business coach who has already reached their goal, in the same area you may be having trouble with, can help motivate and give you direction to help you achieve your own goals.

Which brings us to your next option. . . .

3. Books, tapes, videos

There are numerous books, tapes, and videos available to help keep you motivated. One of my all-time favorites is a cassette tape that I acquired years ago while working with Amway Corporation by George Halsey titled, "A Peep Over the Pail." My understanding is that it is now re-done by Jan Culkins. However, you can find a plethora of information at your fingertips to keep you motivated and focus driven.

4. Baby steps

Perhaps procrastination is your challenge. "Just do it" is easy to say, but at times can be impossible to put into action. Start by refocusing your mind. The key to moving beyond procrastination is learning how to clearly identify what is plaguing you. That way, you can focus on the appropriate remedy. Take baby steps, begin small and do one thing until you complete the task, then tackle the next one. Realize that you don't have to be perfect at something or know everything about a subject to begin. That knowledge alone will help move procrastination to the sideline.

5. Delegate

Don't try to do it all yourself. When you need help ask for it. If you haven't the talent or thrill for doing something, hire someone who does. This eliminates much of the stress associated with business operations and can free you up to do what you do best.

6. Escape

When all else fails, perhaps what you need is to step away and renew and refresh. Sometimes getting up and taking a break is all that is needed. At other times, you may need to find a place of refuge or a total change of environment. While a bubble bath might be all you need, a vacation get away may be the best answer.

I truly hope you have found at least one piece of advice that will help you along your path to business success. Stay focused and working toward your goal. Never, never, never give up, and you too will reach your full potential.

OUTSOURCING: KNOW YOUR LIMITS

Are you an entrepreneur who has been trying to do it all yourself to save a little money? In today's tough economy most of us feel like we are in the same boat. There's just not enough time or money to get everything done. If that is not a problem for you, perhaps it is that you just don't know how to do something that is critical to your ongoing success.

Are you a hands-on entrepreneur? Do you attempt to learn every new technique that comes out? Maybe your issue is Search Engine Optimization (SEO) or even knowing where to start putting together a website at all. Whatever your dilemma, at some point you either have or will begin to feel like you needed some direction or help. Are you taking too much time away from your 'first love' and not gaining ground. If so, take a step back and evaluate where you have come from and where you want to go.

So, how do you know when it is time to consider outsourcing? Outsource when you:

1. Are frustrated
2. Want it done better
3. Need it done faster
4. Want to take your business to the next level

There are definitely people out there that can ease your burden who have a whole lot of expertise in numerous studies. Perhaps you hate doing the tedious chores necessary to make your business thrive. Or could it be marketing as a whole that you deplore? Your time is better spent doing your key task for your business. When you are forced to do things you don't enjoy you won't do them well. Alternatively, when you have to learn something else that isn't your main focus, you lose valuable time growing your business.

Let's look at these reasons through the eyes of, say, a candle representative.

You are trying to learn how to design a graphic or create a video to add to your website but you just can't get it together? After all, you sell candles. You love doing those house parties. But you have no clue where to begin or how to use the graphics or video editing software. Halfway through the project you begin to realize you can't get things to work as easily as the ad said you could. You begin to get frustrated to the point you are ready to quit altogether. You know that your business could benefit if you could just get it done. Hire a videographer or graphic designer. They can most likely do the task efficiently and beautifully in less than half the time it took you to decide to seek help.

Did you see all the reasons that our candle rep would consider it time to outsource?

There graphic design, videographers, coaches and experts in SEO, marketing, blogging, and speaking, and there are also virtual assistants (VAs) that are eager and willing to help you. If you don't know where to begin, ask a friend or trusted colleague if they know somebody that they would or are using.

Learning to delegate is part of the process of growing your business. A word of advice, don't micromanage. Delegate and let them do their job. They know what it takes to get it done and your input, past the original delegation and instruction, will frustrate you and them. Even worse, it could make the end result your quality instead of a professional's work.

DREAM IT, BELIEVE IT, ACHIEVE IT

Success is an elusive animal for many of us. For others it is a daily achievement. Whichever side of this fence you live on we all must admit that true success requires specific mindset and purposeful action. How do you implement these two and integrate them to enable you to live your dream life? The answer is both easy and challenging.

The first thing you must do is to **embrace your dream**. Without a goal or dream you have no purpose. It is like taking a trip without looking at a map and planning your route. I am sure you would agree that when you want to take a trip somewhere you've never been before this is really not a wise decision.

Most likely you would not only want to know the best route to take but also what to see and do once you got there. Toward this end you wouldn't just pick up a map and go for it. More likely, you would want to talk to someone who had knowledge of your destination. Perhaps you would even go to the library or bookstore and get books on the city. At the very least, you would want to go to your local travel guide and ask for any information they might have that would help you find your way. If you happened to be a member of AAA you would get a detailed 'trip tick' (route map) that included the road hazards along the way. Armed with this information these hazards could easily be avoided or at the very least not take you by surprise.

The same goes for your dream. Once you have a clear idea of what you want in life find someone who has already achieved it and follow their advice. If they are willing to mentor you, so much the better. Having gone down this road before you they will be better able to assist you in getting past the hazards that you will encounter along the way.

The next thing you need to do is **adjust your attitude**. Believe that you can achieve your dream. Learn to live each day with a positive mindset. Begin to instill in your mind the unquenchable desire of your heart.

One way to do this is to post affirmations in places where you will see them often throughout your day. You might create a dream board, or even just put a miniature reminder in your pocket or purse that you will stumble across each time your hand goes into it. Don't know what a dream board is? It is a collage of pictures of what it will be like when you are actually living your dream. A very good friend of mine takes this a step further. As a life and business coach, Kim Emerson of the **University of Prosperity** and **Prosperity Mindset** has been creating what she calls *Reality Boxes* for her clients for a number of years. With great care and planning, she puts together her clients dream, places the pieces of the dream within a treasure type box and sends them off for the client to assemble. It is a unique way of capturing the very heart of the vision that her clients express. Eula DeMasi says of her Reality Box, *"What an amazing and grounding experience! This reality box really helped me to re-focus my attention and get a handle on my life."*

Another example I like to use is a new car. Since many of us get so much joy from this one it is easy for many to relate. Let's say you want a new car, don't just say, "I want a new car," decide on the make, model and even the color. Then go and find one and sit in it. Go so far as to have a friend take a picture of you sitting in it. While you are sitting there in it, close your eyes. Sit there and experience, really experience, the moment. Focus; smell how it smells, feel how it feels. Run your hands over the seats, the steering wheel. Picture in your mind actually driving the car, not just around the streets but all the way into your driveway or garage. In this way you will begin believing in your very soul that you can, or better yet, that you have already achieved your dream. Accept no naysayers! Claim it as a reality for you.

If you find it difficult to do this have a friend help you. Another life coach and author of *Bertha Size Your Life!*,[5] Jane Carroll recently reminded me that if you swap dreams with a friend and have them write a vision of you in the future tense living your dream they will often see you more successful than you will allow yourself to become.

For an example, I personally swapped stories with my partner in Jane's class and while my dream is to live in Switzerland, I placed myself in a chalet while my partner had me living in a castle. Give it a try. Not only is this fun, but you might even begin to feel your dream grow bigger. Jane puts it this way, *"We've trained ourselves not to get our hopes up for fear we may be let down. It's so much easier to hold the vision for someone else because we don't view it through the same filters."*

Once you have set your sights on the prize, mapped out your path, and accept the responsibility for your own success, if you continually work at making your dream a reality **you will achieve it**.

---

5   e Carroll. Bertha Size Your Life! www.berthasize.com

DRESS FOR THE SUCCESS YOU DESERVE

Today's business environment is quite different than it was in years past. Thirty years ago, when I first started my surgical business, being in business meant having a physical building and requiring appropriate dress by all employees, all the time. However today, with the world at our fingertips, the Internet has allowed even corporate employees to work from their homes in a much more relaxed atmosphere.

Nevertheless, I have found that the style of dress greatly influences not only how others perceive you, but also how you perceive yourself. Your attire says many things, including how professional you are. It tells your customers how highly you regard them. Dig even deeper and you will find that they feel you are silently telling them your level of experience, or if you are serious or not, merely by the way you look and sound.

Look at your business and what it is that you represent. If you sell sporting goods or are an exercise coach, your 'uniform' would and should be more relaxed. If your area of expertise is anything else, you will want to present a more professional, polished look. Ladies, this means makeup and appropriate attire should be your calling card.

How you dress when you interact with your customers and clients definitely affects your demeanor. When you are dressed in pajamas, you will find the way you sit, stand, and even speak will be a direct reflection of your attire. However, change into a suit and watch how differently you hold yourself.

Here's an example that comes to mind. When a woman has had her fingernails manicured, especially when they are silk nails or that sort, and usually the French manicure for her polish, she begins to hold her hands differently, and move them in such a way as to show them off. She doesn't do this consciously, but she indeed does. I can see you smiling as you can picture that sales girl doing just that.

Now I know you may be saying wearing makeup and doing your hair and nails doesn't add anything to your skill set. Nevertheless, if you look good you will feel and speak with more confidence. Believe me, confidence is an attractor.

When sitting in front of your webcam is your top low cut, or your skirt showing too much leg? Be careful here. You want your customers to pay attention to what you have to sell not how sexy you are. Even modest cleavage can be enhanced by the wrong angle of your webcam. How can anyone take you seriously if you don't present a professional persona?

So, even though you may not be physically in front of your customers or clients, I highly recommend you dress to reflect the style of business you represent. Whether you are typing an email, in a chat environment, on the phone, or in a teleseminar, dress for the success you wish to achieve. Put your best foot forward and you will find that your clients and customers will recognize your professionalism.

I would like to share one parting reminder. Always remember to share the warmth of your smile. Even if you are just on the phone, your customers will hear it in your voice.

HOW DO YOU PUT A PRICE ON THAT?

Do you have trouble charging what you deserve for your services? For most business owners setting a price point is not an issue. Since they sell a physical product, they usually are provided with both the wholesale and the suggested retail rates, at point of purchase. But, what about those of us whose only product is ourselves? A novice service-based business owner usually has no clue how to determine their rates.

Realize that your first consideration should be for time and then for training. Usually, there are also items like software or hardware costs that you should factor into this equation. What is the difference between a $3,000 and $100 design? It comes down to one thing, what's between your ears. How much experience do you already have? Your expertise is gained only after many years on the job. Did you just finish college or are you going out on your own after many years on the job?

As an example, an auto service professional fresh out of college has not yet trained their ear. Whereas, one who has been working with cars for many years will have the ability to listen to a car and immediately know where to look for the problem.

All that said; a new service business owner must begin their research by looking at the range for their profession. You don't want to under value yourself or you will end up feeling overwhelmed and abused. Not only that, your potential customers may become leery of the quality of service they can expect to receive.

For every profession there is a range that has been determined. One good place to find this information is through your profession's society, e.g., Accountants—The National Society of Accountants, Fee Study Report. Another resource you many find of value is in your local college. A recruiter/counselor can usually give you a good idea what rates your field can bear.

Then there is the Internet. Check out Ask.com or eHow.com. Look at your competition. They usually have a rates sheet either online or available for the asking. Don't be afraid to let them know you are doing this as research. They will either clam up, or be grateful that you won't devalue the profession by setting your self-worth at a ridiculously low rate.

Once you know the range how you determine which side of the range you are comfortable with is to look at the other items I mentioned earlier; software, hardware, experience, and expenses. Some will choose hourly rates, while others may work better with flat rates. This choice is up to you. As a graphic designer, I find that a combination of the two works best for my clients and me.

Know that with time and experience you will improve. At that time, you can and should reevaluate your fee structure. I suggest you do this at least once each year.

10 TRUTHS OF
BUSINESS OWNERSHIP

G inger Marks is the owner of a successful family of companies. Writing, Design and Publishing. During her over 30 years in business, she owned a surgical facility and learned how to build a multimillion-dollar business from the kitchen table. She states, "It seems like yesterday," but it was within those 23 years while she ran that business that the Internet was born. Ginger has been designing and writing since then. After helping several people develop their books and eBooks she founded DocUmeant Publishing &Designs, dedicated to assist writers to successfully turn their works into print and digital publication.

It is from her vast knowledge and experience that she shares these ten truths of business ownership with you in the hopes that you too will enjoy your journey to successful entrepreneurship.

1. You are what you are perceived to be

No matter whom you are or what business you are in, the fact is that the image you put forth is not always what you expect. You may diligently work at your business, follow all the gurus' advice, and still not see your business grow.

If you have not yet had your marketing and stationary needs designed by a professional you are taking a huge leap of faith that you will be perceived as a full-time business, in it for the long haul. A small investment now can save you tons of grief later. DocUmeant Designs (http://www. documeant.net/#bonus) will help you design your complete business look at a fraction of what those big design companies charge.

2. You must be teachable

You will be spending a lot of time doing things that have nothing to do with your area of expertise, like bookkeeping, marketing, and IT support! Solicit advice from people who know, for example, other entrepreneurs and reputable small business advisers. The Small Business Administration offers lots of information and support for new business owners.

Whether you are a seasoned or new business owner unless you are open to new ideas your business can stagnate.

3. The Internet can be both friend and foe

Don't get caught in the "Internet Rut!" Why take the time, and expend the energy, to get out of your comfy computer chair to reach the few when the whole world is at your fingertips? The answer is simple, when you attend seminars and conferences it opens the door to the opportunity to build lasting friendships and to learn from others in a much more personal way.

Think about what I just said and you will soon agree. No matter how well you connect to someone online, and I know great friendships can start there as that is where I met my precious husband Philip, you still should consider meeting in person when you can. Take my husband and I as an example, if we had not taken the time to meet face-to-face I venture to say we would not be married today. The same holds true with all our connections. When you take time to meet someone in person, you have an opportunity to know him or her in a real way. Seeing them in the flesh allows you to really see them, read the nuances in their body and voice, and look into their eyes.

The other benefit is also just as easy to accept. In one hall are gathered a host of like-minded entrepreneurs who are willing to learn and share openly with each other. While there, they have the opportunity to learn the latest marketing strategies that they can easily implement upon return to their business. The good news is that the strategies being shared are not untested! They worked before, and they can work again for you. Marketing events are truly a GOLDMINE for your income if you are serious about making a lot of money.

Whether you prefer the smaller group setting or the larger more comprehensive seminar, take the time to attend offline event opportunities, and you will begin to see your business grow in ways you never thought possible.

4. Finding your niche is imperative

I am not saying you can't or shouldn't have more than one business. What I am expressing to you is that if you ultimately choose to have more than one—make sure they complement each other. For example, if you market promotional products you might expand by including greeting cards, but you might find it quite distracting to launch a new business offering an event planning service.

Decide who would benefit most from your product or service. Then take into consideration what would effectively stimulate them to take the necessary action to successfully move from prospect to customer. The more specific you are when determining who your potential customer is the easier it will be to discern what it will take to turn them into customers.

5. Don't be afraid of your competition

When you find someone who is more clever than you, employ them! Look at them as a possible joint venture partner. Take the time to find out what they do better than you do and form a partnership to enhance both of your businesses.

6. Separate your work and personal life

Set your working hours and stick to a strict timetable. When you're not available to clients and customers, leave a message on your answer machine. Let them know when they can expect a reply from you and how to reach you in an emergency. Alternatively, if you use Skype, use the callout and/or the notifications settings. Plan time to do something you enjoy at least a few times a week to recharge your batteries.

7. Develop your customer service skills

Take the time to take courses or hire a business coach if needed, but learn how to interact with people. Whether you are selling a physical product or offering a vital service if you don't know how to relate to people in a way that will help you get your message across you will stagnate your success.

Be sure you develop excellent telephone manners, confirm orders promptly, and react quickly to any complaints or problems in an understanding, rather than confrontational, manner.

8. Stay focused

Focus on a specific goal and work at it until it's achieved. When you try to complete too many tasks or involve yourself in too many functions everything and everyone suffers. Multi-task only to the extent that you can handle. Over-extending your capabilities leads to stress, and stress leads to more than just physical problems.

9. Develop your Business Plan

Not having sufficient capital is a sure fire way to go out of business in the first year according to the Small Business Administration. Be aware that you will go through any initial investment quickly, so ensure you are covered financially until at least the end of the second year.

A properly written out business plan will ensure that your financial goals, as well as your business goals, will remain on the success track. Remember to update it every year.

10. Your time is valuable

Realize that you have knowledge or services that are valuable to others. That is, after all, why you chose to become an entrepreneur. When others come to you for advice, you don't have to give away all your knowledge for free. Finding the balance between giving someone a leg-up and giving away your knowledge is imperative. And don't work for less than you can afford to.

Do others continually ask you the same questions? Put it into an eBook, White Paper, or create a presentation that you can share that will promote your products or services. Consider investing in development of a member's only section of your business site where those who need your assistance and advice pay you for the privilege.

Use the Internet, email, build a website, send out email newsletters, buy online banner advertisements, and register your site with all the major search engines. If you need to, delegate these tasks. You might have to hire a good PA, lawyer, or marketing professional to ensure you will be profitable in the future–DocUmeantDesigns.com offers assistance with design of all your marketing and Internet developmental needs.

Make quality in every aspect of your business your primary focus and aim. If it isn't, you will eventually go out of business.

HOW TO DETERMINE YOUR WORTH

H i Mary, it is so very nice to meet you. Tell me a little bit about yourself. What do you do?"

"I sell handmade products."

"Oh, how interesting; what do you make?"

"Silk flower arrangements."

"Really? That sounds interesting. How long have you been doing that?"

"I just started really."

"What is your business' URL? I would love to see some of your work."

"I am still working on it, really, but here's the link."

Pause

"Very nice, very nice indeed. I love the yellow and green one. What do you charge?"

"Umm. I really don't know, I am so new at this. I am sure we could work something out if you really like it. How do you know what to charge?"

As odd as this scenario is Mary is not so different from the rest of us. As new businesses develop, every day chances are you or someone you know has been asked this same question. Most of the time the person posing this question has set a price, but is not comfortable with their price point, and therefore comes to another business owner in the same of similar business for advice. The likelihood is pretty good that the two business owners, while in the same business, are miles apart in experience and perhaps even talent.

Even if they were willing to divulge their fee structure, it wouldn't be appropriate for the new business owner to charge the same fees. Not only experience but also cost basis could be what sets them apart.

That being the case how do you determine your worth? One of the first things you should do is to go to the library or bookstore. There you will find volumes on standard fee structure for a wide variety of products and services. Then take this knowledge a step further and do some investigation on the web. One place to check is the Small Business Administration. You might also want to check into a business listing service to see what others charge and what the average fee structure is for your product or service.

Depending on your experience and qualifications, you may decide to start on the lower end of the scale. If time is your enemy, take classes either online or at your local college to gain valuable expertise and knowledge quickly.

As you continue to improve, don't forget to increase your prices to reflect your true value. If you don't your customers may wonder why your prices are so low.

The bottom line is you must be comfortable with your fees or like Mary you will find yourself shying away from sharing your business with others. If others have to pry the information out of you then your business is destined to fail. Don't let that happen, take the time to do your research, set your fee structure at a price point that reflects you and share it with the world.

IS YOUR BUSINESS A SINKING SHIP? HOW TO ENSURE CUSTOMER LOYALTY

One of the most important things we can do to ensure customer loyalty is to treat our customers like the VIPs they really are. Failure to do so can be extremely costly. Not only do you lose them, but also any referrals they might have otherwise provided.

As an example of what not to do I will relate a personal experience. After purchasing a sports jacket for my husband as a gift at a well-known menswear store we returned to discuss a possible exchange. The staff was friendly and helpful. The shopping experience itself was pleasant enough.

Although they did not have the correct size replacement, after checking, they assured us that a replacement was available. They took down our information and promised to contact us as soon as the jacket came in.

I hesitate to tell you how long ago that was. However, that is the real issue here. It has now been over a year since this promise was made and we have yet to receive any further correspondence or contact in regards to this issue or any other for that matter. I am sure you fully understand the impact this has had on our customer loyalty to that menswear store.

One of the first things they could have done is to send a note thanking us for our business and perhaps even a questionnaire. That would have acknowledged our visit. Then a week later when the jacket didn't come in they should have notified us that it was either indeed en route or unavailable. For our inconvenience in either caser they might have offered us an additional discount or incentive.

The fact I want you to be aware of here is that although the in-store shopping experience was pleasant enough the promise made and post-shopping service was where they lost our business.

I hope you take a note of how important it is to continue to communicate with your customers. Don't just fill an order and then forget them. Continue to send them cards and perhaps emails or phone calls. Let them know you appreciate them. Don't just send discount notices. Yes, those are always good and should be used when appropriate. But a note thanking them for their business or to just say hi and ask their opinion will have a much greater impact.

Be ever aware that your customer is who keeps you in business. Without them and their referrals you only have a store. Treat your customer like the VIP they are and you will never regret it.

Regardless of how hard you try, things do occasionally go awry. Try really hard not to screw up, but when you do make every effort to make things right. Go out of your way to let your customer know you care and are genuinely sorry. Try to see things from your customer's point of view. Consider not only the error but the ramifications. For instance, when I owned the hair transplant business and a patient was late coming in our personnel was instructed not to make a big deal of it throwing the schedule off to the patient. You never know what they had to go through to get there was the advice we gave our staff.

Use good judgment here. If it was something that was caused by you or your company be quick to take full responsibility for it. However, if the customer is way off base and nothing you say or do will help, let it and them go.

I used to work for someone like that and can honestly say I would see him smile when he "got over" and even when he didn't. He would get a sheepish grin when he got caught. But that never seemed to slow him down. So, know there are people you won't ever be able to make happy and let them go their separate way. Hold yourself to a higher standard and you will continue to be a respected business professional.

My suggestion to you, don't lose your customers because you aren't aware of some reason or another that they haven't shopped with you or used your service. Set-up trigger points that will make you aware when you haven't heard from them in such-and-such a time or at specific intervals. Then use that knowledge to get back with them and find out why. A quality control survey or even a simple phone call can help you accomplish that.

HOW DEEP ARE YOUR ROOTS?

Today I spent the morning watching my tenderly cared for White Bird of Paradise plants being uprooted for transport to their new home. These stately tropical beauties had grown past their estimated height of eight feet to a whopping twelve feet. At that height, the garden home they were originally intended to augment was totally obscured. Therefore, they had to be removed. But that meant cutting them down and relegating them to a sad but necessary end, or so I thought at the time.

However, to my great delight, during a visit to my beautician's shop, Jazz 'n Hair, earlier in the week I was clued into an environmentally conscious online group aptly dubbed Freecycle, by the salon owner, Janette. Similar to recycle, with Freecycle you notify the members of a want or need and then the receiver, once established, is responsible to pick up the item. Yahoo Group is a portal for Freecycle. This service ensures that items that are no longer in use by the current owner don't end up in a garbage fill somewhere down the line. Therefore, the transfer of perfectly good items that would otherwise have been discarded lessens the environmental impact. And since I believe in doing all I can to save the environment and additionally I have a Yahoo ID and account I immediately signed up for my local network upon my return home.

After a very simple procedure, I was admitted to the local group and posted my first "OFFER" and "WANTED" notices on the network board. Within a matter of a very short time I began receiving emails from local residents who were interested in procuring one or two. The easiest thing to do was schedule them all to come on the following Saturday, today, for a "Dig Out Party". Promptly at ten, this morning, they began to arrive and my home began slowly to appear in the swirling dust.

While this uprooting was creating a whirlwind of activity, I began to ponder the depths of the roots that fed those majestic beauties. Just like this foliage, without healthy roots our businesses are destined to die. The roots of a successful business are those key elements that will enable your business to survive even if you are no longer actively participating in the day-to-day operation.

One very important item that is needed is a solid business network. This could include all those whom you outsource work to, whether employee or joint venture partner. If you have the right people, supporting your business venture your network is capable of continuing to service your customer base even when you are on vacation.

Another business "root" is the all-important business plan. It is imperative that you know how you plan on developing your company as well as in what period. This document will come in handy to keep your business growing and for year-end evaluations. Many small business owners skip this vital "tap-root" and that is one of the reasons that nearly sixty percent of all business start-ups fail within their very first year.

Just like my bird of paradise plants without proper tending and the right amount of attention your business "roots" will occasionally need to be tenderly cared for and pruned. An unexpected card or gift may be just the right item for your valued customers or team to ensure their loyalty. At other times a bit of pruning is the right answer.

With proper attention to your business' roots, you will see your enterprise bloom. Take a step back and evaluate your blossoms, are they fragrant and full of life or are your roots so shallow that the least amount of resistance will uproot your business.

EFFECTIVE COMMUNICATION

- Do your customers understand you?
- Do they look forward to your messages?
- Are your suppliers and affiliates listening?
- Is there clear and accurate communications to you and your business?
- Do you maintain a good relationship with your employees and/or your business associates?

This week a most interesting thing occurred. As I was surfing around my usual haunts I came across a message on a board that brought up a very interesting and thought provoking subject. That topic was communication. As odd as it seems, and despite all of our knowledge, resources, and technology, many people today still have difficulty communicating effectively with each other. Some of the most eloquent prose in the English language was written not with the aid of a keyboard and spell checker, but with a goose quill and ink pot by candlelight. The sophisticated communication skills of our ancestors often exceeded those of modern day Americans, many of whose vocabularies are limited to a few score of words, with heavy dependence on the ubiquitous jargon and who have never seemed to master the difference between "your" and "you're".

Why is this a problem for us? Why is it that communication continues to be so difficult to master? After all, we are communicating in one form or another each and every day if not each and every moment? Not only do we interact with each other day in and day out but we have many methods of communicating. If you think about it I am sure you can come up with a few more than the obvious two, verbal and written. What about body language; is that not a form of communication too? And that's just for starters.

Not only are there many ways to communicate but today we have methods of communication that were not available to us a mere ten years ago. Technology offers cell phones, email, chat rooms, message boards and more. One would think that with the many varied methods and modes of communication available we would all be expert communicators. That is just not the case, as any educated person from centuries past would immediately recognize.

Have you ever been in a situation where as you were speaking you felt like what you were saying was not getting through to your listener? What about the all-important issue of correction and criticism? Have you, like I have, ever been speaking with someone and watched them change from receptive to defensive and even hostile to your ideas? Are you able to offer your opinions in a way that they are both considered and received? If you have employees then you need to hone these skills even more than if you are a solo-preneur. There is a reason that corporations utilize H.R. Departments. The people in these positions must have the passion and the skill necessary to effectively communicate with employees and potential employees on many different subjects and levels.

Here are a few suggestions to help you in your quest to become an effective communicator:

1. Listen attentively
2. Ask clarifying questions
3. Listen attentively
4. Consider your audience
5. Listen attentively
6. Think before you speak

and did I say…

7. Listen attentively?

If you take the time to listen to what you are being told instead of thinking about what you are going to say next you will find this one skill will greatly enhance your understanding of what your listener is feeling. Once you know how they think and feel you can easily answer their objections and opinions.

Sales professionals know that if they listen attentively often their potential customer will tell them exactly what they need to say to close the deal. They also know that when someone says, "No," they need to listen and respect their decision. It is only the very young and immature sales or business person that continues to make themselves a pest by their failure to accept and listen to the emphatic NO.

What about the self-proclaimed expert that projects a "my way or the highway" attitude? They are not willing to actively participate in dialogue. Instead of sharing their knowledge openly they try to force their opinions on others. They often come across as rude and uncaring. I don't care how knowledgeable you are on a subject, if you treat your listeners with respect your message will fall on fertile ground. If not you might as well not even open your mouth. It is when you stop listening that communication breaks down.

So listen attentively, ask clarifying questions, and answer objections. If you respect your listener they will be more receptive to your message. They personally may not need your service but that doesn't mean they aren't listening and can't become a valuable source for referrals.

Just the other day I was approached by a client about an "opportunity" that I had no interest in pursuing. I told him right up front in no uncertain terms that I was not interested. Instead of continuing to push his view point on me he listened and accepted my response. Sure he mentioned his desire to share with me a couple of times but then he let it go and no more was said on the subject. Later that same day another friend of mine told me she needed what this gentleman had to offer. I made the referral and they are working together today.

One of the main reasons I gave the referral was that I knew from the way he accepted my disinterest and went on with other things that he would not push himself and his product/service on my friend. So even if you don't make a "sale" don't burn your bridges. You never know who your next referral will come from.

Keep in mind that communication is a two way street. You need to state your message clearly in a way so as to be understood and accepted. Listen attentively to your audience. The bottom line is that *the metric by which the effectiveness of your communications is measured is in the results it produces*. These results are usually multidimensional and may include a combination of ingredients such as more customers, sales, profits, enhancing your audience's appreciation of your endeavors, or even just making a new friend. An experienced communicator is able to evaluate the effects they have on a live audience in real time and adjust their presentation accordingly. It is when you effectively communicate your thoughts and ideas and are willing and open to listen to others that great things happen.

CLIMBING THE PEAKS TO ATTAIN A SUCCESS-FILLED BUSINESS

Christmas time is upon us once again. This means year-end review and New Year planning is at the top of our list of things to ponder. As you begin your business planning, are you considering giving up or are you committed to making this year even better. Stop at nothing, or let nothing stop you; which is your motto? Consider the mountain climber and what it takes to get to the summit.

Like the mountain climber, you must hone your skills by daily exercise. Do something every day for your business. Use the tools you have in your pack. However, if the tool you used in previous year did not result in the goal you chose, then choose a different tool for the coming year. Conversely, if you saw even a modicum of success with the tool of choice, keep it in your tool kit and consider learning how to use it more skillfully in the coming year.

Mountain climbers carefully chose what tools are in their pack. So too should you. What are some of the tools a business owner should have in their pack? Here are just three to get you started.

1. Communication Skills

Without these skills in our bag we can end up saying the wrong thing at the wrong time. When we allow our emotions to dictate what we say, we often say the things we wish we could take back. Also, our sales may suffer as we can't convey our message powerfully enough. This can be evident in our close. Are you afraid to ask for the sale or testimonial you sorely need? Ramp up these skills by hiring a communications coach or taking classes in this sorely needed subject.

2. Marketing Skills

There are many ways to market your business. If you are a writer you have article marketing and press release writing at your fingertips. If you lack the time or skill to do these two very important marketing items then hire a qualified professional. You shouldn't scrimp on your press release writing budget, as a poorly written press release is at best ill-effective. And a press release not submitted to the right sources for you and your area are a waste of good money.

Social media is another area that marketing can play a part. However, if you lack the time to consistently deliver, hire a VA that can do this for you. Again, you will find this well worth your investment.

If nothing else, put ads out there. A well written advertisement, rightly placed (where your target market frequents or frequently reads), can put your business on the proverbial map.

Then there are audio & video. Even if you don't start your own radio show, you can seek to showcase your talents and wares on other's broadcasts. Radio show hosts are always looking for competent professionals who can provide knowledge and insight on subjects that their listeners crave.

I could go on and on about marketing techniques, but let's leave this for another article.

3. Audience

Every business needs an audience. If you are marketing and it isn't paying off, then chances are you haven't done your homework. Surveys are wonderful for uncovering your niche and what they want and need. Also, Googling your keywords can often uncover organizations that will partner with you whose audience is perfect for your products and/or services.

Which brings me to another very important likeness between mountain climbers and business owners. Climbers discover early on that joining with the right team is one of the most important choices they must make. Their life (and your business life), depends on having the right members in your team.

Your team must be able to communicate clearly, be trustworthy, and follow directions. This all requires you to set-up ground rules so everyone knows what they need to do in any given situation. As you develop your business, having these loyal, reliable team members, and policy and procedures readily available is much like having a lead climber holding the rope which ensures everyone's successful climb.

> **Success is the ability to go from failure to failure without losing your enthusiasm. Winston Churchill**

When climbers decide to climb a mountain, they don't just sally forth and begin the climb on the first mountain they find. They first choose which mountain they are going to climb and develop a plan to ensure their success. Sometimes the plan takes many months to develop; or even years. Like them, don't just decide to do something to make your business work; plan what that something is, write it down, and take the time to develop a plan of action that will ensure your successful venture.

In the midst of planning, climbers go through rigorous training. Take their lead and get the coaching you need to help you along the way. This valuable step can make the difference between success and failure. Whatever your need is, I assure you, there is a coach that can train you and thus help you avoid the pitfalls that are sure to be ahead.

Why do climbers and business owners alike fail? Distraction, loss of focus, not taking the climb/business seriously, and failure to plan or even just the wrong plan. Even just one of these can ensure the end before you even begin the venture. But, these are subjects for another day.

FOCUS ON WHAT YOU KNOW

Every day we read about this coach and that coach. This one helps you build a better network; that one helps train you in one area or another. Don't get me wrong; the right coach, at the right time, for the right reason is worth their weight in gold. I have even personally referred my friends and clients to one coach or another when the timing was right for them. The perfect coach can aid your development in an area where you may have struggled before. They can even save your very life or the life of your business.

Nevertheless, some of us float from mentor to mentor, coach to coach, never fully implementing the tools they provide. Why is that? Sometimes it is fear, plain and simple. But most often it is because it's just not something we are capable, or willing, to do at the time.

The best result is the outcome of focus, determination, ability, and action. When even one of these areas is lacking no amount of coaching will succeed in helping you reach your goal. Focus and determination are nearly the same thing; but without ability and action your intended result will never be obtained. Felicia Slattery, Communication Consultant and Coach puts it this way, "Sometimes what many people need is less of a coach and more of a consultant or teacher. Coaching is a fabulous resource for getting you unstuck, but when you don't know how to do something, even the best coaching won't do the trick. You need a teacher, consultant, or trainer; in short someone to show you the how to, plain and simple. And then, you need to follow-up with the plan you create."

Felicia has a wonderful tool on her website that I think is perfect to assist you in determining whether you truly are in need of a coach or not. It is a simple questionnaire that every coach should offer their prospective clients. Be sure to check out her "Are You Coachable" quiz on her resources page.

Your coach can only take you so far. If you don't have the ability to grasp and implement the training your efforts will be futile. As an example, I am very good at math. I can easily grasp most any new concept the first time I read it. However, when it comes to science my brain literally shuts down. You have heard the old saying, "You can lead a horse to water, but you can't make him drink." Well, it's much like that when trying to force yourself to become something you aren't capable of becoming.

So what's the answer? Buck up and admit; there are just some things you have no time, talent, ability, or desire to do. Focus on what you can do instead of what you can't.

One solution is to hire someone, even if only part-time, who can assist you in the areas you need assistance. Then leave it in their capable hands.

Another option is to form a strategic alliance with another business owner who has the knowledge and skill you are seeking. For example, if you want to promote your business through public speaking, but even the thought of it causes you panic attacks find someone outgoing who you can partner with that will promote both of your businesses. Maybe you just can't seem to put pen to paper; the words just don't flow. Hire a ghostwriter or partner with a copy writer/editor who can assist you in this area. You might offer to post the article if they will do the writing.

Carol Deckert, Networking Coach puts it this way, "When you begin your business, it may not be financially possible to hire someone to help you get it all done. You may be forced to do it all yourself with possibly some help from your family. However, if your idea is simply to start a business, take out of this business whatever income it produces, your business won't ever grow.

"In order for growth to happen, you, as the owner, must remain focused on what you want that business to become. Forming a strategic alliance with another business that has a comparable target market could possibly be the best way for your business to grow. Sit down and write a detailed plan, noting the duties/responsibilities each of you will be responsible for, focus on each other's strengths and weaknesses. Exchange of skills between the two of you is the perfect alliance as you each control the growth of your own business but you will have help doing some of the work that you don't want to do, don't have time to do, or simply don't know how to do. The devil is in the details, so be specific and clear in what you expect from each other and then each of you are able to focus on what you want to achieve with your business. Focus on YOUR strengths and a plan of action and you will be able to move forward and grow your business!"

I have used both of these techniques in my 30+ years in business and have never regretted it. Rather than waste valuable time and effort trying to learn something you have no predilection for, you could hire an assistant. Hiring a virtual assistant can be a sound business move. This option allows you to save both time and money, when you consider that you don't have to pay their medical insurance! They can tackle the most tedious chores that you don't have the patience or motivation to do.

Decide for yourself what is more valuable, time spent learning something you neither want to learn nor are capable of implementing, or focusing on what you love. In deciding which method to use, look at the big picture. Is it something that needs to be done or is it an area of your business that will enable you to diversify? If diversification is your answer, then partnering may be your best bet.

On the other hand, if you really want and need the help to learn, a coach or mentor in the specific medium is absolutely your best choice. Drawing from the example of wanting to learn how to improve your public speaking abilities, you might consider hiring someone like Coach Slattery or simply pick up a copy of her recently released eBook titled *Cash In On Speaking*. Another helpful resource and one of my personal favorites is my book, *Presentational Skills for the Next Generation*.

Remember, to gain from your training you will need to commit to learning and implementing the suggested strategies. Their knowledge and experience will enable you to achieve even your loftiest goal only if you put into action what you learn. Otherwise, you should stick to what you know and love and leave the rest to others more capable.

DISCOVER HOW TO DO IT ALL WITHOUT DOING IT ALL AT ONCE— MULTI-TASKING VS. MINI-TASKING

Are you a multi-tasker or mini-tasker? In today's instant gratification society and with the demands on our time from both our job and our family most of us have developed an ability to multi-task. But are you really getting multiple tasks completed at the same exact time or are you simply breaking them down into smaller bites? For those of you who are died in the wool multi-taskers, I applaud you. How you can remember every little piece when they are mixed up with other little pieces I will never understand. I thought I too was in your private club until I stepped back and took a long hard look at the way I was truly getting things done (or not done as the case may be).

When you attempt to tackle more than one thing at a time do you find yourself having to go back and refresh your memory about that fourth from the last thing you were working on? Do you struggle to stay organized or overlook the minute details? Perhaps, like me, you simply are not a multi-tasker but rather a mini-tasker. One quick way to tell is when you are in a group chat setting do you connect with multiple conversations that are going on at the same time or do you have difficulty transitioning from one subject to the next?

As I get older and wiser I realize that multi-tasking is not what it is cracked up to be. You may find it easier and more productive to stay on a steady course and complete one task at a time rather than trying to juggle multiple projects. Often, trying to do too many projects at the same time can lead to miscommunication with others involved with the completion of the task and worse yet your completed project(s) may even suffer from the lack of proper attention to detail. This doesn't mean you can't work on more than one project at the same time. What it means is you, like I, might do better to make a schedule and stick with it. Create a daily planner page or TODO list. At the top of the list write all the tasks you have to accomplish in that day and what part you need to do to make it a reality. Then map out what you are going to do at what time on the schedule. Not only will this give you a road map to success but, if tomorrow you forget what you did yesterday and where you need to begin today, you have it written down and can easily refresh your memory.

According to Russell Poldrack, associate professor of psychology at the University of California, Los Angeles, multitasking's reputation as a timesaving tool is undeserved.

"In general, it's almost always worse to try to do two things at once than it is to do each of those things separately," he says. *"This is because there is a bottleneck in the mind in terms of how people process things psychologically. There are certain things—such as choosing what action to take—that you can only do at one time,"* says Poldrack.

That is why many of us preferred to finish a task that is nearing completion even if it means staying at it past the "bell".

Imagine if you will, the multi-tasker who accomplishes several tasks in the day by doing one for an hour and then switching to make sales calls and then goes back to the previous task. How long do you think it will take to refocus and pick up the ball again? Even if it is just a minute or two, and for some it can be as much at 30 minutes or more, you have simply wasted that productive time. Most of us can actually tackle one or two chores at the same time but any more than that and we begin to lose focus. Even a computer doesn't work in parallel unless it is a special parallel computer. It does one thing and then the next and then the next.

"We humans can do some things in parallel and some things we just simply can't. Humans cannot satisfactorily perform independent tasks simultaneously. Some people are under the mis–conception that they can do that, but what is actually happening is they are rapidly switching back and forth among the different tasks. As a result of the switching process, they are actually only doing one thing at a time with the result that they are less efficient than if they would have done them separately. A simple example of the impossibility of doing just two things at the same time would be to do two long divisions simultaneously and get the correct final answers, for example, dividing 12 by 34 and at the same time dividing 56 by 78. Another example that our younger generation can relate to would be texting while driving your car. To enshrine the perils of muti-tasking our ever vigilant government has made it a crime—driving and texting at the same time." —Philip S Marks, BS Engineering, BS Physics, BS Zoology.

Another way to deal with your multi-tasking needs is to look to others for assistance. Let's say that you are a small business owner and your productive time is spent doing shows and taking care of clients. The time you spend doing activities that are not beneficial to your bottom line are unproductive. Things like creating that website or writing a press release or a number of other business building tasks that you have little or no experience in should be hired out. When you try to do these important things yourself you not only waste your time creating an ineffective end result but you lose the productive time that you could have gained in focusing on your strong points.

To reiterate, become a mini-tasker and you will be much more productive. Make your list, write it down, and be specific. Try this little trick; it works for me. Write at the top of your day's planner page, "I am going to do X and I am going to accomplish Y," for each and every task you wish to complete. Don't allow yourself to overdo it. If you need to research to find a missing link do just enough to fill the need and then move on. Do refer to your notes to refresh your mind as to where you left off if you get interrupted or thrown off track. You'll find this works wonders for getting your mornings off to a quick start. That and a cup of coffee (or tea) will ensure a productive day. We all need as much structure as possible. Develop routines and rituals and stick to them. Don't fool yourself into thinking you don't need them. You do! And lastly, recognize your strengths, and cater to them as much as you can. Ask for help or hire a professional to assist in the areas that you need help.

NEAT AND CLEAN: TIGHT AND TRUE

Running a tight ship and staying on course will keep you on a path to success. Easier said than done, of course; but, you can and must do it to reach your goals. As you consider the economy and its impact on your business we have no choice but to look long and hard at the tools we will utilize.

Do you really need that membership? Did you use it last year to build your business or learn anything of value? If the answer is no, then just perhaps it is time to let it go. As an example, I love Ryze, well, I used to. I spent hours and hours just chatting away, back and forth. But, the last year or two, well, social media has grown and so have I; away from the Ryze community. Therefore, my decision for 2011 was made. Will I continue to pay for their service when so many others are free, or will I let that business building tool continue without me?

What about that newsletter you signed up for? Is it really worth $xx each month? Did you read and implement any of the strategies? If you at least read it, why not commit to implementing some of the suggestions given this year? If you find yourself too busy to read it, perhaps the answer is to set aside time to read it rather than letting it go.

So, how do you tighten up and tidy up? Let's start by understanding what we are talking about. The Idoms free dictionary definition of a tight ship is "to run a ship or an organization in an orderly and disciplined manner." Well, that kind of tells us what we are looking for, but a better realization is probably found more towards the organizational rather than the disciplined. However, being disciplined to read those newsletters and follow through, in practice, is really important in this process too.

Nevertheless, being organized is what we need to do. Organization is not just the executive structure, or the ordering process. It is also looking at the tools you use and those you don't; and that is exactly what we are talking about in this article.

No matter what type of business you have, small; medium; or large, waste is not an option in any economy, let alone in this tough economic condition. So, where do you begin trimming off the excesses and tightening up the ship? Let's look at just a few suggestions.

1. **Impulse Buying**–After you have cleaned house and let go of the unnecessary expenditures, as suggested above, the next step is to put a stop to that impulse buying habit. Think about what you are going to do with the product or service? Will it be useful long-term, or is it something

that will make your business flow more smoothly? In other words, will it be essential to the operation of your business. If the answer is no, then you might want to hold off on making the purchase.

2. **Seek Professional Help**–Don't waste time and money trying to do it yourself. When you need help meeting a deadline, or don't have the skill to accomplish a task, it is better to hire the services of a qualified professional or perhaps a VA (Virtual Assistant).

3. **Clean up you're Accounts Receivables**–Asking for what you are owed is not a bad thing. Rather than letting your clients 'slide' because you don't want to *bug* them, call them and let them know that you are willing to help them work out a payment plan that will fit their budget. You will find that most of your customers have at least some of the money to pay you.

The important thing about running a small business is to know the direction in which you're heading; to know on a day-to-day basis your progress in that very direction; to be aware of what your competitors are doing and to practice good money management at all times. All this will prepare you to recognize potential problems before they arise.

PROSPERITY PRINCIPLE MUSINGS

Recently there has been a lot of press on the prosperity principle. It basically states that if you align yourself with the "Universe" you will attract that which you desire the most. Well I both agree and agree to disagree with this theory. You see, from what I have discovered through diligent investigation is that this theory emerged from L. Ron Hubbard (father of Dianetics). Scientology teachers are subtly trying to convince us that we are in charge of our own realities. However, what they teach us is that each one of us is a god and THAT I can't abide!

I wholeheartedly agree though that it is possible to attract prosperity into your life. The fact is that when you align yourself with God and the principles He teaches us you will see His gentle hand of mercy in your life. What are those principles? Very simply put the lesson is to align yourself with Love! Yes, love. Love of God, family, others and lastly yourself. It is when you have a healthy, loving, relationship with God and family that He is able to share with you from His storehouse.

So, how do I know that this is the case? Well, let me share with you from my own experiences. In my early thirties I conducted an experiment that I recommend you give a try yourself if you doubt the credibility of my findings. For one year I diligently engaged in private devotions. I began with clearing my mind of all hindrances by quietly sitting and meditating on such things as the many names of God. Then after my mind was totally focused on Him I began my prayer time and followed that with bible reading and study. This was the first thing I would do in the morning with my first cup of coffee. It was in that way I didn't have to find time but rather I made time for my devotions. As a result I began to sense God's working in my life.

One particular event that I recall is when I went to bed one night and I felt a gentle tug in the pit of my stomach like I needed to get up and kneel by my beside and pray for a particular pastor and his wife that were heading up a new church plant. As I was already comfortably in bed I tried to lay that thought aside but it just kept prodding me and since I couldn't sleep anyway I got up and began praying.

The next Sunday when I went to speak with pastor Tynsdale and his wife they informed me that at exactly the time I was praying they were meeting with a lady that was applying for the pianist position that turned out to be a Satan worshiper. Coincidence? I don't think so.

The next thing that happened was quite similar yet different. I founded a group of volunteers to mentor new online business owners. In doing so I committed the group to employ the prosperity principles promised in the Bible. One volunteer told me that I needed to tone down the "God-thing" and when I told her I could not she decided that she was going to disassociate herself. Well it was at that time that the group began to flourish and today we have over 100 members.

The third thing that occurred is that I committed my business to the support of a missionary. I promised that missionary before they left on their tour of duty to Mongolia that I would support them with proceeds from my business. With that commitment made I began to see my business grow and flourish, so what did I do? Well, I committed even more of my business income to his support. I set a goal, if I made X number of dollars in a month I would give twice the percentage. Guess what happened next? Right, I had aligned myself with the right relationships and He began to shower blessings on me.

So I say to you, align yourself with the true prosperity principle. Our God is the owner of the wealth of the universe. Aligning yourself with the *universe* is to fall short of your goal. Right alignment comes from putting God first, family second, others third, and yourself last. Remember you can't out-give God. If you don't believe me just give it a try.

RECESSION IS GOOD FOR YOUR SMALL BUSINESS!

Crazy, nuts, totally wacko you are probably thinking to yourself. How could she even begin to think that the current down turn could bring anything but harm to a small business venture? All you have to do is look at the mega-stores that are being affected. Store closings listed in 2008 number nearly six-thousand according to RIS News. The International Council of Shopping Centers reports that in 2008 the closings are up 25% –5,770 compared to a mere 4,603 in 2007. Surging gas prices, higher food costs, and powerful inflationary forces are squeezing consumers and retailers alike.

Just look at the list:

84 Lumber Co. — 30 stores

Ann Taylor — 117 stores

Charming Shoppes (Lane Bryant and Fashion Bug) — 150 stores

Foot Locker — 140 stores

Macy's — 9 stores

Movie Gallery — 160 stores as part of reorganization plan to exit bankruptcy

Pacific Sunwear — 153 Demo stores

Pep Boys — 33 stores

Sprint Nextel —125 retail locations

Wilsons the Leather Experts — 158 stores

Zales — 100 stores

J. C. Penney, **Lowe's** and **Office Depot** are scaling back or delaying expansion. Office Depot had planned to open 150 stores this year, but will now open 75.

CompUSA: All 103 stores will be sold or shut down. After being acquired by an investment firm, the company's business and assets are being sold. The retail stores that don't sell will be shut down.

Levitz Furniture: The furniture retailer has liquidated its assets and closed all of its 76 stores.

Bombay Company: The company unveiled plans to close all 384 U.S.-based Bombay Company stores. The company's online storefront has discontinued operations.

Sharper Image: The company recently filed for bankruptcy protection and announced that 90 of its 184 stores are closing. The retailer will still operate 94 stores to pay off debts, but 90 of these stores have performed poorly and also may close.

Charming Shoppes: The operator of Fashion Bug, Lane Bryant & Catherine's plans to close 150 underperforming stores, lay off 150 employees and reduce the amount of stores it will open in 2009

PacSun 'Demo' Stores: Pacific Sunwear will close its 154 Demo stores after a review of strategic alternatives for the urban-apparel brand. Seventy-four underperforming Demo stores closed last May

Talbot's Kids, Mens: The company reported that 78 stores will close after disappointing sales were reported for the children's and men's apparel stores.

Ethan Allen Interiors: The company announced plans to close 12 of 300+ stores in an effort to cut costs.

Movie Gallery-Stores: The video rental company plans to close 400 of 3,500 Movie Gallery and Hollywood Video stores in addition to the 520 locations the video rental chain closed last fall.

Other retailers facing closures include Rite Aid, Macy's, Sofa Express, Kirkland's, Sigrid Olsen (part of Liz Claiborne), Jasmine Sola and Rent-A-Center.

—According to Christina Zarrello of risnews.com.

So the question remains, if the big retailers are feeling the crunch how could this possibly bode well for the small business owner? The answer is simple! Customer service.

With all these customers looking for goods and services and no place to go why not gear up your marketing to attract them to your business? These customers will still need the items and services, that won't change. With a little bit of careful planning you can secure a completely new group of customers you never could have reached before and therefore increase your customer base.

Here are some ideas that may help you see the light. People are not dining out as much. Why not offer them an alternative—provide low cost-easy to make meal planning services, inexpensive pack and go meals, packaged "You Make" dishes, side dishes and even desserts, alternative dietary choice coaching for those who wish to lose weight and keep it off.

Another thing people will always need is help. Whether it is in the area of financial planning or realizing that they are wasting valuable time trying to save a dollar here or there doing things they really would be better off delegating so they can focus more on what they do best, make the sale. Virtual Assistance now comes in many different forms. Web design, Marketing and Life Coaches, Multi-media providers, and a slew of other service professionals should be a cost-effective alternative.

Put your thinking cap on and I am certain you will find a way that you too can attract these floundering customers.

The tools you will need to succeed in capturing these wayward customers are a solid marketing plan and unsurpassed customer service skills. If you lack in even one of these areas you may be left in the dust with the big retailers.

One tool that can help you solidify your marketing plans is the *Weird & Wacky Holiday Marketing Guide: Your business marketing calendar of ideas.* Beef up your marketing plan with the tools and tips offered throughout this fun and thought provoking guide which is updated annually. Available at http://www.HolidayMarketingGuide.com.

On the customer service end let me offer you a tale that might help you see what I mean by unsurpassed customer service skills that was shared with me a month or so ago in a newsletter by Yanik Silver.

"It seems he was dining with friends at an intimate restaurant called *The Modern* in New York City. About three-quarters of the way through the meal the guests at a nearby table were getting loud and making those in his party uncomfortable the more it impacted their dinner conversation. The waiter came to the table and overly exaggerated to spill a small amount of bottled water on their table. Then in a loud voice (to make sure the other couple overheard) he said, 'Oops, how clumsy of me. I can't believe I spilled water all over the table. We can't have you sitting at a wet table so let me mover you over right away.' Then a team of seven swooped in and moved their table, wine glasses and meal across the dining room.

"What occurred was the staff correctly assessed the situation as being irksome and did something very smart while not embarrassing the other couple." The lesson learned here. Go out of the way to ensure your customers satisfaction and you will have a customer for life.

The key to overcoming the recession talk is to be less distracted by the news and more determined to succeed! Plan today and tomorrow you will succeed.

SALES VS. EXPERTISE

Growing as a business owner is imperative if your business is to survive. With new entrepreneurs appearing every day, your business' success becomes harder and harder to maintain and grow. To stay on top of the pack you must learn the nuances of successful business ownership quickly.

Pushy salespeople may get the sale but being an information provider will guarantee a long and prosperous business success. So how do you make the transition? Before you will ever convince anyone of your superior knowledge on a subject, you first must be wholly convinced within yourself that you are an expert.

As you begin to share your knowledge, others will begin to accept you for the expert that you are. The best way to begin is by sharing through offers. Do you have a white paper, ezine, eBook or some other informational product? If you offer to provide that resource in exchange for their contact information, you not only set yourself up as an expert but you additionally are able to begin list building.

Another idea is to offer free consultations. This allows you to answer the needs of those who 'raise their hand' to your product or service while proving your expertise. This is something that I have found to be successful in building both a multi-million dollar surgical facility and my online business. Be sure you are prepared to answer most of the questions that will arise before tapping into this business-building tool.

One word of warning, when you don't know the answer be honest, tell them, "That is a very good question, I'll have to check into it and get back with you." Never, never, never give advice if you are unsure of what you are saying. It is better to complement the questioner and let them know you will get back to them than to be caught later having said something that turns out to be wrong.

Being a problem solver, information provider will ensure your business will continue to thrive and grow. These powerful techniques will build trust with your prospective customers and your contact list.

SHOW UP BOTH MENTALLY AND PHYSICALLY!

Are you showing up each day both physically and mentally? Are you going through the motions with no joy for what you are doing? Maybe it is just that there are too many distractions. Perhaps you feel like you are being pulled every which way all at once. Are you over-extending yourself? Is your spouse or family competing with your JOB for your time and attention? Whatever you are doing, is it taking you in the direction of success or are you just treading water?

There has been a lot of talk about the power of positive thinking as of late. I am a firm believer that what you think you claim. When you are struggling and find yourself constantly fighting battles step back and take a good look at your mindset and your focus. If you really want to achieve success you have to not only show up every day physically but mentally too.

One sure way for the WAH (work at home) set is to prioritize and organize. Set a schedule and let your family members know what it is. It may take a week or two for them to 'get it', but 'get it' they will. Once the boundaries are set YOU have to learn to stick to them as well. Years ago I had a dog trainer come to my home to teach my dog how to obey my commands. It wasn't long before I realized the one being trained was not the dog.

> **Nothing can stop the man with the right mental attitude from achieving his goal; nothing on earth can help the man with the wrong mental attitude. Thomas Jefferson**

Keeping your thoughts rooted in truth will help you as well. What I mean is to accept the things you know to be true and ignore the rest. If you don't accept the negative comments from naysayers you will not be dragged down by them. Also on this train of thought, if you are a good motivator use that to your advantage and leave the bookkeeping to someone qualified in that area. Yes, delegation will help you as you will not be distracted by chores left undone.

Find other like-minded individuals that are willing to partner with you and expand your offering of services if you must. I have seen my business flourish this past year because I strategically partnered myself with similar business owners that specialize in areas where I am weakest. I have actually partnered with three Virtual Assistants. Why would I partner with those who could be thought of as my competition? The answer is simple by joining forces we each not only expand our list of services but can focus on what we enjoy.

Once you have found your niche and developed successful partnerships encourage each other with empowering thoughts and actions. We all need a pat on the back for a job well done at one time or another. Why not look for the positive in your business relationships? Once you turn your thinking around it is easier to turn your failures into successes.

SWEET OR SOUR
YOUR ATTITUDE WILL MAKE
A DIFFERENCE

From the time we are born until we die we are always learning and growing. One of the things we develop early on is our personality. But one of the most important aspects of our development is the attitude we embrace.

As business owners it is vital that we train ourselves to be people magnets and not sour pusses. We all can relate to the picture of a dour old-maid schoolmarm who clearly represents a sour attitude in its purest form. However, you don't have to look like her to be her.

When you picture this spinster in your mind how does that image make you feel? If you were to meet her in person what would you want to do? For most of us the answer is the same. We would want to avoid her or get away from her as quickly as possible. As business owners we need to remember that truth.

The fact is, if you are a solo-preneneur, it is up to you and you alone to generate interest in your products and/or services. So what can you do to become a people magnet? How can you quickly and easily generate feelings of likeability and trust? Smile. Yes I hear you, your business is online, your communication is mostly written, but believe me your smile will shine through in your words whether written or spoken. Attitude seeps into every fiber of your being. If you go looking for trouble you will most likely find it. A positive attitude generates goodwill and goodwill generates trust and trust is the groundwork for financial success.

Now that you're smiling add enthusiasm to the mix. If you totally believe in what you have to offer you won't have to 'sell' your products. You will simply 'tell' about them. And isn't generating sales while helping people your ultimate goal? Focus on them and what you have to offer rather than you and what you need. If when you meet someone new you remember this one rule you will find it easy to bridge the gap between them and the sale.

Don't be afraid to take this one step further. If you can't help them or don't have something they need at that time but you know someone who can or does, introduce the two of them. Don't just give them an email address or phone number; actually introduce them. This will only lead to goodwill and appreciation for you. You never know where the hand of friendship will lead, but often you will come full circle and you may find it will generate referrals from unexpected sources.

It is when you genuinely care about others, are willing to go out of your way to help them, and believe totally in your product or service that you will endear the people you come in contact with to you. Remember that old saying, people buy from those they know, like, and trust.

TEAM UP TO WIN!

Sandy is a highly motivated business owner. She comes up with fabulous ways to market her business. While others may be standoffish to merging their marketing efforts with other businesses, Sandy aggressively pursues them.

As an independent beauty consultant, she recently contacted a successful restaurant owner in her neighborhood in an effort to woo the female patrons for her upcoming Mothers' Day promotion.

What Sandy saw was the perfect place to find her target market and the best opportunity to win the restaurant owner over to her way of thinking. This out-of-the-box thinking is just the sort of thing that ensures Sandy's successful business growth.

Sandy's proposal is to offer a flower and a card for a complimentary facial to each female patron along with a chance to enter a drawing for a combination of a special basket of products from her and a gift certificate for dinner for two from the participating restaurant owner.

Then on Mother's Day, Sandy will approach each lucky lady, introduce herself on behalf of the restaurant and let her know that she wants to honor her on her special day with a beautiful flower and an invitation for a complimentary facial. Then she mentions the beautiful gift basket that the woman may have noticed as she entered the restaurant and hands her an entry to fill out so she can enter the special Mother's Day drawing.

To close she would mention that the winner will be notified by phone and state, "Happy Mother's Day and thank you for celebrating at *the name of the restaurant.*"

Then the following week all Sandy has to do is call to schedule the complimentary facial and let the lady know she can have a few friends join her if she would like.

Once scheduled, a quick reminder and note of thanks is sent out to her with a free sample. This further solidifies the appointment and makes the confirmation call, a couple of days before the facial that much more pleasantly received. This is certainly a win/win/win all the way around. It's just that simple to come up with a unique marketing approach.

Here is another idea that you don't even have to leave home to take advantage of. Often there are online events that are looking for speakers and/or donations that you can participate in. An added benefit comes from the increased activity and promotion campaign launched and totally done by the organization and their members.

A good example here is a well-established group like the popular WINning Sisters organization.[6] Each year they host a bi-annual Fling. This event is open-to-all and both fun and informative. The Winning Sisters is a not-for-profit group. Their membership consists of women entrepreneurs from just about every nation and country in the world.

Their Fling events are the perfect opportunity to meet a group of small and medium sized business owners. You can share in the wealth of knowledge provided by their special guest speaker and win valuable prizes. Each event brings together a worldwide following, as well as a flurry of activity. This is a unique opportunity for you to market your business for a small donation. When these types of events become available in your niche market be sure to take advantage of their increased traffic and boost your bottom line.

Another event idea is to offer yourself as a speaker, pro-bono. Many clubs and organizations both online and offline are in need of speakers for their meetings. If you don't know where to begin or need some instruction on public speaking you might consider picking up a copy of Felicia Slattery's eBook, *Cash In On Speaking.*[7]

Do you already have the skill and knowledge and need a place to share? Figure out your niche and Google for organizations or networks. Begin by joining social networking sites like FaceBook, MySpace, and LinkedIn. Then search out your target market and offer your services.

Are you looking for offline ideas? Check first with your local chamber or senior citizen center. Then venture forth through club listings in your local yellow pages. Another terrific resource of club listings can be found in your small, local newspapers and publications. These are superb sources as they list not only the organization name but the type of speaker and topics they look for is listed in their event notice.

I hope I have given you at least one idea that you can and will utilize. Think about teaming up with other business owners and create your own win/win marketing campaign.

---

6   WIN and WINning Sisters of Ryze has closed their doors as of 2011.
7   Slattery, Felicia. Cash In On Speaking Communication Transformation, 2008 http://www.communicationtransforma-tion.com/cashinonspeakingebook.html

RUNNING A BUSINESS IN UNCERTAIN TIMES

Unless you are totally oblivious to the state of the worldwide economy, you know that the purse-strings of the average family have been pulled so taut that there is little room for much more than the essentials. Small and large businesses alike are feeling the effects of this economic downturn. We have seen smaller companies and larger corporations close their doors, or merge with another, as a solution to this ever-worsening crisis.

So, where does that leave the small-business owner whose budget already can't support its advertising and inventory needs? What can you do to ensure your small business doesn't fold? After more than thirty years in business, I have experienced both good and bad times. Through it all, I have come to realize that it takes a person of stout character to weather the storm. Yes, a strong will to survive is essential, but that alone oft-times, is not enough.

There is a truth that I would like to share here that is summed up in a trite saying, "It takes money to make money." This is difficult to accept and act upon when times are hard. However, or should I say, nevertheless, this is the most important thing you can do to guarantee your business' survival. Think of it from a different perspective. While others are cutting back on their advertising budget, that leaves those of us who continue to do so the only ones marketing to our potential audiences. And, we all know that if you don't stay active in their minds, you won't reap the rewards in gained customers and sales.

This doesn't mean you have to spend a small fortune on marketing, but it does mean you need to discover avenues that you may not have previously considered.

If you haven't already, get involved in social media. As I have stated before, keeping your name in the public ear is a must-do in these economic times.

Another option is to tap into your local market. The meetings and groups in your area are a viable entity that should be explored. If you are not a joiner, or don't have the budget for membership dues why not consider either splitting the dues with another interested business owner or offering to speak at one of their meetings?

I know of a group of business owners in my area who joined together to enable them to join the local country club. Where it would have cost each of them individually thousands of dollars—it now only costs them 1/10 as much. Therefore, that is affordable—and wise.

How can you employ this principle? Consider sharing a booth at a fair or local event. Better yet, put together a group of business owners and hold your own event. This can be done locally for sure, but done online you will find much less costly. Being a sponsor of an event gets you more media than just participating alone. Again, think about how you can form a joint venture with other business owners to make it more affordable and hence doable.

The other idea I would like to propose, at first, may not sit well with you. Regardless, it also is worthy of mention. Hire competent help. "What? Hire? Doesn't that mean I won't save money by learning and doing it myself? I can't afford to do that!" I hear these comments every time I share this suggestion. Bear with me as I explain.

Let's say you need to sell twelve widgets a month to break even. In order to do that you have to have a social presence, build a website, speak to a group, and design a new marketing piece. Since you, and only you, can do the speaking engagement that is one thing that you can't have someone assist in completing. However, even preparing for your event leaves areas where hiring help should come under consideration. Things like putting together your slide presentation or learning how to use the conference room to its full potential can be done by a capable assistant.

Realize that if you don't have the knowledge or talent to complete a task, you will need to devote many hours more to accomplish your goal than it would have taken you to hire a competent professional to do it for you in the beginning. And, we all know time is money!

While you are slaving away trying to figure out how to use a new program or to put together an attractive marketing piece, your competition has been out there marketing. This puts them miles ahead of you in the market place. Furthermore, if you happen to come up with an end result that doesn't attract your market, all that time and effort is wasted. How much wiser it is to hire someone to do it right in the beginning, and usually in less than half the time it would have taken you. Besides, your time is better-spent marketing, speaking, and networking.

Money is not made while learning, only while marketing. This is not to say learning isn't important. We should all strive to learn something new every day. Think of it more in terms of potential income. Will what you learn help you make a sale? If not, hire it out. Your time is much more valuable!

On this journey to business success, we will continue to experience booms as well as busts, times of plenty and times of lean. However, if you are wise, you will ponder the ideas I have shared and take action, as only action creates income.

UNCOVER YOUR NICHE

How often have you found yourself talking to someone about your product or service to find that they never knew you were even in business? If you haven't had this experience then you are one of the lucky few. Defining your perfect customer can do a lot to help avoid this scenario.

Begin by asking yourself who would best benefit from the purchase of your product or service. Be as specific as you can. ***Don't fool yourself into thinking that your customer is the whole world. Not everyone will need or want what you have to provide.*** Just think about the time and energy, not to mention money, you could save by only marketing to potential customers or clients. Also, discovering where they hang out will be a whole lot easier if you know specifically who your target market is.

Once you discover your target market and find the radio stations or podcasts they listen to, and magazines and ezines they read you will be armed with the information you need to market to them effectively. If you can't afford to advertise in those places why not try marketing to the publication itself. Send them a press release or offer to provide them with articles.

When you know exactly who you are talking to, you know what to say and what not to say to properly inform them. And we all know that a properly informed customer makes a better customer. This will also enable you to speak to the challenges that specifically affect them and provide a viable solution.

Without this information you will have a hard time convincing Mr. or Ms. Buyer that you have the answer they seek. For example, if you were selling financial planning services to young adults you wouldn't tell them this product will help you reach your retirement goals, that is just too far off for them to pay you any attention. Instead, you might want to tell them that starting a savings plan, that you can pull funds from when they need it, will guarantee them a safety net for those unseen emergencies that are bound to crop up. However, if you said the same thing to a group of middle age buyers with a family to provide for the results would be quite different. So you can see, trying to sell to *everyone* is like going for a hole in one with a 9-iron.

To begin think about whom your most likely prospects would be. What specific type of individual would benefit the most by using your product or service? Does information such as age, income, education, sex, geographical location, or some other criteria have any bearing on who would most likely be a prospect? Don't guess. ***Do your homework. A little bit of research now will save you a lot of aggravation and money later.***

Another thing to consider is what you have to offer. Recently I was speaking to a young lady who wanted to provide Virtual Assistance (VA) services. She was confused as to how to effectively market her business. I asked her what services she offered and she replied that she provides a long list of services which included answering phones, press release writing and distribution, and image design. As you see from the list all of her services required a diversity of skills and unless she had employees or contractors most likely what services she did provide were elementary at best.

My follow-up question to her was, "What is your niche? What type of business would benefit from using your services?" Her eyes began to sparkle and a smile came across her face as she proceeded to tell me, "Everybody!" All I could do was shake my head.

If you are not clear on what you provide how can you possibly determine who your niche market is? Besides that, if you have to constantly learn new skills, how can you ever hope to gain the talent and experience necessary to enjoy entrepreneurial success? I suggest you stick with what you are good at and have experience doing rather than trying to be a jack-of-all-trades. Instead of taking the time to learn a new skill you might consider being a source of referral. ***Time spent learning is time taken away from earning*** and that's where the problem lays for many a new business owner.

There are several techniques you can utilize to help you determine your niche. One that I personally believe in is to sit down with pen in hand and write out a list of benefits that you provide. Keep in mind that ***a benefit is not the same thing as a feature***. A benefit is something that your customer is looking for while a feature is what the product provides. If you find yourself having a hard time coming up with this list you might enlist the aid of a few friends or family members to give their opinion on the subject.

Now make a list of types of people who would most likely utilize your product or service. Look for information in trade magazines, talk to people you think will buy and ask friends, relatives and business acquaintances who they think would be interested in the product or service. You might end up with several or just one or two. If you find that your target market is too wide, more than four or five, start out focusing on the first one or two and once you have made a name for yourself in that sphere of influence you can expand out by changing your marketing materials so they will resonate with your next group. ***Never use the same marketing materials for a different target audience*** as I explained above.

Remember, if you don't have the skills, refer out. Chances are that the person you are referring business to will take note and reciprocate in kind. This is what makes for a win-win-win relationship for all three of the parties involved. In this way you will slowly but successfully grow your business and your referral network.

WHAT KIND OF TREE DID YOU PLANT?

This morning, as I was walking around the lake near my home, during my daily exercise time, I began to notice the trees. There were tall, stately oaks and scrawny palms. Some of the trees had dual trucks as if two had been planted in the same hole. The palms are what caught my eye.

What I saw got me to thinking about how we grow our businesses. All of these trees are rooted in the very same mixture of dirt and sand. Yet not only are there palm trees that grow from a tall, skinny trunk with thin branches, there are also those that spread into branches at the base. Then another type of palm grows a solid base and then branches out thick and full.

Just like those palms, we all have the same opportunity to grow our businesses. How we plan determines the eventual growth and success we obtain. Some business owners go it alone with no forethought or planning. These are most like the quick growing, tall, thin, sable palm producing only minimal growth at the top. These business owners continue to do all their business themselves, never even hiring an assistant or Virtual Assistant to alleviate some of the mundane tasks.

Then there are the palms that grow immediately into multiple leaves at their base. These business owners I liken to the saw palmetto with its medium growth rate, they are the most common of all palms. These owners take the time to think through their business plan and then invest just enough resources to develop a good economic and product base. Each year they repeat their successful actions, but fail to diversify. Therefore, they function on a viable, but stagnant base.

Those palms, which were planted so near to each other as to share a common trunk, are like the business owner who partners with another. While they share the workload, they too often grow in opposite directions. Often they even end up parting ways.

Finally, we have the beautiful, pineapple palm. With slow, steady growth each year, it gets fuller and stronger. It has a huge, solid healthy base with lush branches, which spread out from that support. With the passage of time, this palm begins to grow a beautiful fruit shape. Like this palm are those who create a sound business plan, learn about their business, and get the necessary financial backing in place before planting the seeds of their business.

This solid planning results in a business that seems to grow itself. Unlike the single—I have to do it all myself or it won't get done properly—business owner, they are not afraid of their competition. Not only are they not afraid, but they find ways to work together.

While developing their business they realize that in order to succeed they must be willing to work with others. They hire those that will enhance their already healthy business. This helps them to free up their time so that they can continue to expand their business. As they diversify and form joint ventures with others who have a slightly different skill set, they experience a completely new level of success and can offer additional services to their customers and clients.

Because they took the time to develop a solid business plan and their continued commitment, the fruit of their labor is realized. However, it is because of their willingness to let go and to diversify that they flourish.

So, think about where you want your business to take you and the success you wish to achieve. When the timing is right and your business has grown as much as you can take it on your own, consider how you can reach out, and with the assistance of others, accomplish phenomenal growth.

YOUR GREATEST ENEMY

What would you say if I told you that I know the key to happiness? Would you chuckle to yourself and look the other way? Or would you be intrigued enough to consider what I have to say? If you are of the latter mindset I welcome you to follow along on a journey that may surprise you where it ends.

For many of us we consider time to be our worst enemy. Millions, nay, BILLIONS are spent on avoiding and restoring the toll that time takes on our bodies. Just look at the numerous industries that have sprung up to this end. First we have cosmetics, and cosmetic surgery, followed up with diet and stomach stapling, then what about exercise and personal trainers. If that isn't quite enough, we can look to the time robber restoring industries. To that end we are provided with time management journals, training, coaching, clocks, alarms, secretaries, and Virtual Assistants who help keep us on time and focused to name just a few. If you think that time is your greatest enemy read on. That could be just the tip of the proverbial iceberg.

Now we have education, knowledge, and credibility. These three are really just one. Do you lack the proper experience or training to give you the competitive edge? If so perhaps you should consider enhancing your education by taking online coursework or even sitting in on your local college classes. This leads me to the question, "At what point do I become an expert in my field?" The simple answer is when YOU decide you are! But even this is not the greatest of all enemies.

OK, so if not these what about funding. Could that be the big bad wolf? Not having sufficient funds to properly build or market your business is definitely a problem for many small businesses. However, proper planning and a sound business plan can make a difference here. With these tools you may even be able to establish a small business loan to jump start your business. Besides these possibilities there are many resources available to the small business owner through government grants and such. So, obviously financial burdens are a big sore spot for many of us, but they still are not the worst of the worst.

Lest I get carried away, there are numerous pebbles in the road to business success but the greatest enemy of all is YOU! Yes, *you are your worst enemy*. When you fail to employ all the resources at your disposal or to properly plan you stand in the way of your own success. As an example, the lack of utilizing the simple act of follow-up is not the root of your problem it is merely the result of the fear in you that is holding you back.

When you set your fears aside, no matter what they may be, and take a step outside of your comfort zone you will gain far more than if you allow your fear to overcome your desire to win. If your fear stems from the inability to properly communicate your thoughts you should seek a counselor who can help you to see where and how to correct your communication lacks. One such book I found extremely helpful was JoJo Tabares' book on just this subject, *Say What You Mean When You Are In Business*.[8] This is one I highly recommend. Whereas if your fear stems from public speaking, my own book on this subject, *Presentational Skills for the Next Generation* might be the ticket.

Most likely the fear that separates you from success is in itself keeping you from taking action. So the action itself is not the problem, rather, it is YOUR lack of action that is the problem. What about inflexibility? Again, this boils down to YOU! Are you beginning to see the root of the problem? Once you recognize wherein your enemy resides you can begin to develop ways to overcome the thing that is keeping YOU from becoming the best that you can be. Take a moment or two to contemplate just where your strengths and weaknesses lay and seek out the assistance or the information to help you overcome the fears that lie in wait to prevent you from reaching your desired potential. Procrastination won't get you there. Do it right now and you will forever be thankful that you did!

---

8   http://artofeloquence.com/

REFLECT, EVALUATE, AND GROW

There comes a time in every business when you need to reflect back on where you came from and where you have in mind to go. We all experience lulls in our business. Some businesses may be geared to seasonal spurts, while others enjoy a steady stream of income. No matter which type of business you own, evaluating the different parts of the whole, separately, can be of profound benefit.

With marketing, the key to success is found in reflection and evaluation. However, when was the last time you evaluated your products or services? Are they all making you money or could you update or eliminate some to make room for new?

As an example, I offer MaryKay products to a few select friends so that I can buy them wholesale. One thing I can tell you for certain is that MaryKay's products are always being updated and improved. Perhaps it may be their packaging only, but at every turn, their makeup is being tried, tested, reviewed, evaluated, and updated. This has been one of their key tools to success.

In my graphics and publishing businesses, my products are always changing. Each client deserves unique and custom designs and books. As I learn new techniques and gain experience my products improve and change. However, sometimes evaluating the need to offer a particular style or to learn a new technique must be carefully contemplated. You must prudently consider whether your clients or customers would benefit from an update of your product line. If so, take the initiative and learn a new skill or technique or try out a new product. But when you don't have the time or talent, seek joint venture partners who have both the talent and skill to provide these new techniques.

Reflect on how much fun you will have when you have something new to offer. Besides that, think about what a great opportunity it will be to promote your business, in a new and unique light, your new product or skill will present.

ARE YOU FOLLOWING YOUR COMPETITION OVER THE CLIFF?

I often hear business owners say, so and so is doing it, so I need to do it too. Or, "This is how we always have done it." These words make me cringe. As a business owner and designer, I relish in my ability to come up with workable solutions that bring out a business owner's uniqueness in all their design and marketing materials.

Whether you need business stationary, or a website built, keep in mind that what sets you apart from your competition is what will spur you on to success. (Yes, your business stationary is a marketing tool.)

Just because your competition is using one form or look, doesn't mean you have to use it too. If, in their marketing, they are hosting Podcasts, or using TV ads it doesn't necessarily mean you have to use these mediums.

Discover Your Uniqueness, then Let the World Know What It Is.

Perhaps your business marketing model includes Google Ad Words, then again, maybe it doesn't. The same applies to print materials, a website's design type, giveaways, social media and every other form of marketing mediums.

So as it is with every aspect of your business, look at what your Unique Selling Perspective (USP) is and use that information to your advantage. Use your talents and experience to come up with a new and better way of doing things. Have the competition following YOUR example, not the other way around. Don't be afraid to try something new.

This statement by Chuck Green of DesignLikes puts it all in perspective. "Follow the leader marketing and mirror-the-competition tactics ignore that all-important fact. The best marketing approach (we all know) is one that is invented for one specific organization and its unique circumstances. Ideally, it even includes some elements that competitors are not using at all."

Think about Pepsi and Coke. They have similar products, yet their marketing and even their logos are unique. While one company's marketing is youth oriented (The Pepsi Generation) the other focuses on taste, (the Real Thing). So too, you must find your USP and use the tools at your disposal that will best share that information with your customers.

TO BE OR NOT TO BE A "REAL" BUSINESS

That is definitely the question. Have you been 'playing' with your business? Is it viable and alive or are you still struggling after months or even years? Do you desire to finally, once-and-for-all, to see your business grow? Then this article is for you. As you read on you will discover what is holding you back, and hopefully how to move forward.

The foremost thing to do is to **change your mind set**. Right now, this very moment, decide to succeed! Until you do so you will be stuck in the quagmire of neglect and self-doubt. Having a positive direction and commitment can be life changing. When you 'try' to do something you are already setting yourself up for failure. So, make a promise, not just to you; put it on paper and hang it up in a prominent place, somewhere you will see it often throughout the day. Tell your spouse, sister, brother, business partner, or anyone else who will hold you accountable. Buddy systems are great for helping to keep you on track. Now that you have the decision made and are firmly committed to your business's success let's look at some fundamentals of entrepreneurship.

The key to any successful business is to **run it like a business**. *Set your hours and stick to them.* You'll get a lot more done and come quitting time your family and friends will be there to refresh and revive you for the next work day.

Some of us have such a strong work ethic that we forget to stop and refresh and renew for the journey ahead. While a strict work ethic is imperative you'll be no good to anyone if you allow yourself to become overly exhausted.

Another concept that must be completely ingrained into your being is that **it is perfectly permissible to satisfy your clients and customers and make money at the same time!** By learning how to be a better, more responsible business owner you can accomplish this and more.

While pursuing the daily tasks we often get immersed in providing our services and talents to our clients and customers. *We have trouble making the shift from employee, provider, to business manager.* If you never ask for fair compensation you will never get it. Your customer expects to pay, but will naturally accept *over-service*. Don't make this critical mistake or you will find yourself discontent and overworked and your clients will come to expect what you regard as extras service as the norm.

This brings us to another valuable lesson. When the time is right *don't be afraid to increase your rates.* Given time and experience, knowledge and training, your skills should be increasing. So too should your rates. Go ahead. Take a deep breath and moving forward; ask for what your services are worth. I can assure you that if your customers value your service they will be happy to grow with you. Yes, you may lose one or two along the way but inevitably they probably would have moved on anyway.

In every growing business venture there comes a time to hire help. When you do so there are some tried and true ways to successfully make this change. The first rule is to *keep your total payroll at or below 50% of your revenues*. For example, a business with net income of $150,000 should not allow their payroll to exceed $75,000. Anything over that you should consider as coming right out of your own pocket; because it is!

Therefore, another rule in this regard is to not automatically hire new employees when you generate more business. This mistake is one that even major corporations fall victim to. When you are sure that your income is stably increased, and not just enjoying a temporary influx, then it is time to do the hiring, and not a moment sooner.

One last thought in this direction is to *know your choices*. Will you form a partnership; hire an employee; or a sub-contractor. Each has its merits. While a partner will be willing to share expenses as well as profits you may decide that an employee is a better choice for you and your company.

Here in the US, when you hire an employee you are required to provide wage, tax forms and accounting. This can be expensive and requires a bank account set-up just to hold the 'withholding' until your quarterly payment comes due to Uncle Sam. If you aren't up to keeping sufficient records I highly suggest you hire an accountant before you hire your first employee.

The other option is to hire sub-contractors. Through the years and many businesses this has been my method of choice. While the negative is that they may come and go as they like, they also know that to make money they need to work when and where the work exists. Therefore, this has always been a non-issue for my businesses. Even when I employed doctors and nurses in my multimillion dollar surgical clinic it was never an issue. When it was time to do surgery, everybody showed up and stayed until the work was done.

The other key benefit of hiring sub-contractors is that they and not you are responsible for all taxes and record keeping. Not to speak of benefits you don't have to pay. This has been a real advantage to business owners for many years. And did I mention your relief from medical insurance and retirement plan sharing requirements for their employee counterpart.

So the takeaway here is, keep your pretax profits under control regardless of the size of your business. Follow the 50-25-25 rule. 50% of gross net to payroll, 25% overhead, and 25% profit. If you hold to these benchmark parameters, you will be assured that you are providing adequate and appropriate levels of service to your clients, keeping your payroll within a sustainable range, and pocketing a good and fair return.

WHO ARE YOU BEING INFLUENCED BY?

"You are the average of the five people you hang around most." –**Jim Rohn**

This quote got me to genuinely consider, who am I hanging around that I should be avoiding? Am I spending time with naysayers; people that are constantly discrediting my business? Or are my closest companions forward thinking people that are adding to my knowledge base? Do my friends share the joy with me in action by recommending me and my products or services to their trusted companions?

How quickly would my business expand if I made a promise to make this one little change? Would I start to genuinely think and therefore act in a more positive light? I believe the response to all of these questions is a resounding YES!

Who are you hanging around that you might require to rethink your association with?

Relatives—ok so you may not be able to choose your relatives but you can limit your interaction with them if need be, except of course for your immediate family.

Best friend—if your best and closest friend is not your ally you may have to find another more in tuned with your positive direction. Don't burn your bridge, you never know if and when they will seek a change for the positive.

Friends—close friends at work and play have a huge impact on your thinking. Find like-minded individuals to hang around with.

Business Associates—your up-line and down-line and even the partners you choose can significantly affect your attitude and business growth. A positive association will provide a solid support system and direction. When they share creative ideas for developing your business do you listen and take action or do you merely let the

> **Ideas and direction are only as good as the decisive actions that you take to implement them.**

relevant information go in one ear and out the other? Why not take heed to just one suggestion and see if it is an effective tool?

Look for people who have a positive direction in their own lives. Those that are seeing prosperity and are where you fervently hope to be may be just the ticket to your success. Find someone willing to mentor you or just accept you in their circle of influence; the energy that they emit may rub off on you. Keep moving in a positive direction with positive influences propelling you to implement the necessary action to ultimately succeed and you will achieve your pinnacle of success.

LIFE ON THE EDGE

Are you on the edge of success or in the middle of mediocrity? What is it that is holding you back? Is it time? There is no better time than now. Is it talent? Just do it! Is it lack of education about your product of service? Find a mentor or get a good book on the subject at hand. There is always a way to get around a problem if you really want to.

Take a look in your success mirror. What have you been doing that if you made a little effort to enhance could catapult your business over the edge of mediocrity into the very real realm of success?

Sometimes we look at others and demean ourselves instead of realizing that out there to some we are the expert. There is always someone who could benefit from a close business relationship with you and your business. Find that person that fills a gap where you have a disadvantage. You might mentor each other or even better form a partnership.

Come on, take a step over the edge of mediocrity and join those of us who choose to take charge of our life and business. Take responsibility for your success and take the action that will break the hold mediocrity has on you today.

FROWN YOUR WAY
TO SUCCESS!

H a! I knew that would get your attention! Now that I have it I want to encourage you to adopt this thought as your very own. Why? Simply put, unless you are uncomfortable with your circumstances you will never take the initiatives to make a change.

Take a moment to reflect on the reason you began your business. Most likely you did your due diligence and found the perfect match for your needs and goals. Your choice also needed to be based on a line of products or services that reflected who you are and what you believe in.

As time went by you may have lost your passion. You may have let the naysayers that came across your path deter you from your goal. Are you happy with where you are and what you are doing? If this is not the case go back to the "box" and take a peek inside once again. Talk to your support group. Attend your group meetings. Do whatever it takes to get back your enthusiasm.

Become totally disgusted with where you are in your business or life; disgusted enough to change. Whatever is keeping you from sharing with the joy of first love, look it square in the eye and let it know that it has no control of you any longer.

Change is uncomfortable but growth never comes without it.

Consider the acorn. It must first die to spring to life and then it must be nurtured to eventually become the grand oak that is contained in that tiny seed.

DO IT NOW

We all procrastinate at times, me included. While only 20% of us are chronic procrastinators, we all have temporarily avoided doing something that we knew we needed to do.

Before you know it that deadline creeps up on you, and zap, you go into frenzy mode. The outcome can be quite ugly, given that you don't have time to really think things through. E.g., Writers have deadlines and if they don't get the article written in time to get through the editorial process it gets published errors and all—or not at all.

We aren't born procrastinators; we learn this bad habit from our parents and social circles. For example, if a child has a controlling parent it may be that they will rebel by choosing to put off rather than do.

Why is it so easy to choose self-sabotage over self-regulation? Let's reflect on why we procrastinate. Just what causes us to put things off that we know we need to get done?

1. **Arousal Type**—I work better under pressure. Have you ever heard yourself or someone else say, "I work better under pressure"? That is a sure sign that they are a procrastinator. My husband uses this excuse all the time. Do you?

2. **Avoidance Type**—This isn't important. Convincing yourself that what you should get done is less important only aggravates the problem.

3. **Decisional Type**—Distractions. Looking for other things to do instead of tackling the issue is a common response. Things quickly done take the limelight, in this scenario. E.g., cleaning out your inbox, getting a snack, etc.

"Telling someone who procrastinates to buy a weekly planner is like telling someone with chronic depression to just cheer up," insists Joseph Ferrari, Ph.D., associate professor of psychology at De Paul University.

Realizing what type of procrastinator you are will better help you understand how to cope with this bad habit. You can indeed change your behavior, but it may take more than sheer will power. If you can't overcome this maladaptive habit, seek help from a cognitive behavioral therapist or life coach.

When you put things off you lose more than productivity, you actually harm yourself—mentally and physically. It takes just as much energy to avoid a task as it does to do it. Procrastination saps power; completion gives relief.

Don't rebel against doing, no debate, no delay. Do it now!

THE INTERNET RUT

Why would you take the time and expend the energy to get out of your comfy computer chair to reach the few when the whole world is at their fingertips? The answer is simple, when you attend seminars and conferences they open their door to opportunity to build lasting friendships and learn from others in a much more personal way.

Think about what I just said and you will soon agree. No matter how well you connect to someone online, and I know great friendships can start there, after all, that is where I met my husband, you still should consider meeting in person when you can. The same holds true with all our connections. When you take time to meet someone in person, you have an opportunity to know him or her in a real way. Seeing them in the flesh allows you to really see them, read the nuances in their body and voice, and look into their eyes.

The other benefit is also just as easy to accept. In one hall are gathered a host of like-minded entrepreneurs who are willing to learn and share openly with each other! While there, you have the opportunity to learn the latest marketing strategies that you can easily implement upon return to your home. The good news is that the strategies being shared are not untested! They worked before, and they can work again for you. Marketing events are truly a GOLDMINE for your income if you're serious about making a lot of money.

Whether you prefer the smaller group setting or the larger more comprehensive seminar, take the time to attend offline event opportunities, and you will begin to see your business grow in ways you never thought possible

DARE TO BE DIFFERENT

Leaders don't always fit the mold. As business owners we need to be aware that we are already different than 90 percent of the population. We are motivated and hard working as well as goal oriented. We aren't satisfied to accept what we are given as employees. Our ability to face the challenges of entrepreneurship head on and stay focused on our goals sets us apart from the norm.

However, to reach the top in your chosen field, you must break out of your complacency and blaze the uncharted trail. Think "outside the box." Find new, or better, ways of providing your products or services.

If you take a minute to think about those who have achieved stupendous success, you have to admit that they were definitely not the normal entrepreneur. Henry Ford, Bill Gates, Donald Trump, Mary Kay, and Doctor Ruth just to name a few, all found a new way of doing, living, or designing that was different than anything that had come before.

Now, I am not saying you have to be cut-throat to achieve unique success, just highly motivated and unique. You can make 'nice' work for you too. The current economy requires you to find new and unique ways of doing business. Learning to balance kindness with assertiveness could be the key to moving your business in a positive direction. After all, there is a reason someone came up with the idiom, "You can catch more flies with honey than with vinegar."

I am reminded of a business owner I once met online who was in a similar business to mine. He was rude, obnoxious and just plain unpleasant to interact with. He had a 'know-it-all' attitude. Frankly, in the field of design, you can never know it all. This business, like many others, is constantly evolving and you must be willing to learn new techniques or you'll be left behind.

So, how can you find this balance between nice and aggressive? You must realize the 'nice' means being respectful, authentic, and understanding of others. However, don't forget there is a time and place for assertiveness, when used in an appropriate fashion.

Being nice, rather than cut-throat, will gain you a reputation of trustworthiness. What is that saying we hear over-and-over again? "People do business with people they know, like and trust." You need to learn how to have candid conversations with others. Be honest, but not blatant. Your purpose is not to hurt the other person's feelings. *Note: If you don't know how to communicate effectively, I highly recommend you seek professional help.*

Whether you like it or not, the business world is highly competitive in nature. Knowing how to communicate your ideas and opinions in a way that they are accepted, rather than putting the other person on the defense, will gain you a reputation of trust and respect.

Thus, you can easily see the value of learning how to blend the positive attributes of nice with the candid communication techniques that will effectively resolve your potential customers and client's challenges. Don't approach them in a manner of holier-than-thou or with a know-it-all attitude. Rather, take them by the proverbial hand and show or explain, in a candid but caring manner, how your business will benefit them. Remember always, that your customer is looking for what your product or service can do for them, not what your product or service does.

In *Nice Guys Can Get the Corner Office* by Russ Edelman is a list of eight strategies for getting ahead without being a jerk, which I would like to quote here.

1. **Self-awareness**—learn about yourself. Know your strength and weaknesses.
2. **Speak-up**—learn to express your opinions and be heard. ₁
3. **Set boundaries**—learn to set clear, strong and appropriate parameters.
4. **Confront**—learn to confront issues directly and without fear.
5. **Choose**—learn to make choices without guilt.
6. **Expect results**—learn to hold others and yourself accountable.
7. **Be bold**—learn to take chances.
8. **Win**—learn how to finish first- respectfully and fairly.

All of these strategies for getting ahead in the workplace are sage advice for the business owner who wants to make 'nice' work for them.

One last piece of advice I can give you is to always look for new ways to add value to your business. Be innovative, creative, and a good communicator. Remember, your business is a reflection of you. Make it one that others want to praise. There is no better way to grow your business than referrals. So, don't be afraid to ask for them.

HOW TO KEEP YOUR BUSINESS ON TRACK DURING 'SUMMER VACATION'

Helpful hints from moms who've been there

How DO you keep your business on track during summer vacation? As if it isn't hard enough to keep your focus on a growing home business when the kiddos are in school most of the day; now we have to entertain them ourselves for the next several months. I can just imagine what it is like with preschoolers! Each age group acts and reacts differently and their demands on your time will vary.

For the *work at home parent* (WAHP) life is always a mixed blessing. When our children are infants and toddlers remaining focused on our daily business building activities is a rocky road, to put it mildly. At this age children demand our constant care and attention. How do you keep your business on solid ground during these demanding developmental years? The ways may vary but the means seems to be the same for all age groups. One young mother, Wendy Cooper of Freelance VA, tells of sitting her two-year old son Kaius on the kitchen floor with a bowl of flour and a spoon. "Makes for easy clean up," she states.

To find out what WAHMs find the most helpful I recently polled a group of online business owners and WAHPs and the top three suggestions were:

1. Try to take it easy and not stress out over your own expectations
2. Include your children in your business activities
3. Scheduling playtime both with mom & friends

In a recent article by Aimee Kraus in Pink™ Magazine Aimee suggest that if your child is overly adventurous you might sign them up for a specialized program in lieu of the stoic summer camp. For older children you might enroll them in a SAT prep class.

Audrey Okaneko, a successful online WAHM since 1983, mother of two, and currently with Leaving Prints states, "I was beyond fortunate, in that my husband (now ex-husband) truly supported me and my business. When he got home at 5 pm, he always took over so I could work.

"Over the summer, with kids over 5, I had them in various camps. I had to have daytime hours I could make calls, make home visits, etc. We had science camps, Girl Scout camps, park and recreation camps, zoo camp, etc. When the kids were preschool age, their preschool had a summer camp program.

"If I got up at 5 am and began making calls to the east coast and the kids didn't get up until 8 am that gave me 2 1/2 hours of working time. Then if they were in camp for 3 hours, I had another 2 1/2 hours of working time. It's only 1 pm and I've already put in 5 hours. If their dad took over at 5 pm and I worked until 9 pm, I could put in a 9 hour day, with a toddler.

"I never did paperwork while the kids were gone. When they were gone I was on the phone and talking to others. I took full advantage of them not being home.

"Most camps were out by 1 pm and so we would hang out until 5 pm, go swimming, go to the park, take a walk etc.

"My beliefs might be different from other 'business owners'. I do not believe you can run a business with young children under foot 24/7, nor do I believe you can run a business while the kids nap.

"As a consumer, I don't want to only be able to reach you from 1 pm to 2 pm, nor do I want to hear screaming kids when you and I talk. When folks would learn I had a two-year-old, they were amazed. They NEVER heard her in the background."

Remember, you need to take your business seriously if you intend to be successful. I know you may think it is cute to allow your children to answer the phone or to include your child's photo in your business image, but these activities may do more harm than good!

So, now that summer is here don't let your business and yourself down. The facts confirm that you CAN keep your business on track even with the kids under toe if you simply find a way to keep them occupied while you work.

Marketing

HOW TO GET NOTICED WITHOUT BREAKING THE BANK

With the economic condition getting tighter and tighter as time passes business owners from all genres need to tighten their proverbial belt. Nevertheless, marketing is not one of the areas that should suffer. Cutting back on your marketing will ensure an untimely demise for your business. However, there are ways to promote your business without breaking the bank. In my thirty plus years as an entrepreneur I have been though times of boom and bust. It is through this experience that I have come to realize that throwing money at a problem only is not the most profitable means of business promotion.

I have listed below several ways that you too can promote your business, products and services without incurring great expense. I hope you too will find these suggestions useful.

Reward Loyal Customers

One of the best ways to market your business is to let your loyal customers know how important they are to you. Something as simple as a quick note—not an email—or as complex as a gift sent in a timely manner will do two positive things for your business. First, it brings your name back to the forefront of their thoughts, and second, it solidifies their loyalty. Yes, an email may suffice, but a card in their hands will have a greater impact. In your card you could offer them an incentive, or not. The choice is up to you.

When considering what type of thank you gift to send, whether it is a discounted event ticket to one of your events or a physical product, think like your customer. What would they be more apt to remember you for sending them? What would they find useful? Sometimes a branded pen or other item is exactly what is called for. While for the very best customers you might consider a box of yummy chocolates. If your gift is from a fellow small business owner or joint venture partner, so much the better. Which brings us to the next suggestion; joint ventures.

Joint Ventures with Cross-over Business Partners

Joint ventures (JV) are one of the most overlooked marketing ideas in the small to medium-sized business owner's marketing arsenal. Why this is the case is simple, they are often thought of as competition. However, you might be surprised to learn that even similar businesses often don't offer some of the services or products that you do. Therefore, consider not only cross-over businesses but similar ones as well when looking into the possibilities of participating in JV opportunities.

As an example, often I JV with writing coaches, marketing firms, video production specialists, and editors. While I offer publishing and design services, over the years I have discovered my dislike for editing. I spent many years search for qualified editors. Then, one day about two years ago, I was approached by an editor and not too long after that we formed an alliance. She now refers me to her writers, and when I have the opportunity I reciprocate.

Offer Referral Incentives

One easy way to take advantage of the aforementioned JV experience is to offer referral incentives. For many years now I have offered a bonus referral of 10 percent off first invoice. This has been both beneficial for the referring person and me. Giving back, in a real and tangible fashion is an excellent way to genuinely show my thankfulness for referrals and often generates additional referrals. In the last couple of years, I have noticed a marked increase in business; do in great part to referrals.

Put Your Business Card on Bulletin Boards

Have you been out and about and seen a bulletin board in a business, college, or library with business cards tacked on it? Have you ever taken one down to use? I have personally done both. Even the restaurants in my local area have tabletop business card promotions that I have asked the waiter for a card or two more than once. These are excellent free and inexpensive ways to market your business. Don't let this opportunity pass you by. Put your card or flyer up and check back often so you can replace it when you see it is missing.

Become a Joiner

Online and offline alike, there are many groups and organizations that the business owner has at their disposal. No matter what your business or interests are you will find a plethora of choices. When you get an email that mentions one of your 'keywords' do you sit up and take notice? As you read the email do you decide that it isn't worth your time? We all have to pick and choose wisely, but when you join groups that include your target information or audience you might be pleasantly surprised by the content and opportunities that arise.

Participate

Just joining is not enough. Once you join, if you don't participate you'll have wasted your time and money. Get involved, offer to help in any way you can and you will soon find the members more inclined to include you in their circle of friends. Think about the clubs and organizations in which you currently participate. If you aren't making headway, is it due to a lack of participation, or is it just not working? Clean house, chose again, and participate.

Provide Quality Content

Good content is paramount to good marketing. Misspellings in your marketing pieces, no matter where they are found, only make you look sloppy and unprofessional. After all, who would hire you if they see the lack of care in your own information products and ads? Yet, typos and grammar errors are not the only things that can count against you. Stale or overused content too can create a sense that you aren't providing your reader with the information they seek. Yes, do your research, quote sources, but keep the content relevant and fresh.

Write Articles

Article writing is an excellent way to promote your business, products, and services. Not only is this cost-effective but your contact information will always be included. However, you aren't getting the full benefit of article writing if you are only submitting them to online article houses. Your local newspaper or magazine is always searching for good content. Why not consider submitting articles to them? First, find out who the contact person is for the section of the newspaper or magazine you want to provide articles for and then jot them a quick note, or better yet, call them to find out their production schedule and required format. Then as mentioned before, provide well written, production ready articles on a timely basis.

Get Active Online

Facebook and Twitter, Google+ and Pinterest, Four Square and LinkedIn, just to name a few, social media has taken hold. If you aren't participating you are missing the mark. Each time you comment or post you have the chance to go 'viral'. But, if you don't participate, you never will! Yes, these things take time. Schedule an hour a day to post on the forums and social media; that would be a good start. If you truly don't have time to get involved it is well worth your marketing dollars to hire a virtual assistant that specializes in social media to do it for you. You can even use tools that are available to automate your posts. Seek and ye shall find!

Update Your Blog

Speaking of activity, it is imperative that you keep your blog fresh. If you can't come up with content yourself why not invite others to supply content for you. Hosting an author or business owner interview or blog tour are just a couple of ways to bring new visitors and keep your blog fresh. And, whatever you do, make sure your content is free of grammatical and spelling errors. Before you publish, read and rewrite your content. It isn't going to do you any good if your content is not relevant or of high quality.

Comment on Blogs

Here again is another oft overlooked marketing method. When you comment on another person's blog you usually have the opportunity to include your website link. These unreciprocated links are seen as some of the best SEO (Search Engine Marketing) boosters. Not only will you enjoy this benefit, but you will be opening your business to a whole different set of eyes. So, go now and search for blogs where your comments will be welcome and useful. Then, comment yourself into a new community of readers who just might become your best fans.

Google and Visit Online Marketing Sites

Good Marketing Ideas and Small Business Association are just two of the terrific websites offering business owners marketing and business advice. With a simple Google search you will discover that there are a whole host of websites that can help in this regard. Spend some time reading their content and take advantage of their advice. You'll find it well worth the time taken.

Spruce up your Website

When you look at your web presence does it make you smile? Is it well designed and easy to navigate? If you can't see beyond your current website or think it can't be improved, ask your customers. Their feedback may clue you into changes that you may not be aware of that need to be made. Sometimes, just updating or adding another page is all you need to do. At other times, you may want to give your site a complete makeover. Just like getting a new dress, a website makeover takes time and consideration, but once the choice is made the thrill can be invigorating. Besides which, it gives you the reason to have a press release written and distributed, which is your bonus marketing suggestion.

Never Give Up

If you are in need of additional ideas to either implement or just to spark your imagination, I highly recommend you pick up a copy of the award-winning, annual, *Weird & Wacky Holiday Marketing Guide* (http://www.HolidayMarketingGuide.com). In it you will find a whole year's worth of marketing opportunities and even the tools and tips to implement them. Remember, winning new and potential customer's business is an ongoing battle. It takes time and effort, but in the end you will reach your goal. Figure out what works for you and repeat the process.

YOUR BUSINESS' BEST KEPT SECRET WEAPON

We all know that in any given group ten percent are the active members who keep things together. But, what does this mean to a business owner? It equates to your bottom line being sustained by ten percent of your client base. Sure, you generate income from all your customers or they wouldn't be your customers. However, repeat purchases are made by a select few.

We have also heard that retaining a customer is more profitable than acquiring one because a loyal customer is easier to market to and less costly. *On an average a business owner will spend six to seven times as much to gain a new customer than to reinvigorate a current one.*

What these statistics say to me is that staying in constant contact with your existing client base is a 'must-do' for any savvy business owner. The easiest, and most cost effective, way to do that is to use an auto responder. An auto responder is your business' best kept secret arsenal.

For those of you who are unfamiliar with auto responders let me explain briefly what they are and how they work. An auto responder is a means of setting up notices to be delivered on a set schedule to your mailing list. This may be in response to an event, such as purchasing a product core service from you or even just signing up for your company newsletter. You do have one of those, right? If not, I highly recommend you start one.

There are numerous providers of auto responder software. However, I won't get into those in this article. Check into the available sources and choose the one that is right for you and your business.

As you can see this is an excellent marketing tool. With them you can send out sales letters, confirm receipt of a customer's email or order, and even follow-up with past customers. Then there are always customer surveys to consider.

The best part is you "set-it-and-forget-it!" This allows you to stay in communication with your client base while leaving you free to grow your business, rather than running it.

> **A business owner typically will spend six to seven times as much to gain a new customer than to reinvigorate a current one.**

Here are some quick ideas on how you can use your auto responder to stay in touch with your clients.

1. Confirm a subscription or purchase
2. Send a thank you note
3. Offer an incentive to 'come back'
4. Send out a discount voucher
5. Remind them of an upcoming event or sale
6. Send a short survey
7. Ask for feedback on a product or service
8. Offer a helpful tip on product usage
9. Send tracking information on products they have ordered
10. Set-up a FAQ email and give them a way to contact you if they have a question that has not been addressed in your FAQ

I could go on and on but by now I am sure you can see just how beneficial an auto responder can be to the livelihood of your thriving business. Once you begin using your auto responder you will be amazed how easy it is generate additional income, just by sending follow-up promotions.

SAGE HOLIDAY PLANNING ADVICE FROM A WISE OLD OWL

Holiday marketing ideas for a successful and stress-free season

The holidays will soon be upon us. How they will impact your business and your life will be directly related to the actions you take today.

You might be saying to yourself that the holidays are a long way off. You may even believe it is simply way too early to begin your holiday marketing planning. On the contrary, after thirty years as a successful business owner I have found that planning and putting your marketing strategies in place prior to the frenzy is sound business building advice. A secondary benefit rests solidly in the benefit that your holidays will be much less stressful. When you don't need to focus every moment on your business you will happily discover the freedom to spend quality time with your friends and family.

So what can you do towards this goal so early in the season? Simply map out your holiday marketing plan and develop it now. This way when it comes time to launch all you have to do is implement it.

What are some ideas you should be considering? Whether you have a product driven business or offer a service you should begin now to align yourself and your business with other like-minded business owners. A strategic alliance can benefit you in more ways than one.

Some things that you could consider doing together are joint marketing campaigns. Things like writing testimonials, articles, or interviews about each other's business. These can be submitted to article marketing websites, press release sources, and your local media. It is much better to have these articles finished and ready to publish long before they are needed.

Another thing you might consider doing is setting up a referral program. Offer a percentage or specific dollar amount for every customer or sale they send your way. Depending on your business you should also consider what you could do that could give your business a holiday boost. For example, if you are a Virtual Assistant (VA) be prepared to offer "Santa Letters" or something similar. Not only will this increase your bottom line but it will significantly impact the lives of the children receiving your special letter.

So, what if you are not a VA? How about getting involved with a charity organization. Even a simple donation can be a blessing when delivered in the right spirit. These activities can easily be used as promotional tools for your business. Donating items as seemingly insignificant as pencils, with your business imprint on them, to the local school and writing and submitting a press release surrounding these activities can be a beneficial marketing tool for your business.

I am certain by now your marketing neurons are singing and dancing. Whatever you decide to do to market your business this holiday the best advice I can give is to pull it together now so that when it is time to launch you aren't scrambling around trying to pull the pieces together instead of enjoying quality time with your family and friends.

HOW TO ENSURE CUSTOMER LOYALTY

One of the most important things we can do to ensure customer loyalty is to treat them like the VIP they really are. Failure to do so can be extremely costly. Not only do you lose them, but also any referrals they might have otherwise provided.

As an example of what not to do I will relate a personal experience. This happened at a well know menswear store. After purchasing a sports jacket for my husband as a gift, we returned to discuss a possible exchange. The staff was friendly and helpful. The shopping experience itself was pleasant enough.

Although they did not have the correct size replacement jacket, after checking, they assured us that one was available. They politely asked for our contact information which we quickly provided after which they promised to contact us as soon as the item arrived.

I hesitate to tell you how long ago that was for fear you wouldn't believe me. However, that is the real issue here. It has now been over a year since this promise was made and we have yet to receive any further correspondence or contact in regards to this issue. I am sure you fully understand the impact this has had on our customer loyalty.

One of the first things they could have done is to send a note thanking us for our business and perhaps even a questionnaire. That would have at least acknowledged our visit. Then a week later when the jacket didn't come in they should have notified us that it was either indeed en route or unavailable. For our inconvenience in either case they might have offered us an additional discount or incentive.

The fact I want you to be aware of here is that although the in store shopping experience was pleasant enough the promise made and post-shopping service was where they lost our business. I hope you take note of how important it is to continue to communicate with your customers. Don't just fill an order and then forget them. Continue to send cards and perhaps emails or give them a phone call. Let them know you appreciate them. Don't just send discount notices. Yes, those are always good and should be used when appropriate, but a note thanking them for their business or just to say hi and ask their opinion will have a much greater impact. Besides which, we all love to share our opinions.

Be ever aware that your customer is who keeps you in business. Without them and their referrals you only have a store. Treat your customers like the VIP they are and you will never regret it. Try really hard not to screw-up. But when you do, make every effort to make things right. Go out of your way to let them know you care and are genuinely sorry. Try to see things from your customer's point of view.

Consider not only the error but the ramifications. You never know the inconvenience, or worse the heartache, you may have caused them. Use good judgment here. If it was something that was caused by you or your staff be quick to take full responsibility for it. However, if the customer is way off-base and nothing you say or do will help, let it and them go.

I used to work for someone like that and can honestly say I would see him smile when he "got over" and even when he didn't. He would get a sheepish grin when he got caught. But that never seemed to slow him down. So, know there are people you won't ever be able to make happy and let them go their separate way. Hold yourself to a higher standard and you will become a respected business professional.

My suggestion to you, don't lose your customers because you aren't aware of some reason they haven't shopped with you or used your service. Set-up trigger points that will make you aware when you haven't heard from them in such-and-such time or at regular intervals. Then use that knowledge to get back with them and find out why. A quality control survey or even just a simple phone call can help you accomplish that easily.

TELESEMINAR SECRETS

Teleseminars are fast becoming a viable tool for marketing our businesses offline. Many of us are finding that working our business online is good but adding the offline component adds that extra oomph that online alone fails to provide.

There are many ways to market your business offline such as print ads, attending seminars and direct mail. However, by far the least expensive way to market your business is through teleseminars. Not only do they allow you to grow your customer base, but you can also create resale products.

One simple idea to turn your teleseminar into a product is through transcripts. These are typed copies of your teleseminar that contain information that others want and need to know.

Another simple idea is to hold your teleseminar with just a small group of folks. Have them ask you questions about your business which are commonly asked of you. Questions that when you meet up with others and they ask you about what you do, you routinely have to answer. Then create a CD and hand it out like a business card or simply sell it!

Now that you have a couple of ideas, let's talk about the five mistakes most newbie teleseminar hosts make.

1. Not starting on time
2. No mute control
3. Failing to record the call
4. No call to action
5. Selling before adding value

Avoid these common mistakes and you will be ahead of the game.

Number one, not starting on time, can equate to lack of trust to your participants. Remember, their time is valuable too!

Number two, the problems are obvious. Know how to use your service before you host your call. If you are using it for the first time, go through their training, if they offer it, or do a test call.

You may not feel like a 'guru', but you are to someone.

Number three, failing to record the call, will cost you money in the long run. We have just briefly touched on a couple of examples on how you can profit from teleseminars. That is just the proverbial surface.

Number four, no call to action. Use every opportunity to clearly state what you want your listeners to take action on or they won't take any action. However, be careful about number five. . . .

Number five, selling before adding value. Always provide valuable content. Show your expertise. Remember, you may not feel like a 'guru', but you are to someone. Then after you have proven your credibility you will find your listeners, when given clear action steps, will take the desired action.

It's all about building relationships. So be natural. Speak like you are speaking with friends. Add a touch of enthusiasm and you will have more fun and so will your listeners.

ARE YOU A NURTURER

Gleanster Research estimates that 50% of leads who are qualified to buy are not ready to purchase immediately. Ask yourself these questions, "How long does it typically take a lead to become a customer after his or her first inquiry?" and "Does the sales cycle vary for different types of purchases?" The answers to these questions will assist you to determine how to interact with your potential customers.

You need to build an auto responder email campaign that will fully satisfy their need; not what you think they need, but rather what you know or have learned from experience or surveys. Once you have the answers, group your leads by categories. Some categories you might have could be new leads, inactive leads, and those who have purchased from you in the past (xx) months. On the other hand, maybe your lists include work-at-home-moms, life coaches, and people who love to travel. Taking the time to segment your lists will ensure the highest ROI (return on investment) for your time and money.

I have been told that the promptness of my replies has been the key to opening the door to work with several of my customers. They complain that other companies just aren't efficient enough for their liking. So, don't hesitate; get them into your auto responder campaign right away.

Typically, the best course of action is to begin by educating them. However, you could and should mix it up just a bit. Maybe start with an educational slant and throw in a promo or giveaway. Your freebee doesn't have to cost you anything. Why not consider putting together a tool that you found useful; a resource list and a keyboard shortcut sheet are two I have used in the past. Weekly activity sheets is one that I am working on now. If you want a copy just let me know, I'll be more than happy to share.

Never hit them with 'buy now' in your first email if you know that it typically takes a month or more before they take action. Remember, it's all about relationship building and your email campaign is the perfect tool to accomplish that task. Not only will you build rapport, your campaign will keep your business in their 'radar'. Even if they don't need your product or services, they are more apt to tell someone else they might know who does when the opportunity arises.

In the course of communicating with my clients, I have found that when I repeatedly offer the same discount sales dwindle. They see this as routine and disregard those messages. For example, how many of you have gotten your hands on the *Weird & Wacky Holiday Marketing Guide*? It is mentioned in every newsletter, but I can count on one hand how many of you have this annual edition. The lesson here is, make your offer for a limited time and make it enticing. Know what they want and give it to them.

This brings up another point, nurturing your leads is not relegated to email only. Newsletters, postcards, cards and what I call "bumpy mail" can also be used to communicate with your interested bystander. There are many tools available to you today to stay connected besides even these; consider social media, if you haven't already. A word to the wise, don't send mixed messages on your social media sites. If you want to share personal information on a business site, keep it to a bare minimum. Sharing that you are in Bermuda is okay, but what you ate while there, well less is more, if you get my drift.

By now, you probably see how important staying in touch with your prospects can be to the life of your business. Moreover, I hope you will take the time to get started, if you haven't already. Lastly, remember to evaluate your campaign and tweak it to keep it working. When you test and retest, tweak and polish your campaign by evaluating it as time goes by, you will find your efforts will pay off in the end.

A SIGN OF THE TIMES

Jeff Jarvis advises journalists to concentrate on producing content with high value added: "Do what you do best and link to the rest."

This is not just good advice for journalists, but for the small business owner it is imperative that we adopt this principle. If you want to grow a substantial business, stay in touch with your customers, and learn what they perceive as valuable.

Consider the web and how it influences, not only what you provide, but how you provide it. Look at the newspapers and books as firm examples. There was a time when people only sought and bought printed materials. Today things have changed. With the advent of the web people are getting their information and information products digitally. This is very cost-effective for the author as there are no more printing costs, making it the cheapest and quickest way to obtain the books and magazines, as well as news.

For the business owner this means two things. First, provide only that which you are spectacularly good at and either joint venture or give referral commission to those who recommend you to their friends. Put your money where their mouth is! Word of mouth is the best type of referral that there is, so why not give your customers and friends a reason to talk about you and your products or services.

The other thing we as business owners need to keep in mind is 'added value'. This is so important to the overall health of your growing business. When you listen to your customers, they will tell you what they find valuable or that they would like. Then fill that need. If you don't know where to start to find out just what those things are why not send out a survey. Sure only a handful of people will fill it out, but realize, that *for every one person who does, ten more feel the same way.*

Listen carefully: for every one person who complains, ten more may feel the same way.

This is one thing it took me many years to comprehend. If you have a customer who complains, listen carefully to what they say. They are speaking the words of many, not just themselves. Listen with an ear to what they are saying, not how to counter what they are saying. Then mull over their words carefully and you may just be able to turn them around and gain valuable information that you would not have obtained in any other way.

Once you give them their chance to talk, think it over, you will more than likely come up with a solution that will make them even more endeared to you than before. Then implement the changes necessary so that those who never spoke up and those who come after won't have those negative feelings either.

AFFILIATE MARKETING: WHAT'S THE BIG DEAL?

Most everyone is talking about affiliate marketing these days. But, not everyone is embracing this golden opportunity. I hear the questions pouring in now. Questions like, "Why do you say it is a "golden opportunity?" and "What is the big deal, anyway?"

Well, to begin with, affiliate marketers on both sides of this fence know that talking about a product or service, such as the superior service InMotion Hosting provides, is easy to do. Moreover, when you can make a profit from doing so … well, let's just say, "it's a no brainer!"

We as humans tend to shy away from tooting our own horn, but when it comes to our experiences, whether good or bad, the words seem to fall off our tongues like water over a cliff. We have no problem sharing raves about our favorite restaurant, our children's after-school program, and yes, even the last e-book we just finished reading. Imagine how great it would be to earn even a small bonus when someone takes action on your words of advice? Well, that's what affiliate marketing is all about and why I call it the "golden opportunity."

Now you may be thinking, why would a company pay 'me' when they don't have to? The answer is easy. First, chances are greater that you will go to a restaurant or use a product or service that you have been told about. That equates to the company benefiting financially. This is why they embrace affiliate marketing, which gives you an added incentive to speak their name at every opportunity by literally putting money in your pocket.

Second, besides this fact, we have been told countless times that it costs less to keep a customer than to find a new one. Even though this may seem a bit cliché, this truth has been well studied and documented. In fact, RightNow.com informs us in its 2005 report "The Loyalty Connection: Secrets to Customer Retention and Increased Profits" the cost to replace these departing customers is €122 million or about $162.3 million... in new customer acquisition (40 percent) much higher than customer retention. In Customer Winback: How To Recapture Lost Customers—And Keep Them Loyal., Griffin and. Lowenstein cite a 2002 Marketing Metrics study, which found that the average company has 60 to 70 percent probability of a successful sale to active customers; a 20 percent probability of a sale to lost customers, and only a 5 to 20 percent probability of a sale to a prospect. Therefore, it makes perfect sense for a business owner to use affiliate marketing in its business marketing toolkit. One of the smartest things a company does to show its appreciation is to put real, cold, hard, cash for referrals in your pocket. In doing so the chances of your migrating to some other service provider becomes infinitesimally small.

Whether you call it a referral bonus as I do in my business, or you fully embrace affiliate marketing, this is one sure way to solidify your customer base and grow your bottom line at the same time. Ultimately, affiliate marketing is a tool you should incorporate both as a service provider and customer. It is the ultimate win/win situation.

ARE YOU A LANDMINE
OR A GOLDMINE?

Recently I was in the midst of transferring my business domain to a new server and when it came time to discuss payment I was told I could use one of two ways. I could either pay with a check, which meant spending the time writing it out, locating an envelope and making a run to the post-office, or I could simply send payment through an online payment service.

All that sounded fine to me and I was ready to pay for the service online when unexpectedly the young man informed me, "If you pay with the online service they take a portion off the top so I don't know, I think it would be better for you to pay by check.

Now I don't know about you but for me I immediately started seeing red flags and skyrockets going off all around me. What was I doing? What was I thinking? Do I really want to do business with this company? I had been thinking of all of my clients that I could refer to them, but in the blink of an eye all that changed.

How many times have you automatically made a similar mistake? Do you invest all of your time and energy building your business and then when you begin to sense success you undermine that success with one wrong move? Maybe you have been building your "baby" and are seeing a modicum of success and know it is time to hire or designate someone to do some of the routine tasks, but once they are hired you impede them in completing the jobs you hired them for.

What can you do to prevent yourself from being your business' own worst enemy? Think about what you specifically desire from your company. Do you want to have a mom and pop business that is totally hands on forever? If so, maybe what you are doing is enough. By the same token, if you hope to create a successful business you have to grasp a couple of fundamental rules to learn to stay out of your own way.

One of the things that you need to do is, **be aware.** Listen to what you say and how you say it when speaking to others. Sometimes we as business owners tend to have so much on our minds that we don't take the time to effectively listen when others speak to us. When we do *listen* our minds are moving at such a fast pace that we find ourselves thinking about how to respond instead of truly listening to what the other person is conveying. Worse yet, perhaps you suffer from the habit of expecting others to be mind-readers. I recall an employment ad I read in a local newspaper it essentially said, if you are a mind reader this is the job for you. Stop and really listen next time. Really listen to what is being said.

Another landmine that we often lay in our path to success is ego. What I am intimating is that when you start to think more of yourself than others do, you run the unavoidable risk of becoming overbearing and forceful. As a consumer given the option would you prefer to deal with someone that knows their business and shows a genuine interest in you and your needs or would you seek someone who is disrespectful of you and constantly letting you know how superior they are. When the person I am dealing with begins to act like a know-it-all or comes off crass and rude I tend to look elsewhere for the services I need. Most certainly you should display your professional competence but be careful about the presentation.

These are some of the pitfalls we fall prey to in the course of our business lives. When you learn to avoid them you will begin to witness the floodgates of success open wide. Not only will your business reap the rewards but your relationships will too.

ARE YOU GETTING IN YOUR OWN WAY?

L ife is a strange animal when you think about it. We are all given certain talents and the ability to develop specific skill sets yet many of us just exist on a day to day basis instead of striving to be our best.

What makes one so uniquely different from another is the drive to doggedly achieve our goals. Why is it that the person on the top seemingly arrives there through no effort of their own? That's not actually the case, just ask any successful person and they will tell you it wasn't always easy.

The main theme you will hear when they speak is how they had to learn to remain focused on their goals rather than their failures. They had to learn to "stay out of their own way."

What is the #1 excuse we have for not accomplishing our true potential? Fear. Fear is the primary obstacle we put in our own path to success.

So what can you do to get out of your own way and step over this nasty dragon named fear? First you should acknowledge what it is that you are actually fearful of. What makes you hesitate to take the actions necessary to achieve your goal? Is it the fear of rejection that is haunting your success? The fear of public speaking? What about the fear of success itself?

No matter what your answer to this question is, naming it is the first step. Once you have put a face on your dragon it's time to begin to slay it.

Now that you are looking at your dragon eye to eye let's look at how you react to that fear. I once was told that if you ask for something and the person tells you "no" what have you lost? But if they say "yes" what have you gained? The answer to the negative response is you actually haven't lost a thing; whereas, if you get a positive response you have gained what you were seeking. How you react to the "no" is what makes all the difference.

If you are affected by the negative answer you probably find yourself falling into the arms of your old friend *fear* again. The negative feelings that you experience and whether you accept your fear or face it head-on will make the difference in your success or failure.

This is what is known as 'self-destructive behavior'. This friend fear tells you "see I told you, you were going to fall flat on your face." However, what I realized when I perform, whether singing, playing the piano, or just public speaking is that generally, only I know I flubbed up! That's right.

Also, I realized that my audience isn't there to witness my failure they are there to learn from me. What this means is that they not only want me to succeed but they expect me to. Hmmm, novel thought, eh?

So, it's time to look at your fears, confront them and release them. Repeat after me, "Out with the bad; in with the good!" You must alter your mindset! You must kick those fears aside and take that first *step* outside of your comfort zone. I challenge you to change the way you think. Focus on the positive and don't look back! You too can be successful if you are willing to kick your fears to the curb and keep on keeping on.

ARE YOU STILL HOT?

In today's fast paced business world everyone is looking for honesty and integrity with those they do business. It is a well-known fact that you have a mere three to ten seconds to capture your customer's attention. But, after you capture their attention, what do you do next?

If you love what you do it will show. If not, then search your soul. Are you still enamored with your business venture? If not, why not? What has changed? Is it the service? Is it the products? Maybe it is the support you receive from those who have gone before. Can you honestly look in your customer's eyes and enthusiastically share the products or services you represent? Do you stand behind what you sell? If any of these questions produce a negative answer then perhaps it is time to move on. Otherwise, you will be stuck in the quicksand with other failing business owners.

No matter what the reason, come to terms with it and decide if you should move on or merely rediscover what it was that drew you to the enterprise you chose in the first place. Rediscover your first love! After all, the level of enthusiasm that made you fall in love with your products and services is what draws your customer to you.

Your attitude, demeanor, and poise along with a good dose of belief in your product line will shine through when you speak. Think of it this way, when you fell in love for the first time you probably thought of nothing or no one else. You ate, breathed, and talked about him/her at every opportunity. It is this feeling that you need to rediscover about your business in order to succeed.

So, rev up your creative juices. Break into a sweat and get out there! When you are geared up for success things will begin to happen; doors will open; opportunities will appear.

CONTAGIOUS INFLUENCE

So, you passionately desire to have a successful business. You've bought all the tools, read all the books, joined all the associations and you're still struggling to break even. This scenario is all too familiar for many small business owners. But, how do you change all that? How do you help people recognize that what you have to offer is what they have been seriously looking for? Become contagious!

No, I am not talking about going out and passing around that flu bug. What I am recommending is the art of presenting yourself in a manner that attracts others to you.

Let's look at the facts. Nobody wants to buy anything that they haven't already bought-into. If they don't believe they won't buy. So how do you successfully develop a contagious personality if you weren't born with one? The steps are clear and simple. I call it the C++ principle.

C + C + C = CI.

The first C stands for Commitment. You have to be committed to what you have to offer. You have to genuinely believe in your product or service to be able to persuade others of its potential value. How many of you have a product or service that you don't believe 100% in? Have you lost your enthusiasm for what you have to provide? How do you expect others to conclude they just can't live without "it" if you don't believe what you have is truly the best answer for YOU?

The second C stands for Communication. Be ready to share! What do you share? The best way to communicate your faith in your product or service is to merely "tell your story"; yet, so many of us are trying to master those pat sales lines. We have become convinced that if we say just what everybody else says we can be as successful as they are. Truly, it took them years to develop the "sales process" but when you hear it you know you are being *sold!* Simply tell your particular story. It is much more powerful than any sales tactic that you may have at your disposal.

What would you rather have a salesperson say to you? "Our widgets are the best widgets in the world! We have sold over 1-billion widgets." or "It will alleviate all your aches and pains with just one application!" or "When my spouse died unexpectedly, I found myself in financial ruin. I quickly learned that if I had just set aside a small amount each month I would not have been so financially devastated. That is why I determined to become a Financial Advisor, so that others won't have to go through the same pain I did." (This IS my story.)

Communicate with them; help them understand what you have and why they absolutely need it. Share your precious time with them. They won't listen until they perceive that you honestly care. Share your before and after story with them. Make it personal. Make it real.

This brings us to the third C, Character. Be genuine in your compassion and offer it with gentleness and respect. Don't "hit them over the head" or come on so strong that you push them away. You need to be respectful at all times while showing them your passion. Honesty is a moral virtue, that's true. It also is the best evidence of a strong character. Remember to always be truthful and sincere. Those that offer empty promises will soon find that they have nothing but headaches to fall back on. It is when you humble yourself and share genuine concern that you command the attention of others.

Remember the formula; Commitment + Communication + Character = Contagious Influence.

Walk in wisdom. Commit to be true to yourself and honest with others. Show compassion in your speech and your actions. Help them understand that you sincerely care. Then and only then will you have developed Contagious Influence.

THE MOST COST EFFECTIVE MARKETING ACTION PLAN FOR THE SAVVY BUSINESS OWNER

Cutting down on your expenses is imperative in these tough economic times. Everywhere you turn businesses are closing their doors and corporations are cutting back. It has been reported that the job loss rate is the highest it has been in over thirty years. But, don't get caught up in all this negativity. Keep focused on the opportunity that is presenting itself. Realize that people still need products and services. Now that the path has been cleared for you to approach them, you need to let them know you exist.

So, how can you do that in an economical and cost effective manner? Let me give you a couple of ideas that might just light a spark of creativity to your marketing dilemma. One simple idea that comes quickly to mind, when I think economical, is targeting your current customer/client base. It is easier to generate sales from this group and costs a whole lot less than trying to capture a new customer. Actually, I have read the statistics to be six to seven times more costly to acquire a new customer as compared to keeping them.

Sending out a card or postcard is about the least expensive way to market to this group. Of course emails are less expensive than even postcards, but they don't have the same impact either.

So now that you have a plan of action let's look at how you can make them into an effective marketing tool. The first thing to consider is the design. Use a design that brands well to your business. Invest in a custom designed card cover. It will pay off in a big way as compared to a generic card cover. This is where a designer like me can help you pull it together. However, if you can't work this into your budget, all is not lost. Merely find a cover that carries an image that speaks to your message.

Just what do I mean by that? Well, simply put, this means that it is a picture that evokes an emotion. Make sure it is the emotion that your message or your business brand calls for. As an example, a pet care supplier might use a sad or happy puppy, while a determined youngster might strengthen a message geared towards a coaching program for children. Or, what about your message itself, I would think that if your message is about your overstock sale, a photo of a cluttered closet might do nicely. Try to think about what would tie well together either your business or your message and go from there.

Make your message compelling. Don't just say we're having a sale. Use action words; tell them exactly what you have and what you expect them to do to be able to take advantage of your offer. People need to be clear what you want or they won't take any action. While you are at it be sure to include a deadline and make it a short deadline. People are apt to put off ordering until the very last day and if that date is two months from now, that won't help your month end report too very much.

What if you were to use your card just to touch base? Why not send a thank you note? If not handwritten at least make it hand addressed. Make sure to include something specific to the individual in your remarks. These can be sent after a purchase, after they have been away for a while, or when you've added a new service or product. How about using them to find out how to better serve their needs? Whether they have not used your service or purchased from you in a while or not, if you ask them they will tell you. Then you need to figure out how to 'fix' things so that they will be a satisfied customer once again.

People need to be clear what you want or they won't take any action.

Here's another terrific reason to send a handwritten note, to thank them for a referral. This last one is extremely important! Be sure to always thank them for their word of mouth referral. This is your gravy! And they are your biggest cheerleader, so let them know you appreciate them. Better yet, why not send an unexpected gift to let them know how grateful you really are for their recommendation.

I like to give a 10% referral bonus on first invoice. This works well because it is something I know will be accepted and put to good use. However, if you are a cosmetics company you might give 'hostess bonuses' for example, like Mary Kay reps do.

Another idea in your mailing is to find a way to give your mailing piece dimension. Anything that bulks up the envelope will almost certainly cause your recipient to open it. That is half the battle already won. Once your marketing piece is open they are more apt to read your card or letter if for no other reason than to find out why you sent what you did.

One last piece of advice, if your note is a thank you type, try to refrain from selling. Just let them know how you feel and leave it at that. They may faint, but they will be grateful and most likely will use your services or purchase from you the next time they have a need rather than going to your competitor.

HOW TO HARNESS THE POWER OF VIRAL MARKETING

Marketing is the number one most important thing we can do for our businesses. Every day we are bombarded with it in one form or another. Since the advent of the Internet we are now capable of marketing to a worldwide audience. We receive offers from not only our local retailers and services but from distant lands we may not have thought possible to reach before.

The Internet has closed the gap that miles and oceans once previously separated us by. With the click of your mouse you can be chatting with someone in a whole different country.

This being the case a new term has emerged in the world of marketing. That term is "Viral Marketing" or "buzz marketing". Just what is viral marketing and how can you take advantage of the opportunities it provides.

Viral marketing is, simply put, word-of-mouth. Nearly half of all online marketers engage in viral marketing in one form or another each and every day. So, how do you stimulate others to create a "buzz" about your business?

The first and most important thing to remember is that viral marketing exists because of others. When you treat your customers/clients well they will not only come back but they will tell others about you. When you treat them poorly they will still tell other. Therefore your viral marketing is based on customer loyalty. Once you endear your customers to you your next objective is to create genuine enthusiasm surrounding your product or services.

Begin by asking yourself one simple question, "Why would my customers refer their friends to me?" You need to be creative in your marketing efforts. Create something that is interesting enough that your "loyal customers" will want to talk about and share your products and services with everyone they come in contact with.

People love discounts and specials. When offering these types of incentives be sure you put a limit on them. I recently heard a story that was shared by Dan Kennedy, one of the top online marketers, about a promotion his medical sales company did early on in his marketing career. He put a distant expiration date on his advertisement and it wasn't until the very last day of his offer that he began to receive orders.

Not only should you offer your clients/customers a discount but why not consider offering them an additional bonus or discount for every referral? You may even want to create an affiliate program.

Another way you can harness the potential of viral marketing is to ask your customer for a testimonial. Better yet, send them an email, card, or letter offering an incentive for them to write a brief testimonial or fill out a testimonial form.

Other techniques you might consider are games, white papers, contests, parties, and email or greeting card campaigns.

One of the hottest new marketing concepts is that of the 'viral video'. A quick word or two welcoming your potential customer, done in your own voice and allowing your customer to put a face to the voice, will do wonders for your marketing efforts.

Video clips can bring attention to a specific product or service or simply share your latest special. You may want to create a forwardable link to make it even easier for your customer to share your "viral video" with their friends. These links can even be embedded in your newsletters and emails.

Whatever you decide to do be creative in your planning; make it as easy as you can for your customer to interact and share and you will see the referrals come pouring in.

HOW TO OVERCOME YOUR FEAR OF MARKETING?

For many small business owners just the word marketing sends chills up their spines. Is even the word 'marketing' uncomfortable in your mouth? What is it that causes these feelings?

For many of us our fear stems from our own reaction to sales. Be honest, when I say the word marketing is your first thought the dreaded phone sales person or the pushy salesman at the department store? Regardless of your answer, what you need to remember is that marketing is a necessary part of any successful business. It is the main tool to successfully grow your business.

It has been proven time and again that marketing is a process, not just a onetime fix. You market to gain new customers and retain old ones. This process is never ending. Done properly it results in healthy profits and a successful business venture.

Once you embrace the need for marketing and venture outside of your comfort zone to promote your product or service you will begin to see exponential growth. You don't have to market in ways that make you totally uncomfortable, but you have to begin. Choose methods that you know will improve your bottom line and that you are a bit more in line with doing.

If you want to let go of the strings and hire a marketing company to assist you to get your marketing efforts underway, do so. However if you want to be effective in your marketing you must first believe in your product or service. Simple believe will do a lot for your marketing efforts. When you believe in what you are offering you will find it easier to share your belief with those you come in contact with. As a matter of fact, you probably will find yourself trying to STOP talking about what you have to offer rather than START!

Besides word of mouth, which is a very effective marketing method, there are many online marketing methods that help you gain new customers, as well as retain or revive old ones. Create a strategy that encompasses several methods rather than focusing on just one. It is evident that when marketing is done in this way you create multiple income streams, which results in healthy business growth.

You should create an online and offline marketing strategy that draws your target customers to your web site and your door. Your task is to draw people who are already interested in what you have to offer even before they come to your web site or store. It is much easier to sell to people who already want and need your products or services.

Consider things like mailings and coupon books to gain both new and repeat business. A well thought out marketing plan will look something like this:

- Coupon Book Ad to target market area
- Email campaign, spread out over one month, sent 3-days apart
- Phone campaign follow-up
- Greeting Card or Postcard mailing, sent as thank you or promotional to both existing customer base and new prospective customers who have shown a minimal amount of interest.

These are just some suggestions and in no way am I stating that you have to use this exact solution for your business. The point I am making here is, simply put, start somewhere, follow through, and then start over again. With each specific marketing effort you gain confidence and skill making it that much simpler to undertake the subsequent campaign.

Marketing is not about being a sleazy used car salesman; it is about drawing in your target customers who are already interested in your products and services.

As stated earlier, if you don't have the time to manage your marketing efforts or you simply cannot bring yourself to take that proverbial step outside of your comfort zone, a marketing company may just be the answer you are seeking. EMSI is the company I use and highly recommend. Marsha Friedman's Public Relations Company is the first ever *Pay for Performance PR Company* in its field. If you want to reach a vast audience, including TV, radio, and social media I would be more than happy to formally introduce you. Just send me a quick note at publisher@documeantpublishing.com.

THE SECRET OF SETTING UP A SUCCESSFUL REBATE/REWARDS/ INCENTIVE PROGRAM

Many vendors offer special reward or incentive programs for making purchases from their company. These rewards take many forms including gift certificates, prizes, clothing, etc. When considering implementation of such a program for your business, there are things you need to consider.

Terms—Clearly indicate the terms of the program. Be transparent in the language to avoid problems on the back end. Terms such as 'one rebate per household' or 'valid through June 2013' are some such terms you may want to include.

Eligibility Requirements—If there are eligibility requirements state them clearly. Here you can state things like, "You will earn cash-back for every qualified retail purchase." Then go on to explain what those qualified retail purchases actually include or point them to the paragraph where they can read those requirements. The following are some ideas on how to state your requirements.

Yearly Purchases	Rebate Reward
$1,000 and below	0.25%
$1,001—$2,000	0.50%
$2,001—$3,000	0.75%
$3,001 and above	1.00%

- Your monthly statement will list your beginning rebate balance, month-to-date rebate earnings and ending rebate balance. The ending balance may include any cash-back credits.
- Qualified purchases do not include items returned.
- Adjustments will be posted to your ending rebate balance total for retail purchase returns (credits) posted to your account.
- Rebate Reward credits are neither transferable nor exchangeable.
- Your account must be maintained in a positive status during the entire program period.
- Members will automatically forfeit any earned Rebate Rewards if your account becomes two or more cycles delinquent or if your account is canceled, terminated, delinquent or otherwise not available to use for charges at the time the Rebate Reward credits are posted each year.

- (Your Company), at its own discretion, may modify suspend or cancel this Rebate Rewards program at any time without restriction or penalty.
- Cash-back credit may be forfeited due to violations of these rules. This program is void where prohibited or restricted by law.
- The member is responsible for any federal, state or local income tax or other taxes.

To make it a worry-free, trackable rebate, rewards, incentive program and to increase loyalty and traffic consider setting up a member's only section on your website where members can track their eligibility and progress towards their next goal. Many companies offer these sections and with WordPress membership sites they are easy to include and implement. If you are unfamiliar or need help implementing a membership site, there is always a WordPress Virtual Assistant close by who will help you get started.

While these are all good ways to track and sustain a rebate program, you might not want to get involved in the onset with such a complicated system. This is when and where you can offer your reward at the time of purchase. A gift certificate might fare well here. Alternatively, you can do as I do, for every referral who hires DocUmeant Publishing & Designs the referee receives a 10% (10 percent) bonus reward on first invoice. This makes it easy to track and maintain. All that is required is keeping track of or knowing who the referee is.

If you want to give a gift certificate, you can do this digitally or physically. I highly recommend you send them a physical gift certificate and keep track of the certificate number and who it was given to in case they lose or misplace it before it expires. Yes, expiration dates are important to include as well as tracking information. An open-end expiration may be nice for the customer, but when there is no deadline, they are not motivated to use it in a timely manner. They may even set it aside and forget it altogether.

When setting up your rebate, rewards, or incentive program the knowledge of what motivates people is wise to keep in mind. According to a study done by Ran Kivetz (2006), people are more motivated as they get closer to a goal. In the study, they gave one group a frequent buyer card that had two stamps already, and the other group got an unstamped card. While both groups were required to purchase the same amount, the group that got the two pre-stamped card took a shorter time to receive their bonus. This shows that people focus on the accomplishment and not what they have already completed, according to Kivetz. Does that give you any ideas you can use when setting up your own rebate, reward, incentive program?

For rebate, reward, incentive programs to work the main thing you need to remember is that the reward must be something your specific audience values. What does your particular audience want? Do you even know? If not, perhaps you should send out a survey to get the answer so you know what and how to set-up your program.

KICK UP SOME DUST

With the recent downturn in the economy, everyone is feeling the crunch. The US dollar hasn't been worth so little since the great depression in 1929.

So what can we, as business owners, do to ensure our continued success? How can we market our wares in a way that will be cost effective? Creative thinking and cost efficient techniques are what are called for.

Since acquiring a new customer costs six to seven times more than keeping them, this is the group you should consider targeting with your marketing budget. Begin by asking yourself, "How can I best serve their needs?" How do you find that information out if you don't have it already? The easy answer is to ask them. Two things can happen when you ask. First, you will get the answers you seek and second you may stimulate additional income. The mere act of getting your name in front of your customer may remind them of their need for your product or service, or it may result in a referral. Either way everyone is better off.

Here are a three cost-effective ways to get those queries out there:

1. Phone
2. Email/Surveys
3. Mailings

If you are like most people, your fear of the phone is greater than your fear of failure. Realize you're not alone. Most of us either have, or have dealt with, this malady. Seek help to overcome this fear as soon as you can. Once overcome, you will enjoy an added measure of success that you never dreamed possible. If this is the case and you can't talk yourself into picking up the phone, for now, try one of the other less aggressive contact means. Surveys and emails are both good options if this is your plight.

Ensure that they are equally eye appealing and copy edited. One misspelling can cause your reader to discredit your whole business—not just the piece. Even a missing link can do hefty damage. So, be sure to check and recheck before you send out the final piece. You may want to consider hiring an editor to assist you. The money spent on a copy writer/editor is money well spent.

Never, ever, under any circumstances should you attempt to edit your own writing. I can't stress enough how imperative it is to get someone else to edit your copy. Even I, a professional copy writer/editor, have missed a typo now and then when proof reading my work. This happens due to Repetition Blindness.

This is the mind reading what you know should be there but isn't. For this reason, I always have someone else proofread my copy and the text on my design work before I call it press-ready.

Another option to consider in these lean times is postcard marketing. For several reasons this is truly an impactful and affordable marketing strategy. Receiving a beautiful card in the mail is something that we all appreciate. The tangible card is more likely to generate results than email, not by a huge margin but enough to consider the cost of design and mailing to be of value. In addition, there is the fact that postcards cost less to mail than letters or greeting cards so you can save a little here too.

Another thing to consider is the retention factor. A beautifully designed postcard may gain the coveted refrigerator space, keeping your name in front of your customer/client several times per day. Talk about the 'shelf-life' of a marketing piece!

If your piece is branded to your business, so much the better. Hire a competent designer to ensure your piece is both attractive and professional. Don't try to do this yourself unless you have the skill and experience to produce a professional looking brand image. Remember, what you put out there, whether branded to your business or not, is a direct reflection of the quality of products and services you provide.

Another cost effective tool is the all-important eBook. The costs involved here are time, copy editing, layout and design. If you want to cut your overhead here, utilize eBooks that offer re-sell rights. One really good source for these is through Digital Mom Team (DMT). They offer both low cost eBooks by the piece and membership options. Rhonda of DMT has this to say, "DMT is a cost effective way to have tools at your fingertips for growing your knowledge, as well as adding to your income!"

Submitting articles and press releases are one last idea I would like to offer you to market your business as a cost efficient and effective strategy. The well-written article or press release could easily generate free publicity when submitted to the right sources. We all know how valuable media coverage can be. Cost cutting here is in direct relation to the assistance you require. The more you do yourself the less it will cost you monetarily. However, if you don't know where to submit them or how to write them the money you save will be in direct proportion of the response you receive. So consider wisely how best to monetize here.

If you are willing to invest the time, you can save a lot of green. Nevertheless, be sure you evaluate thoroughly your time, talent, and skill prior to deciding where and how to cut your costs.

MAKING ENDS MEET

Now that things are slowing down and our business budgets are tighter than ever, most small business owners are struggling to make ends meet. We still need to keep stock, maintain a social media presence, and market our wares. Even those of us whose wares are our services, rather than physical products are being affected.

While you may have used a virtual assistant to keep you in the social media limelight, with this tightening you may have had to cut this service out of your budget. I certainly hope that if you did that you are keeping it up yourself. If not, I can assure you that you need to rehire and rethink. Some things can be done away with, but a good virtual assistant is worth their weight in gold.

Jodie Burdette, the owner of TheOSP . . . puts it this way, "It takes a lot to maintain your business and your brand's visibility. After all, keeping your name out there is how you advertise your products or services AND attract clients. You have a blog to maintain, newsletters to write, a social media presence to maintain and more. On top of that you have your current client's needs to take care of, marketing to attract new clients, and you need to work on creating new products and launching each one. If you try to take care of all of this yourself your business is going to suffer and you are going to burn yourself out.

"A good VA can take care of much of this and in way less time than you would spend trying to do it yourself. Plus, an experienced VA has seen it all (good and bad) and can offer suggestions to improve your products, unique ways to market them, put you in touch with potential joint venture partners you didn't even know existed, and more. A quality VA is not just an assistant she (or he) truly is a partner in your business and is invested in your success. Making you look good, makes your VA look good."

Now let's look at other ways to make your budget while marketing your business. During your time socializing I am pretty sure you've met other business owners in compatible or even the same field. These entrepreneurs are most likely in the same predicament as you. Why not consider working together? You can even hold a seminar, tape it, and sell the replay and transcripts. Talk to other business owners and get started right away.

These are just a couple of marketing ideas, but I also have a suggestion, or rather a comment to make. Price it right and

Action left undone reaps no reward.

reap the rewards. No matter how good your product or service is if you don't price it right you are only hurting yourself. Overpricing is just as detrimental as underpricing.

When setting your prices, consider not only the time and costs, but also software and education. If you are fresh out of college or a twenty year veteran in your industry just going solo, your rates should reflect that experience. Yes, be consistent with your industry, but establish a fair price within the industry norms. Cut-rate products and services are often thought of as inferior. So don't under value yourself or your products if you want to be successful. And, don't be afraid to raise your prices as you gain knowledge and experience. Sure you may lose a client or customer along the way, but that is bound to happen regardless.

As you continue to seek ways to reweave those fraying financial cords, consider carefully the lessons and insights shared. Remember, action left undone reaps no reward.

EFFECTIVE MARKETING: THE HIDDEN TRUTH BEHIND MALE VS. FEMALE MARKETING

What is the greatest difference between marketing to men and women? With the women you have to explain everything. Women question everything and suggest alternatives. With the guys, it's the old Nike saying, "Just do it!"

That answer may seem harsh but it is also very true. Men are a different animal than women and the way they approach things is quite the opposite of how a woman sees things. Often we allow ourselves to become emotionally attached to our projects while men, on the other hand, tend to look at their course of action with a blind eye to the emotional implications.

So how do you effectively market a product or service to both groups? To get a better handle on this concept let's look at the ever popular world of ezines. Whenever I see an ezine that just goes on and on, blabbering over and over, repeating the same facts in different ways I know that most likely it was created by or for a male. **Men's decisions are based strongly on their perceptions of usefulness.** In contrast **women are more strongly influenced by ease of use.** Women, with their busy schedules, juggling family and career, just don't have time for all that fluff. They want the facts and the emotions all neatly presented.

Now I know you are saying to yourself this is just the opposite from what I just stated but if you look closely you will see a definite connect. While women tend to need to know the why's men need only the grit, they just need it over and over.

Studies have shown that female marketing professionals demonstrate higher research ethics judgments than their male counterparts. One of the reasons for this that is noted in the social psychological literature is that the **male counterpart tends to be self-confident and goal-oriented, while women lean towards being more communal and well-balanced (socially oriented).** It was discovered that while women tend to focus on maintaining group cohesion men remain effective at task-oriented behaviors (i.e., those focused on getting the job done).

A blend of the ideas from these studies suggests the premise regarding which factors should be most influential to male and female consumers in determining customer satisfaction with service encounters.

This is of great interest to marketing professionals and should also be to you as a business owner. The findings from three separate experiments provide support for the hypothesis that women may be generally more sensitive to relational aspects of a service encounter and men to core aspects.

So, to effectively market to both the answer seems to be to **separate the marketing campaign into two gender oriented groups.** Marketing products that would attract the female audience i.e., lipstick, would probably not bring the male audience pounding on your door. Where you might capture the man's attention would be if your product offering were of masculine nature, i.e., a lawnmower. Remember there is always an exception to every rule; however generally this concept holds true. This rule can best be evidenced in advertisements for items like the family car.

The world of marketing is a highly competitive one and unless you focus your attention on the audience you are marketing to you will find yourself spinning your wheels. Most assuredly the first step in creating a successful campaign is to do your homework. Decide just who your product or service is geared towards and then look at the market area to uncover if there truly is a need. You may find that the idea you have has already been thoroughly exhausted in your market area or that it is an open arena. Either way you will need to do your homework.

Once you have uncovered the need, and established who your target market is, you can to begin to put together your campaign. Remember, **when marketing to women keep it short and full of the facts of not only what your product or service can provide but how it will effectively make their lives easier or better.** While with the male market you will need to **incorporate the bells and whistles of what you have to offer and not so much the reason they need it.**

MARKETING IS BIG BUSINESS

Marketing is a business' most important activity. However, it is also one of the most dreaded for most small business owners. Regardless of your business type, if you don't market your business you won't have a business. Therefore, you should constantly be looking for new marketing opportunities even as you are in the midst of running one. Actually, that is the BEST time to discover new ways to market your business. You have heard the proverb, "A rolling stone gathers no moss." Well, opportunity comes to those who seek, as well. Time and again, you will be sending out marketing materials when out of the blue another opportunity will either come to mind or be offered to you by one of the very people you are marketing to. So, to give you a jump on your competition here are a few ideas to get you started.

The number one thing you can do is to **create a marketing plan**. Ya, easy for me to say. Really, it isn't that difficult. When you know the definition of a marketing plan, and see how easy it is to create one, you will laugh to yourself that you ever dreaded writing one. Wikipedia says that a marketing plan is nothing more than a list of actions. See, it's not the how to; it's more the what. Of course the "how" must follow the "what," but start with the "what" and go from there.

So now for the what; some ideas to get you started? Okay, I can help with that. **Start with the annual** *Weird & Wacky Holiday Marketing Guide* (**http://www.HolidayMarketingGuide.com**) available online. It is chocked full of marketing ideas developed around unusual holidays that happen every year. Not only is it a terrific resource for your business for ideas, it contains tools and templates to help you get started on a few select ones each and every year.

Another idea is to **conduct a survey** or **start an "Elite Group"** of your own. A simple survey will tell you what your customers would like to see, while a private group will help you come up with ways to implement those ideas.

Is it time for you to **create a brochure or update an old one?** Yes, these are important tools for marketing your business too. Another one I have used is helpful information pieces that you can digitize and make available for free or a small fee to help build your customer base. If you look at my online sites you will easily find some tools that I have designed to do just that. There are eBooks, reports, a US State Abbreviation & Keyboard Symbols sheet, and even a new offering, My Weekly Activities sheets. All of these types of tools should contain your contact information so others who happen across them will know how to find you. Heck, you can even give them away at networking events. People love free and now your business contact info is in their hands.

Take it offline. This is a very often overlooked marketing tool. So often we get caught up in our comfy computer chair that we forget there is a local market for our products and services. Get out of your chair and go out and get some fresh air. Even at a park or grocery store you have the opportunity to connect with a new prospective customer. However, a word to the wise here, don't push it. If the conversation doesn't go in the direction to allow you to hand them your business card then don't. Speaking of which, you do have a nice professional looking business card, right? Not the one you personally designed and printed on your desktop printer.

Register for a conference. Do something to get out there and meet other people. You never know when you will run into someone who either needs your product or service or knows someone who does.

Offer an incentive to your current client base to send you referrals. This is one of the best ways to market your business. I have been offering a 10 percent referral bonus on first invoice to my clients ever since day one. This one marketing medium has increased my client base and my bottom line. Give it a try the next time you get a chance. You have to tell them so they will know.

How about sending out a snail or email to start the ball rolling? Everyone knows any reason to touch base with your customers is a terrific way to get your business name back in their mind's eye.

There you have it; seven plus simple steps to market your business. Use one or use them all. The choice is up to you. The more you do, the easier it gets. Success is within your grasp; but grasp it you must.

MARKETING: IT ALL BEGINS WITH A PLAN

Now, more than ever, you need a marketing plan. One that will catapult your business to the top of the minds and hearts of your potential customer base. Without one in place your business will not thrive and grow. The economic downturn that we are experiencing is no excuse. People are still spending money and are in need of products and services. The question is how are you going to get them to spend their money on what you have to offer? Your marketing plan is your roadmap to getting them to do just that. At the very least, they will learn that you exist. And that is the first step to making the sale.

Begin by doing your homework. Find out what it is that sets your product or service apart from the competition. This is called your USP or Unique Selling Perspective. These are the 'features' of your wares.

This is important to know, but remember, customers don't buy 'features' they buy if and when the 'benefit' is of value to them. So, after you determine the features spend some time in thought about how these features can become beneficial to your target market.

Speaking of which, you have already pinpointed your 'most likely to buy' or target market, haven't you? If you haven't, then go back to square one and narrow your market down. In these trying times, you don't need to market to the whole of humanity. If you are selling tools, what kind of tools are you selling? A mechanic's tools wouldn't do a hairdresser any good. Nor would a car accessory be of much use to a chef. Sure, if you are lucky, the chef may want your chrome plated side step panel for their monster truck, but you will probably sell a lot more at a car show. And, if a dealership see the benefit to offering their customers your accessory…need I say more?

OK, let's say you know who your target market is and you have developed your list of benefits. What is your next step? Check out the competition. Find out where they spend their marketing dollars and how they market their goods and services. Radio is good for some businesses, while print may be a better medium for another. Perhaps you will find seasonal differences in advertising mediums will affect your bottom line.

People on the go, during the warm summer months are more apt to turn on a radio, because they just happen to be out and about more often that time of year. While in winter they may snuggle up to a warm fire or bed with a newspaper or magazine. This is something I both learned and employed in my surgical clinic marketing practices.

My suggestion to you is try different mediums and change the wording on your contact key so you can track your responses. Unless you can sort out which ads work and which don't you could end up spending your entire marketing budget on ineffective ads.

ENTREPRENEURIAL EXPRESS: OBJECTION STATION

Congratulations on your decision to get on board the Entrepreneurial Express. You have considered carefully and chosen the business association or career path that is in proper alignment with your lifestyle choices. Now it is time to look to the future and focus on your destination.

I hope that you have written out your goals and mapped out your plan to ensure you're on the right train; if you are lucky enough to have found a mentor, so much the better. Irrespective of what vehicle you use, you will experience obstacles along your trip. It is how you react to these obstacles that will ensure your ticket to the end of the line.

The first station on the success track is a make or break stop over. It is almost always arrived at early on in your trip. This station we'll call the "Objection Station" and this will be the focus of our discussion.

When you arrive at the "Objection Station" the choice is yours to either get off permanently or make it just a brief layover. Some mentors teach you how to deal with objections and others to avoid them. It is obvious that one way or the other is not sufficient to ensure your re-boarding pass will be stamped. In order to continue on your journey you need to be prepared to utilize both techniques.

Of the two tools at hand, the new business owner's first choice is to learn how to answer objections before they are even asked. I don't mean knowing a pat set of answers to respond if the objection is made. What I mean is to narrow down the objections to what they ultimately imply and handle that 'base objection' up front. This will take some due diligence on your part. You may want to research the completion and know what they are saying about your product or service. Do your homework. As an example, if you happen to know your price is higher than the competition find out why it is so. Knowing what sets your product line or services apart will enable you to bring out the facts and allay these objections up front. One way to do this is to listen to the people that utilize these types of products. Knowing what your customers are saying as well as what the competition's customers say will enable you to answer these objections from a point of knowledge instead of opinion. If you happen to have been sponsored into your business, ask your sponsor to assist you in this area. They will be a rich resource of knowledge and support and are there for you when you need help, but you have to ask or they won't even be aware that you have a need.

The other solution to addressing objections is sure to be put to the test. Even the most experienced sales person runs across objections they haven't considered before. For this reason it is important to know how best to deal with your lack of knowledge to an unexpected question. Rather than ramble on, avoiding the issue all together, or worse yet giving your opinion rather than fact use this easily learned tool. Repeat after me, "That's a really good question. I don't know the answer but I assure you I do know who to ask and will get back with you soon with the answer. Thank you for bringing that to my attention."

Two things are accomplished here. First, you have built trust and credibility. Your potential customer is now aware that you are not only listening to them but also not going to tell them something just to hear yourself talk. Absolutely do not, under any circumstances, give an answer you aren't sure is correct. It is better to say nothing than be caught in a web of half-truths later.

The other benefit of utilizing this method is found in the very first statement and the last. "That's a really good question," and "Thank you for bringing that to my attention." Both of these statements subtly compliment your prospect and we all know what that can do for your potential customer's ego.

Utilizing both of these techniques at the right time and delivered in a sincere manner guarantees that you will be able to sufficiently address any objections you may encounter. Now, grab your ticket firmly in hand and get back on the Success Train, it's headed in your direction.

POPCORN IS NOT JUST FOR EATING

The other day I was making some of popcorn on the stove, for the novelty, and began to think about the similarities between what I was doing and sales and marketing. The very first thing that I realized is that it all started with a desire or hunger. That desire needed to be strong enough for me to recognize and act upon it in order to get any satisfactory result. When you work for yourself the need and desire to succeed are firmly established. All your marketing efforts are encased in the hull of that desire just as the corn kernel is encased in its hard outer shell.

Selecting just the right pot is the next challenge. If I were to select a pot that is too shallow for the amount of corn I wish to end up with it will spill over and others will gain the benefit while I may end up with nothing but a mess. Conversely, if my pan is too big it may never heat up sufficiently to allow for maximum results no matter how much effort I put into it.

In the same way your efforts need to be measured and your marketing specifically targeted to the right audience. If you put the time and money into marketing to the wrong group or you use the wrong marketing tactics for your targeted market your results will be just as costly and ineffective; which further reminds me of the need to put the perfect amount of corn into the pot.

Let's say I want huge results but I only put one kernel of corn in the pot. What if that one piece doesn't pop at all? Where would that leave me? So too your marketing needs to be numerous and varied. If you send out just one press release and never do another type of marketing it would be like that lone kernel of corn in your pot. No matter how long you wait that one kernel is never going to create a fluffy white bowl full of wonderful popcorn.

OK, so I put several pieces together in the bottom of the pot with a little oil and put it over the flame. I am sure you can see the correlation here. The oil could be your initial investment or it could be an incentive for your potential customer. Without one of these in the pot you may not see any result at all.

Now, onto the stove with the readied pot; turn up the heat and begin to agitate. With just the right amount of heat and non-stop action the corn begins to pop. Ever so slowly at first until it picks up speed from its own momentum and heat, until the popping eventually subsides.

When I finally sit down to enjoy my bowl of hot buttery popcorn I notice that all the kernels are not popped. But the result is sufficient to have made my time and money worth the initial effort and investment. So the next time you begin to formulate your marketing plan, think about that bowl of corn you want to pop. Put all the pieces together in your pot, turn up the heat, and keep up the action until you get to your desired result. Then sit back and in satisfaction and remember popcorn isn't just for eating anymore.

TOP 5 REASONS TO START A REBATE OR REWARDS PROGRAM

Everywhere you look companies are offering a rewards or rebate program to their customers. So, the question is, have you implemented a rewards program for your customers? If you haven't considered doing so, listed below are a the top five reasons you should consider for doing just that.

Reward programs are designed to grow your business in at least five important ways.

1. **Attract New Customers**—Who likes getting something back for a purchase you are going to make? I would say that would include all of us. Therefore, it is easy to see how offering a reward for purchase is incentive enough, in and of itself, to incentivize your potential customers to purchase from you rather than from your competitor. So, what are you waiting for? This reason alone is worth the time and effort it takes to implement a rebate program for your business.

2. **Dispose Inventory**—While you are looking at what you can give as a reward for purchase why not consider that overstock you have been wishing you could move? You don't always need to give cash rewards. When you give an extra product it does two things, first it makes your customer happy and second it introduces them to a product they might never have considered purchasing. What that means is that they have a chance to experience another product in your inventory and may even fall in love with it and therefore purchase it in the future.

3. **Increase Sales**—As I have already stated in disposing of inventory, trial products can and often do increase sales. If you are a service based business, as I am, you might consider offering a free service or service discount to your customers.

4. **Promote Products**— Even your most loyal customers may not be aware of all of your products or services. Merely offering them a reward for purchase might just be enough to get them off the fence and hire you for a project they have been toying with developing.

5. **Build Customer Loyalty**—This is what every business owner should strive to accomplish. Customer loyalty is important to your thriving business. You probably already know that the

cost of client retention is much less than obtaining a new client. Therefore, building customer loyalty any way you can is just plain good business! When you offer a reward for services or products, your client or customer is more likely to purchase from you over-and-over again.

So, there you have it. The five top reasons to implement a rebate or rewards program for your business.

SOCIAL MEDIA: ARE YOU USING IT RIGHT?

Social media is the hot new way to generate money for your business. However, if you aren't using it properly, you'll never see those dollars mount in your account. How are you using this incredible, wealth-building tool? Have you been spending all your free time making sure you get messages posted on your Facebook, Twitter, and all the other myriad of networks to which you belong? If you have discovered Tweet Deck and are using it, congratulations. You save yourself countless hours. However, what sort of messages are you sharing?

If you are posting personal things like, "I made spaghetti sauce from scratch for dinner," "I feel totally out of it today," or "My child made honor roll," then you are wasting your time, just making friends, not money. It's high time you separated your business from your personal. Go now and set-up a business profile. Then, use it as it was intended; for business!

As you begin sharing on your new profile, you need to follow one simple rule; share, don't sell! I don't mean to say you should never let your network know if you have a service or product that fills a need, just keep it to a 70/30 ratio, or less. Offer tips, articles, resources and the like and you will build a much more valuable following. Moreover, which would you prefer—a network of millions of friends or a few hundred interested prospects and clients?

Another plan you might consider is to find another business minded poster and cross promote each other. People tend to respond better when they hear someone other than yourself singing your praises.

Think about it. When you find something that is really terrific, not only do you want to tell others, but when you do, if it is something they are looking for, they listen. Wouldn't you?

So, stop wasting your time trying to use social media to make money by posting personal messages. Make your communications something noteworthy—something others would want to re-tweet. Build a loyal business following, even if it's a smaller group, and watch your efforts pay off.

HOLIDAY MARKETING 101: TASTEFULLY SIMPLE

Marketing has hit an all-time high. The shopping frenzy has begun. With less than three months until the gift giving season is here every day wasted counts heavily towards your income potential for the year.

I cannot think of a better time to make use of your marketing dollars than to put your money where their mouths are. That is why when your customers insatiable appetite for a deal has been raised to an all-time high, I ask you, why not take advantage of their desire by offering a taste of things to come.

You might assume that what I am suggesting only applies to you if you have a food oriented business. This is just the tip of the proverbial iceberg. Businesses of all venues can make use of this "teaspoon" marketing style.

If you have been in business for any length of time at all I am sure you have received the card friendly catalogue with the sample card enclosed. So how do you turn this buying frenzy to your advantage? How about following the trend of the retail stores that offer you buy one get one free deals? Then there is always the free shipping offer that you could make. You might set it up as a minimum purchase required to make it worth your investment. I would classify those as samples too. I have even heard of service oriented businesses offering the first hour free. Now there's one I can sink my teeth into. How about you?

If neither of those appeal to you why not try offering a before you buy choice? This is a win-win offer; better known as Risk Reversal in the marketing world. Are their people who have raised their hand in interest throughout the year? Maybe they contacted you, or even purchased a product or service, in the past; they might be good sources of new or repeat business? It has been proven that people who buy once are more likely to buy from you a second and third time if you merely market to them. The Boston's Consultant Group states in their article Retailing Online: Coming of Age, "Retailers, on average, generated $7 in revenue for every dollar invested in acquisition and $25 for every dollar spent on retention, each nearly double the previous year's averages of $4 and $13, respectively." Now how can you not like those stats?

We all love contests and prizes. Do you know of an event that is accepting prize donations? Be the first to step up and give a little taste of your wares as a prize. Not only will the winner enjoy your gift but think of the free publicity! Haven't heard of any? Start your own. If you need or want help, partner with another like-minded business owner and make it a joint venture. You have just doubled your exposure by marketing to each other's lists.

There are many marketing techniques that fit into this category. No one marketing technique will work for everybody. Find the ones that fit your business and personality and utilize them again and again to ensure your business success. Every once in a while stretch your taste buds and try something just a bit different. Hey, you might just find something that works even better than a system you have used in the past.

These are just a sampling of how you can increase your bottom line with a few simple solutions. So before it's too late get your holiday marketing plan set and in motion. Consider your customer; if you were trying to decide which product or service to use and one offered a sample or trial and the other didn't what would you do? Think like your customers and your marketing results are sure to fill your plate.

TELESEMINARS: ARE THEY A GOOD FIT FOR YOUR BUSINESS?

Anyone who has a business and has toyed with the idea of sharing their product or service in a large group setting eventually comes to the topic of public speaking. With the advent of the Audio/Video (A/V) capabilities presentations are now being given from the comfort or our homes and offices. If you are considering how to take advantage of this marketing trend for your business but don't have the financial resources to rent an online A/V chat room, perhaps you should consider offering teleseminars.

Teleseminars are fast becoming the hot new marketing trend. A well thought out promotion can be organized in a short time and with very little effort. If you have a customer base that you have developed from offering an ezine or newsletter you can create a simple email to let them know when and where to call in to access the presentation. If not, I recommend you begin to compile your list today.

Once you know who your target market is you next need to decide on a topic that will interest them enough to set aside time from their hectic schedule to attend. You might want to offer them an incentive to join you such as a product sample or information source. As an example, when I began my ezine, you may remember, I offer a Resource & US State Abbreviation List. Also, presentation notes or audio copy of your presentation given after the fact can increase your credibility as well as your customer base.

Don't feel like you have to provide this service free. Your customers know that there are fees involved with hosting a teleconference, just like there are for hosting any conference. Figure out a reasonable fee that will cover your expenses and confirm the value of the information you will be providing. You might even surpass your expectations and earn a profit from your teleconference.

Recently I read a testimonial from Barbara Thompson, the author of a weight loss book. She states, "I sponsored my first teleseminar called 'It's All About Food' and 114 people signed up at $19.95 each. That's $2,274.20 in revenue. I recorded it, so I have a brand new product that will go into my shopping cart. I couldn't have done it without you!" There you have two good reasons for considering adding teleseminars to your list of marketing plans.

Deciding on the conference host can be the most important decision you will make when planning your teleconference. Be sure to select one that fits your intended audience number. Don't over extend yourself here; limit your available 'seats'. This will do two things for your marketing efforts, first it will keep you within budget and most importantly it will give your target market an incentive to register early.

Also, be careful that you hire a company that offers several choices of available services. You will need to decide if your presentation and your pocket book afford the use of a moderated teleconference lines or un-moderated one. Don't skimp on quality though, free is not always cost-effective. When selecting your provider poor quality connection can do more harm than good. One company, e-Teleconferencing (http://www.e-teleconferencing.com), charges $75.00 for a one hour conference with 100 lines. This includes recorded mp3 file. They also have lower end services that run about $35 for 10 lines. Check around, do your research; there are plenty of companies available.

If you are unsure how to put together a presentation that will demonstrate your product or service in a way that will prove valuable to both you and your audience, you may want to pick up your copy of *Presentational Skills for the Next Generation*, available now at http://www.amazon.com/dp/0978883144/.

THE POWER OF EMAIL MARKETING

What is Email marketing? Why use it? Does it work? How do I set one up? I am asked these questions and more by business owners both new and seasoned alike.

To begin with, there are a couple reasons you should consider implementing an email campaign in conjunction with your other marketing mediums. Primarily, email is the number one easiest and most cost effective way to stay in front of your customers. The main cost involves time; time spent to set-up and evaluate its effectiveness. The other reason is that they work! How do I know they work? Well, let me give you a recent example.

Between sips of coffee, while winding my way through my emails, I came across a message that caught my eye. It was from one of the sites that my design business, DocUmeant Designs (http://www.DocUmeantDesigns.com), is listed on. They were offering a one-month free top position listing for every design business that generated ten or more reviews from their clients posted through their website. Why were they doing that? Simple, increased traffic to their site, which in turn would elevate their Search Engine rating. A win/win for sure.

That isn't the entire story though. I immediately set to work creating my own email campaign. When done I would have at least ten new letters of recommendation that I could use in my promotions and a free top position listing with this company.

I wrote up a nice email with offer included as a thank you for writing the review. The next step was to test market my email to ensure it would accomplish its goal. With the results in hand, I was confident that I had a well-designed and written piece that would get the job done.

The next step was to prepare to send it out to my customers. To accomplish this task, I used a tool already at my disposal, Constant Contact. There are many good Contact Management Systems (CMS) (http://cjaffiliate.roving.com/?AID=10296666&PID=2121146) available, such as AWeber, Ingeniux, and Joomla, besides Constant Contact. However, since I already had a CMS in place all it required was to upload my customer list to a new database in my existing account.

The next item on my ToDo list was to make a copy of the previous text campaign and link my new database to it. Once that was done, I generated a Thank You email that gave them a link to a bonus eBook that was in line with my services and would be something that my clients would find both beneficial and useful information for their own businesses.

If your CMS happens to be an auto-responder, which most are, the task of generating your follow-up email is just a matter of linking. Look for a CMS which is an ideal fit for your business. AWeber is a fine system, but it may be overkill for the small business owner. That is why I use and recommend Constant Contact. It comes with everything your small business, associations, or non-profit needs, is easy to use, is priced in the low to mid-range, and they provide expert personal coaching on their system.

Now that all the pieces are together, the next thing on the ToDo list is to decide how to track the results. Most CMS companies offer this service, which makes the evaluation process a simple task. If however, you are doing your campaign through your email server you will need to create a spreadsheet to track your success. One important thing to remember when using your email server is not to send to more than 50 email recipients with a single email. Your server may view more than that number of addresses in one email as spam and shut your service down. I always advise my marketing clients to check with their provider to find out what those limits are before sending out the first 'blast'.

Another tip is to put ALL of your email addresses in BCC: (Blind Carbon Copy) instead of TO:. This will generate each email with "Undisclosed Recipients" which protects your customers from spam-bots.

See how easy that was to set-up?

When we began, I promised to tell you how I know email marketing works. Remember I told you I immediately accepted the offer I received? That, in itself is evidence they work. However, their offer was not the only benefit I enjoyed. What about my own campaign?

Email is the number one easiest and most cost effective way to stay in front of your customers.

In evaluating my results, Constant Contact reported that of the emails I sent more than half of the recipients opened them, well more than half of those took action and 10% of those who took action hired me to do additional work for them. I would say that was a successful and worthwhile email campaign.

Now you know how easy it is to set-up and why you should implement your own campaign as part of your overall marketing strategy. What are you waiting for? The next step is up to you. If you're still hesitant, and want assistance contact me and we will be happy to provide you with the tools necessary to assist you to implement your own email marketing program.

THE SEASONAL SLUMP?

Everyone who has ever been in sales has heard it said that the holidays are the down time of the year. That is the reason that many businesses close for the season. Some will close for a couple of days while others close for the entire two weeks between Christmas and New Year's Days. I have even heard of businesses closing for the entire holiday season beginning Thanksgiving and lasting until Valentine's Day. Now that is what I call *Death Valley Days*.

Do you agree? Do you allow yourself and your business to succumb to this mindset? Do you close down the shop and invariably end up losing business because you believe in the seasonal slump? I beg to differ. I believe that there is **NO Seasonal Slump!** OK, pick yourself back up off the floor. Shake the wax out of your ear, you didn't hear me wrong. I did say there is NO SEASONAL SLUMP! Bear with me for a minute or two and I promise I will tell you why I so resolutely deny this mindset.

How can I even begin to form those words? To begin with I believe, as in life, time is what you make of it. If you tell yourself it is going to be slower than molasses in January then that is what you will get. However, if you go into the season with the intention of making it the most profitable you have seen in decades AND you *take the action* to make it so it will be so!

Times have changed. There are new rules that have taken root. This has become *the season of promotion.* Now is the time to promote your product or service in ways that have **double the impact.** Double the impact? Yes double! First you send out your initial campaign via advertising or mailing and when it is over you offer a 'second wave'. This second promotional wave cost you nearly nothing. Make use of the addresses you gained from the first promotional run and you can easily target interested consumers with a discount on the item they initially showed an interest in. Now how's that for making your advertising dollar pull double duty? Words like *'final offer'* and *'deep discount'* will definitely make your interested consumer sit up and take notice.

Without evalution of your marketing plan you'll never know what whether your plan is working.

Another truly unique marketing opportunity that gains additional impact this season is charity functions. I recommend that you could align yourself with a charity. *This type of marketing has even more impact on your consumer than they will admit.* This time of year news reporters are seeking out these types of stories. When you align yourself and your business in charitable ways it places your business in the fortunate position to allow you to get free publicity through multiple media streams. I said allow here because you still have to let the media know what you are up to so the story can be picked up. I am sure you have noticed not a few large corporations take advantage of this seasonal marketing tactic. Why shouldn't you follow suit? What is stopping you and your business from taking advantage of this strategy?

Are you afraid because you don't know how to write? Hire a press release writer? Are you not sure of what to say or how to get your press release in the hands of the media? Again, hire a press release writer. The minimal expense you incur will be well worth the cost if you hire a writer that has proven results. Don't be afraid to ask for confirmation of the results from previous releases. Any good press release writer will have at least one or two happy customers that can share stories of being called or having their story picked up by one news source or another.

We have just scratched the surface as to how you can effectively market your business this holiday season. I am sure you will agree, now is not the time to sit back, but to stand up and get noticed! Happy Holiday Marketing Days are just around the bend.

3 RULES FOR SELLING SUCCESS

Selling or Telling

In today's online environment we all have our share of marketing nightmares we could relate. One that immediately pops into my mind is the store that uses pushy sales tactics. I don't know about you but for me these stores tend to push me right out their door. I cannot think of a better example than this to teach us how to avoid losing potential customers. Let's compare this live shopping experience with our online counterpart to gain some valuable insight.

The basic thing they do is **attack** you the minute you walk in the door. So how do you avoid making your customer feel 'pounced on'? At your first contact do you enter the chat room or offer your first message in the "it's all about me" frame of mind? Do you tend to share about what your do before you have barely even introduced yourself? Stop for a moment and consider how this could be perceived? How would you react if you were on the receiving end? How can you turn this around? How do you tell your shopper what you have to offer without causing them to want to turn and run?

The first thing you should do is kick that old "me" out of the door. Keep pushing; sometimes "me" wants to hold onto the doorposts. If you listen to what you are saying and concentrate on correcting this attitude you will succeed. Hang in there. You can and must do it for the sake of your business success.

Now that you have kicked "it's all about me" to the curb, welcome in "it's all about THEM!" This one simple change can have a tremendous impact on your marketing efforts both on and off line.

To effect this change take the time to figure out what you have and how it will make your shopper's life easier or better. Start off by evaluating your product or service. Make a list of *features* and then try to figure out what *benefit* can be provided by the use of this feature.

Features Inform—Benefits Sell!

What does your product or service do for your customer? If it is a kitchen tool you might say it will help them get out of the kitchen faster. Then digging deeper this will allow them to have more time to spend with their family and friends. So now you can introduce yourself and tell them, "I help enrich your life!" How that makes them feel is what will take them to the next level. I am sure you will agree that the automatic response is "Oh, tell me how." With this one small change you have introduced yourself and your business in such a way that has them asking for more information rather than looking for the exit sign.

The next thing our "model" store does after the "pounce" is to **lurk**. What this means to us is that they either stand at a distance waiting to pounce once again or they follow you around the store. This is best avoided by asking them what they do. You will find people like to talk about themselves and if you listen you may even learn something.

Two things can be accomplished if you take the time to really listen to what they say. First they will tell you by what they have to share where their interests lay. Second, if you listen carefully enough they may even tell you why they need your product or service. Perhaps they will go so far as to tell you what objections you need to overcome to convince them of their need. If you are selling children's toys and they don't have children or grands you will know you can't help them personally. However, I guarantee you they will have at least one friend or family member who does. So don't write them off quite yet. Befriend them and once you build a relationship they may share their referrals with you. So rule number two is Listen, REALLY listen!

These two rules put to good use will be the beginning of untold opportunities. Start with a brief introduction; then stop and listen. If your visitor is interested they will surely let you know. Simply step back and get to know your customer and their needs. This will be your opportunity to learn and show them you genuinely care. Be willing to give and ready to answer questions. Participate in the discussions.

Don't just hit and run

That is rule number 3. Let me say that one more time. **Don't just tell them what you sell and then leave.** Stay and learn about them, build relationships and the business will come. After all we all know we buy from people we know, like, and TRUST! Building a solid relationship will not only bring you new business but repeat business too. Repeat business will in turn open new doors through referrals. That is after all the ultimate goal, is it not?

THE SCIENCE OF MARKETING

Fundamental marketing concepts, as well as marketing as a discipline, have evolved into a whole new group of ideas. Micro-marketing, maxi-marketing, database marketing, new marketing, wrap-around marketing, value-added marketing, relationship marketing and neo-marketing are but a few of today's marketing options. The very fact that there are so many off-shoots, illustrates and illuminates the eventual disintegration of the science of marketing as we know it.

In decades past it was absolutely imperative to consider your customer orientation in order to hone in on your local market. However, today's over-informed, over-stressed, contemporary market has expanded into a new horizon, the Internet,—a worldwide audience.

Consider the fact that exchange value is now based on customer use and loyalty to a product or brand. This is contrary to the opinion that exchange value is completely based on the 'point-of-sale'. Therefore today we must emphasize the customer experience.

Traditional theory tells us that segmentation, targeting, and position are how to identify customers. Yet, demographics alone is no longer the whole picture, you must also consider how your customer reacts.

Recently I listened attentively as a very young, Jonah Lehrer explained how the brain works and what stimulates us to make the leap from uninterested browser to customer status. Jonah asks, "How do we decide?" In his new book, *How We Decide,* he answers this question. His answer, "The sum of our desires and preferences are largely centered in the unconscious, which actually drives your behavior and shapes what you do, unbeknownst to you. Most of the time," Lehrer further explains, "your customer's emotions drive what they do."

Analyze and quantify, if not qualify, your target market.

To better understand who your customer is and what spurs them to buy, try looking deeper. Analyze and quantify, if not qualify, your target market. Consider polling their opinions, whether they purchase your products or services or not.

If your business has grown past the niche' or segmented market you may be ready to grow faster with the mass-marketing techniques available through purchased lists or online marketing techniques such as tribal marketing, cross-marketing, email marketing, and yes, even RSS feeds to name just a few. Now, you may also want to consider affiliate marketing or 'many-to-many' marketing to use and 'old-school' term.

The bottom line, marketing as a whole has evolved since the advent of the computer and marketing techniques have expanded past the traditional 'old-school'. The Internet has evolved and expanded the very basic methods once thought all-encompassing.

Yes, use the Internet to market to a wider audience, but more importantly, use it to brand your business in the minds of your customers and create a loyal customer base for life.

STAYING ON TOP OF THE SEARCH ENGINES

When was the last time you looked at your business' website? I mean, really looked at it. Since you had it built, or built it yourself, have you updated it? Are you keeping up with technology or are you convinced your business is different and doesn't need all those bells and whistles? UK Web hosting provider Streamline.net's latest "Small Business Bytes Survey" has revealed some discouraging information.

"Despite two thirds of those surveyed having had a business website for 2 years or more, only 1 in 10 firms made updates on a daily basis."

That is a pretty sad statistics for the small business owner and their online presence. This means that most small business owners aren't taking full advantage of the Internet or the opportunities it provides. Even sadder still are these additional survey findings:

- 1 in 4 companies admit to updating their websites on a monthly basis
- over half (54 per cent) admitted to making technical tweaks only 'infrequently'

If you are a small business website owner, you need to update your website with new content on a regular basis. Though you may feel that once you get your site up and running, that is the end of your job and now "they" will come, this is not necessarily the case. To maintain a strong web presence you need to give the Google web bots something new to search. Stale content is the number one worst marketing faux pas'. When was the last time you made a content or even a technical tweak?

You don't need to update your website every day, but getting into the habit of making frequent changes is a best practice. Even just a minor update is better than no update at all. Don't get left in the dust of your competition. Hire outside help, if you don't have the time or willpower to make these revisions.

If you don't know what to change, ask your customers for their input. Put up a survey; find out what they want to know and how your business can help them achieve their dreams and goals. Do your own web search. Find pertinent information you can share, learn a new technique and share some 'how tos' with your visitors.

If you have a blog site, start a new discussion with your customers. Look for topics that interest them and then help them find the answers they seek.

There are many ways to keep your content fresh and the bots visiting your website. These are just a few that quickly come to mind. I hope you will take advantage of this information and outwit your lazy competition!

7 HOT TIPS FOR A PROSPEROUS YEAR

This is your year! Up until today you have been madly writing article after article trying to promote your business. You are past ready to begin reaping the rewards for all of your efforts. So, how do you make this year different than the previous year? Where should you start?

1. Evaluate

The very first thing you need to do is to evaluate what worked and what didn't. Resolve never to do those things that were of no benefit and to duplicate, as often as possible, those that did. However, even before you can take this step you need to be honest with yourself. You must know what you wish to accomplish.

Do you want to learn to write better? If so, you need to dig a bit deeper and discover what type of writer you want to be. If you want to write fiction, you will need to find different resources than if you want to write for magazines; if you want to write marketing copy you will need still different sources for inspiration.

Perhaps you have a book in you. If that is the case, before you even begin you need to put a marketing plan soundly in place and begin promoting it. I know that sounds funny, but even if you are going with a conventional publishing house you will want to promote the book yourself. If you rely on the publishing house alone for sales, you may be in for a rude awakening when your commission check arrives. Even celebrities with a large following don't always get the promotion that the publisher makes them think they will before they sign on the bottom line.

2. Attend and participate in events

Now that you have an idea of what worked and what didn't where do you go from here? Take a look, once again, at your list. After each successful event, did you follow-up? Right about now you are probably thinking, "I know I should be doing follow-ups. I have heard that said a million times before. That's nothing new!" Maybe so, but do you DO IT? If not, I highly recommend that you make it a habit in the New Year. If there is one thing that separates the successful writer from the struggling one it is FOLLOW-UP! Let's look at some terrific and simple follow-up ideas that are sure to get results.

I hope that at your event you made a note of the people who attended. What event? Oh dear, if you haven't been involved in events as a speaker then you really need to consider offering them. When you share your knowledge with others, they will see how much they want or need to read your materials. If you are frightened at the mere suggestion of speaking to a group I highly recommend you pick up your copy of *Presentational Skills for the Next Generation* available through (http://www.amazon.com/dp/0978883144/) or contact me personally and I will be happy to direct you.

3. Follow-up

If you have been involved in events but don't know your attendee's contact information ask the host or hostess of your event. They should be more than happy to assist you. Realize that those that were in attendance were at least mildly interested or they wouldn't have been there. Don't let this knowledge slip by unnoticed or unused. Write them a quick thank you for attending email—or better yet, if you can get their mailing address send them a card or postcard. With all the junk mail we receive today the timely postal piece makes a substantial impact on your eager audience.

Another idea that I don't want you to miss is to include a 'thank-you' gift in your correspondence. You will be pleasantly surprised how beneficial a discount or bonus is in getting an interested shopper off the notorious *fence*. All of the most successful companies use some form or another of this technique and you should too!

4. Share your knowledge

Yet another helpful piece of advice I would like to impart is to share your knowledge through the numerous resources at your disposal. Begin with a blog, articles, books, and perhaps even ezines. All of these will help you in three ways. One, it will keep your name in front of your interested consumer; two it will multiply the number of unreciprocated links to your business website, (you do have one of those I hope), as your articles and links are picked up and forwarded. When search engines find these links they increase your ranking. Unreciprocated links are given more weight than reciprocal links. When search engine bots find numerous unreciprocated links they see you as an expert, and that gives you *even better* ranking in the search listings. Speaking of expert, this is the third benefit; you are perceived by, not only the bots, but by people as an expert!

5. Stake your claim

The reality is YOU determine when you are the "guru". Every expert I have ever talked to claims this to be true. When they started believing they were an expert and started calling themselves one is when others started believing they were too. This is not a title you earn; it is one you must CLAIM!

6. Build your list

While you are doing all of this writing don't forget this tip, build your client base by creating a subscriber opt-in list. Don't miss the boat here. This is a very easy way to differentiate the interested browser from the non-interested ones. Two words of advice here, FREEBEEs and EVERY PAGE! OK, so that was three. To increase the chance your visitor will opt-in, offer something of value to them and make it easy for them to sign-up.

If you only have your sign-up form on only one page you lessen the chance that when your visitor is ready to register for your newsletter they will find their way back to do so. In today's immediate gratification society, you must be there when and where they need you. By simply putting your opt-in form on every page of your website, you increase your chances of gaining a new contact for your business. So put your sign-up form on ALL your web pages; yes, even your blog!

7. Stay focused

One final tip is NEVER GIVE UP! Stay focused on your goal. It is when you jump from one thing to the next and don't give your best effort, or you quit because it is too hard, that you fail. Take a tip from the Olympic athletes. They don't win the gold by entering multiple competitions. The gymnast doesn't train for both gymnastics and skating, and the skater doesn't train also for skiing. Although these sports may seem similar to you the Olympic athlete knows that to win the gold they must *focus on one and only one goal*. Then they focus all their energy, learning and practicing on a *daily basis*. Did you catch that one? Do something for your business DAILY!

Be careful here. I am not saying you shouldn't diversify. What I am saying is wait to diversify until you have conquered the one business that you want to see succeed. How well I remember in my hair transplant business, years ago, that when I jumped off into another business venture before I should have my main business suffered. Luckily, I saw the error and closed the second venture until my bread-winning business could stand on its own.

Make this YOUR year to WIN! Decide what you want and go for it. Reach for the stars. If you only make it to the moon you are a lot better off than if you had not tried at all.

MARKETING FUN AND EASY

We are well into the New Year. Is your marketing plan on target? Or, like the rest of your New Year's resolutions has it too lost its momentum? Would you like to get back on track? In this article, I will offer you a couple of ideas on how to do so.

First, **change your mindset**. Most likely, your marketing is boring and just plain work. Truth be told, marketing is FUN! When you consider ways to market your business, why not incorporate some frivolity? Two things happen when you break out of the norm. First, you will actually enjoy putting your marketing in action and second your customers will take notice. Boring marketing materials are destined for the round file. Is that really where you want yours to end up? If you are at a loss for fun and unique ways to market your business I suggest you look first at the annual *Weird & Wacky Holiday Marketing Guide (http://www.HolidayMarketingGuide.com)*. It is updated with new ideas and the tools to implement them every year. This is a marketing resource you'll find yourself turning to often.

Now that your marketing is no longer following the path of the normal and boring let's turn our gaze to your actual marketing plan. You did write one down, right? Well, if not there is no better time than now to do so. Before your heart rate elevates to an out-of-control level, and you throw up your hands let's take a quick look at just how easy it is to **write a marketing plan**.

Wikipedia defines a marketing plan thus, "A marketing plan is a written document that details the necessary actions to achieve one or more marketing objectives." So, a marketing plan is merely a list of ideas and when and how you plan to use them. Dare I say, not the scary monster you imagined.

Once your plan is written down to stay on track you can use what's known as a **tickler file** or just click here to download my free two-page Weekly Activity List sheets.[9] Print them out and use them daily to help you stay focused and on track.

Remember to keep your business growing a good marketing plan is needed. However, unless you implement, at the least you'll stagnate. Action is needed to succeed.

---

9   Weekly Activity List, http://documeantdesigns.com/PDFs/Weekly_Planner_Sheets.pdf

10 SUMMER MARKETING IDEAS FOR YOUR BUSINESS

Summer is now upon us and the kids are out of school. For some of us this means gearing down our business activities to make room for the added distraction, or should I say joy, of summer follies and family. Others of us are taking vacations or increasing our mini-vacations, like visits to the museum, parks, picnics, beach and other fun activities.

Wherever you find yourself, your business, unless it is on auto-pilot, will falter if not properly attended to during this season. So how can you find the right balance of family and business? There are many things that you can do to keep your business from faltering during the summer. Let's consider just ten of the over fifty ways I can come up with off the top of my head.

1. Offer a summer sale

This is the most reasonable and first thing that pops into my head, and probably yours. Not only will this bring in unexpected business but it allows you to pump up the promotion to those who may be "sitting-on-the-fence," so to speak.

2. Cut the fat

This may be a bit more difficult for some, but it is certainly worth considering none the less. Perhaps you have been building your stock, or maybe investing in an educational program. If you can cut back in any way you will find that keeping more of your money, even just 10-15% will increase your bottom line and make for a more profitable summer.

3. Observe & pinpoint summer businesses

Swim suits and t-shirt sales both take a huge leap in business during the summer months. Do you have a business that can take advantage of a partnership with a business like these? If your products would enhance the lives of health conscious individuals then these storefront operations might just be where your target market hangs out. For example, do you sell organics, or health supplements? Why not partner with a swim wear store or even your local health food store? Even if you only are able to leave your business card with a sample attached or a flyer in the window you will open up your business to a new and targeted audience. Put your thinking cap on. This one will take some brain power.

4. Involve your kids

If you are lucky enough to have kids old enough to write ask for their assistance. Begin a marketing campaign with their help. Have them write a short note to your target market inviting them to visit your store. Everybody love kids and their hand-written note could be just the thing to get your potential client or customer to take action.

5. Teaspoon Marketing

Your local deli and ice cream shop have this technique down pat. Take a hint from them. Offer a sample of your product or service.

6. Buzz Marketing

What better way to promote your business than having your satisfied customers toot your horn. Not only will you gain new customers but your old ones will remember their interaction with you and might even need to use your products or services again, which brings me to #7.

7. Create a keeper

Design a tool your customer/client will hold on to or share. How about a time management or perhaps an appointment setting tool. Be sure to put your business contact information on it. One tool that I created that you may remember that has been very successful for me is the State Abbreviation and Links list that you receive as an incentive for signing up for my Words of Wisdom ezine. These are great list building tools.

8. Repeat past successes

Did you do something before that turned out as well or better than you expected? Why not do it again, not just once. When you use proven success strategies you are guaranteed results.

9. Teleseminars

Teleseminars are being used by successful entrepreneurs every day. There is a good reason for that; they work. Why not consider adding this valuable marketing tool to your arsenal? Not only are they cost effective but they will help you build your list since those who attend have already raised their proverbial hand.

10. Cross-promotion

Have you used a product or service that you have totally fallen in love with? Why not contact the business owner and suggest cross-promotion. While they recommend your business to their customers you can do the same for them. This is what I call a win-win scenario. When others speak your praises for you people listen more carefully than when you do the speaking yourself.

There you have my ten favorite summer marketing ideas. Choose one or two and utilize them. I would love to know which ones you use, why and how successfully they work for you.

EARLY PLANNING FOR YEAR-END MOMENTUM

Every year when the holidays roll around many business owners feel torn between our business and our families. How do we keep both on an even keel and retain our sanity? Impossible, some of you are saying. Ya right, others express. The truth of the matter is that with proper planning your business will propel *itself* while you enjoy your holidays with friends and family.

Rather than waiting for the last minute to figure out how to sustain both your family and your income while also trying to include all the extracurricular activities beginning mapping out your strategies and implementing them now.

For example, if you don't already have a business blog consider how one can benefit your bottom line and get yours started today. If you already have one, why not write all your posts early and then when you want to publish them you will only have to hit the publish button. Don't have the time to even do that? Hire a competent Virtual Assistant (VA) to handle these mundane tasks.

Many of you have already worked with auto responders. These tools can be put to good use during the holidays. Early planning of your marketing efforts will pay off generously when utilizing the scheduling sequence that auto responders offer.

There are many tools that fit in this category. You can set-up your whole biz as a big automated machine. Here's a list to get your creative juices flowing: Google ads, landing pages, email messages, videos, audios, interviews, and live chats with you and your staff. These can all be set-up so that your visitors will move from one stage to the next with little or no effort on your part.

Take advantage of these tools by planning, writing, and preparing all your holiday specials way before they need to be implemented.

These are just a couple of ideas to keep you and your business on track while others are away.

THE #1 MOST POWERFUL MARKETING TOOL

Whether your business is storefront only or has an online presence, you must have a marketing plan in place to succeed. This may entail a budget set aside annually or as you can afford to advertise you commit the funds at that time. Sometimes the best approach for a new business owner is a monthly budget. No matter which approach you use, marketing should be your number one priority.

It is through your marketing efforts that your customers and clients find you. Therefore, without it your business will eventually die. Moreover, for a business start-up lack of marketing can prevent you from even getting off the ground.

I wonder at how so many new business owners invest their resources in stocking their shelves only to close-up shop within their very first year.

According to the U.S. Small Business Administration findings on business survival rates shows that 66% of all business started between 1992–1998 were still in business after two years. Out of those surviving 50% lasted an additional two years with only 40% of those remained after six years. Could *lack of investing* in their business through marketing campaigns *and evaluating them* be one of the reasons for this high failure rate? More than likely.

Marketing not only requires a monetary investment but an investment of time as well. To properly market your business you need to do two things. Before spending a dime, you must *do your research* and after you've concluded your marketing, *evaluate the results.*

Research where your potential customers are going and what they are reading. You might start by looking at where your competition is spending their marketing budget. Then put together a catchy campaign that will attract them to your business. On the other hand, you might try the buckshot approach if you have an unlimited budget. Either way, if you take the time to evaluate your marketing campaign results, you will have a better idea of how and where to focus the next go-around.

Regardless of how or where you market your business, the results from personal contact is the most lucrative.

Going where your potential customer goes and personally interacting with them will work wonders for your bottom-line. Think about how you felt the last time you went out to dinner and the owner or manager came up to you and showed he/she cared about your dining experience. This personal interaction sure makes me want to come back.

If your target market is women business owners search for events catering to this market, if your market is single parents, seek out parenting groups, etc. These types of online activities can be beneficial for many business owners. With the opportunity to interact with other like-minded business owners, you gain valuable insight and experience.

Events like these offer the savvy business owner the chance to market their business in a non-threatening environment. The simple act of donating a valuable prize can garner free publicity. Not only do you benefit from your sponsorship, but oft-times these types of events are promoted through press release, word of mouth and other marketing means. This brings in "unique visitors" which see your sponsorship prize donation or ad and can end up becoming your customer for life.

Being there in person gives you a chance to mingle while getting yourself known. Look around, find out where your target market is and what magazines they are drawn to, and you will find the time spent involving your money and your time in these places to be most fulfilling.

So what is the #1 most powerful marketing tool? The answer is YOU!

OFFLINE VS. ONLINE MARKETING HAVE THE WINDS OF MARKETING CHANGED?

As I ponder this question, as I am sure you are too, there are many thoughts that whip around in our minds. Students of marketing are no longer only being taught the standard marketing strategy. The shift to online marketing has gained such strength that those that had never considered the Internet a viable choice are now including it as an important part of all their marketing efforts. One of the reasons for that shift is the vast amount of monies that are saved on printing costs vs. online set-up fees.

In the past business owners had no choice but to pay out the hefty fees necessary to print hundreds of copies for their ad runs only to find that the ad campaign failed or had at most a small response rate. If they were tracking the response they had to go back to the board and create a new ad campaign and print and mail the new ad, significantly increasing their initial investment and decreasing their profit margin. On the contrary, once their website has been created the expense of changing the look or feel of their campaign is minor.

Both online and offline the length of time that it takes a browser to become a buyer may not be much different. But how do you turn a browser into a buyer? As marketing professionals and students alike know very well, it takes **seven to ten contacts** with a customer before they become the sought after buyer. *Familiarity is the key.* You have to build trust and that only comes with time. After the sale that trust must continue to increase or the new buyer may not come back and certainly won't refer their friends and family to you. However, I am getting ahead of myself. We'll save this discussion for another time.

Some of you may think that your business is different. You don't have a product that would benefit from an online presence. Perhaps you think that traditional marketing is the only way to go. I would like to offer an example if you will indulge me. Let's say you own a bakery. We'll call it My Little Taste of Italy. You are located in a small town in southern California and have a loyal, local, customer base. As you sell perishable goods how can you possibly benefit from an Internet presence? I will now show you just how viable the Internet is for a business such as this.

Our first step is to put together a web presence. This will take some marketing dollars that you may feel are better spent in the local market but realize we are now talking global marketing. As you know very well, as your market area increases so does your potential customer base. When putting together your website you will need to optimize your web presence with every available means. So what you need to consider is not only your keyword density but what keywords you should even use. This is done by checking out the competition. Look at the words like, bakery, Italy, Italian, and perhaps some of your product line biscotti, rosettes, cakes, cookies, muffins, brownies, and any combination of those words. After checking out the competition you will know whether you should continue to use these as your keywords or look for more specific ones.

Once your site is complete and your online presence is there you need to begin your marketing efforts. One thing that you can and should do is to link the offline with the online markets. Perhaps you can send a custom postcard to make your offline market aware of the convenience of online ordering. Continuing to mix the two marketing arenas is always a wise investment. As I have heard it said many times before, putting all your eggs in one basket is asking for trouble, so don't close the doors, but open another; your Internet store.

Your press release communicates a newsworthy story and should not be a blatant ad.

There are specific steps you should take to optimize your web presence. Having a website is just the beginning. Lead generation, customer acquisition, 1st transaction, subsequent sales, delivery of content, and back-end sales marketing efforts should be interlinked both online and offline. If you are not doing this you risk leaving sales unrealized and money on the proverbial table.

It is well known in marketing arenas that spending minimum amounts of money to obtain leads will result in minimum, low quality leads. So, what I am suggesting you do is to narrow your lead base by qualifying your buyer. If a customer is really interested in what you have to offer they WILL take the time to learn all they can about you. One of the things the bakery we used as our model, My Little Taste of Italy, does is to network effectively both online and off. You are your best salesman; let others know you are there. If your product is as good as you believe it is your customers will come back again and again.

Besides networking what else does My Little Taste of Italy do? They have products of the highest quality, yet if others don't know they exist how are they ever going to win new business. Let's see what else they do to further promote their goodies? One idea they might try is adding a little something extra in outgoing packages. Why would they spend hard earned income giving away goods for free? If they truly have the best products around, then giving out samples can only increase the chance of customers trying something different in their next order. The more they try the more they will buy. That is why samples have been such a profitable investment in many businesses efforts over the years.

Another point I would like to make here is presentation is priceless. No matter how good your product is you want to wow your customers. Make sure when your customers receive their packages they are satiated with all of their senses. Remember the eye is the window to the soul and the presentation is as important as the offering. For this reason the bakery we have chosen as our example, My Little Taste of Italy, packages with care each and every outgoing shipment.

Now you have your product and packaging, your web presence, and a few customers. Let's see what we can do to increase the customer base. Article marketing has been proven to be an effective tool. Use the media, whether offline or on to grow your business. Be sure the information is such that the media will even care. A holiday is a good time to send out an article or press release to announce an event, new product, or business expansion that you are promoting. Again we turn to the bakery.

One thing that My Little Taste of Italy could do is put together care packages for the soldiers stationed overseas. That would be a good idea for promoting their business while serving the community. The media loves the holiday angle. One of the benefits is that any coverage you gain by making the media aware of your efforts costs you only the time and effort to put the information in-front of them, if you have the ability and talent to write an effective press release or article.

Your press release communicates a newsworthy story and should not be a blatant ad. Once crafted, you will need to disseminate it to the right audience if you expect it to be picked up; this is where a press release copywriter becomes invaluable. The amount of money you will invest to have a skilled press release writer send your release out is one of the wisest investments you will make. In addition, once you get picked up by one media source the possibility of being picked up by another increases exponentially.

While you continue to market your business in non-traditional ways—and traditional alike—you should always remember that with marketing the terms are always changing. What I mean by that is look at the telemarketers, email marketing, and such. With the ever changing tide of laws governing how we can market and what we can do to avoid spamming, our marketing efforts should never be stagnant or single-focused. In other words, use several types of marketing, not just a single email campaign. Varying your efforts guarantees you won't suffer huge losses in revenue if what you are doing is affected by these changes.

WHERE DO YOU TURN FOR INSPIRATION?

As business owners, we all know we have to market our wares if we are going to make an income. However, most of us just do the bare minimum or copy the status quo. Nevertheless, in order to be successful you have to break out from the crowd and get noticed. We regard those whose marketing campaigns are unique to have the key to creative, innovative, out-of-the-box thinking. So, why aren't we all creating successful, attention getting promotional marketing campaigns? The answer is simple; we don't think we can.

How do you come up with ideas as to what to say or do to let others know about your business? Do you just follow the crowd? Do you always use the same mediums or words? Are your advertisements filled with facts with an image or two thrown in? If you have taken a novel approach to your marketing you probably noticed a spurt in business. Using catchy verbiage, images, or colors may be all that is standing in the way of your success. On the other hand, maybe you would benefit from trying a unique approach, something you haven't attempted before.

If you always write articles but never create incentive products to spur or challenge your audience you could be leaving money on the table. Have you considered partnering with other likeminded business owners to hold a local or online event? Why not give it a try? You might be surprised who you will talk to who needs or knows of someone who could use your expertise or products?

For other inspirational suggestions, I often turn to the *Weird & Wacky Holiday Marketing Guide* (Amazon ASIN: B006T8IQZS). This resource is filled with not only the tools you need to open your mind to new and fun ways to market your business but also the templates to accomplish a few of the suggestions found within its covers.

Other sources of inspiration may just be an arm's length away. Browse through a magazine, look at what catches your eye. Is there something that attracts you in all the ads you espy or is there one that truly stands out from the rest? Why not emulate that in your next ad? If you don't find anything that stimulates your imagination, then it may just be you need to take a break, get out and get some fresh air for a new perspective. This has

Be certain to follow the rules and/or hire a compamy that will also when creating your SEO ranking program.

been proven to be an effective way to open your mind to allow fresh ideas to flow. "There is something about being outdoors that lends to a more open discussion and broadens our thinking," said Reno City Councilwoman Sharon Zadra. She dubbed it her 'Fresh Air, New Ideas' walk.[10]

Whether your inspiration comes from meditation or a trip to the bookstore. Whenever you change your surroundings, you give yourself a chance to expand your horizons, which in turn may just inspire you to greater heights.

---

10   Nevada Today, http://www.unr.edu/nevada-today/news/2009/city-councilwomen-seek-fresh-air-and-new-ideas

GIVE THEM WHAT
THEY WANT!

As business owners one of the most important things we can do is to make our voices heard. What better way to do that than to re-purpose our content? Recently, I set out to do just that. And now I will share that information with you.

Like me, you may have written reports, articles, and/or books. Most likely, you already know that there is a great need for your information, but you are at a loss for how to get it out there. Having gone the press releases route I will not bore you with those details. This after all, is not re-purposing, but rather promotion. However, if you need help in that area let me know, and I'll be happy to share with you that information. On the other hand, if you can't wait, go get a copy of the *Weird & Wacky Holiday Marketing Guide*. This annual ebook contains a sample press release and many other outstanding ways to promote your business and have fun while doing so.

What I discovered and intend to share with you is taking your current content and turning it into an audio book! If that is of interest to you, read on.

Sit back for just a moment and think about the busy people you see every day. Both our youth and adults are plugging in. Everywhere you look people are listening to audios while exercising, driving and even just walking down the street. Therefore, it seems to me that the demand for audio, of all kinds, would far exceed that for any other medium. And, for those of us who already have Kindle ebooks available the process of creating audiobooks is already partially done.

Another good reason to consider re-purposing your content into audio books is the fact that those who purchase your audiobook, if they enjoy it, are far more likely to purchase it in another medium or even other products you have to offer. It is definitely a rapidly growing market place. According to the Audiobook Publisher's Association audio book buyers are higher-income earners than non-listeners, which translates into more sales for you if they like what they find, and they're better educated, which means they know what they need when they see it. That said; if you plan on taking on this challenge make sure you only offer high-quality content!

It used to be that only a select few were even allowed to create audio books, but today things are changing for the better in this arena too. Considering the fact that digital books are only a few years old and already far surpassing print books in sales, it is a logical progression for our plugged-in society to embrace audiobooks.

If you have a good voice and can read well, you too can produce your own audiobooks with just a couple of pieces of equipment and a quiet room. If you don't like your voice you can always hire a narrator. Some narrators will even work for split royalties, which equates to no out-of-pocket expense.

So, what is stopping you? Why not join me in offering good-quality audiobooks to the starving throng that will eagerly devour your content, if you only just make it available.

COMMUNICATION SKILLS ARE A MUST FOR THE ENTREPRENEUR

We are now into October, and the holiday season is just around the corner. It is during this time that business owners will be ramping up their marketing efforts; letter and email writing is in full gear.

Now is not the time to relax your writing skill, but rather to learn better how to write what you are trying to communicate to your readers. Once learned and applied you can use these skills in your oral communication too, and gain a modicum of respect that you would not have with your common spoken language.

How you communicate your point is as essential, even more so, than your actual message. Lee Iacocca said, "You can have brilliant ideas, but if you can't get them across, your ideas won't get you anywhere." Another quote that lends credence to the importance of careful communication is one I recently read by Mark Twain "The difference between the right word and the almost right word is the difference between lightning and the lightning bug."

For example, here's a tricky one. When you are trying to say that something caused you to act a certain way, do you say it affected me in an adverse manner, or it effected me in an adverse manner? I hope you said the primary rather than the latter. First of all, affect is always a verb. It means to bring on or cause a change, or to cause emotion, to provoke feelings (good or bad). It can also mean to adopt a false characteristic. Effect can be either a noun or a verb. As a noun, it means the result of something (cause and effect). E.g., unemployed workers are a direct effect of factory closures. But, when used as a verb, it means the same thing as the verb "effectuate", which means to bring about, to accomplish. E.g., when the government effected tax cuts, everyone received a larger paycheck. Pulling them together to make it even clearer to you, it could be stated this way, "We were all deeply affected when the government effected a tax increase." You can remember it easily the same way I do; effect is causative while affect is resultant.

Simple errors like this in communication are not only bad grammar, but can even end up communicating something totally different than what you intended. I have seen relationships severed and business lost on the weight of a single missing or wrong word. A misplaced or missing comma can change the whole meaning of a sentence. Even if you add a wink, or LOL, that may not be enough to ensure your communication is understood as you intended. So, be very careful what you say and how you say it. Another good rule to remember is, if you wouldn't write and **sign it**, don't say it.

When speaking or writing try to stay away from clichés. Sometimes, a saying you are used to hearing day-in-and-day-out may be never used and therefore not clear to your reader. Did you see that lazy way of writing in the last sentence? Would it not sound more professional to say, "Sometimes, a saying you are used to hearing daily may be unused by your reader?" Much shorter, to the point and without the "pat" cliché, don't you agree?

Now let's talk a bit about words that 'communicate' in marketing. When you write an ad (not an add) do you tell your listeners about the benefits of using your product or service, or do you talk about the features? What is in it for them is what they are looking for. So, why would you waste their time on the features of your product? Yes, the features are important, but it is the benefit that sells. There are plenty of examples that show the right and wrong way to write your next advertisement. Google is a good place to start.

Then there are the words that spur your reader or listener to take action. Do you use action verbs? If you do, you will increase your sales. Your audience needs to be told what action to take or they won't take any at all. Therefore, in the next ad you write be sure to use words that evoke powerful thought and action. Most advertising that is professionally written contain at least one *power word* and one *action verb*. Here's one I wrote recently to give you an idea of what I mean.

The art of public speaking has never before been so easily within your grasp as it is in the newly released book, *Presentational Skills for the Next Generation*. Discover the secret to spur your listeners to take action. *Presentational Skills for the Next Generation*, the ultimate guide for public speakers and those who want to be, reveals all this and more. Get your copy today at your local or online bookstore or directly from the author at http://www.GingerMarksBooks.com. That's G-I-N-G-E-R-M-A-R-K-S books dot com.

Does this ad excite you? It should if you ever wanted to be a public speaker. The key phrases used, in case you missed them are:

- Art of
- Easily within your grasp
- Newly released
- Discover
- Secret
- Ultimate guide
- Reveals

Then, at the end I tell them exactly what to do and where to go to get their copy. Try using some of these key words and phrases in your next ad and see what happens.

Once you master the art of communication you will reap the rewards of success and avoid the pitfalls of poor grammar and lost revenues. If you need more help with developing your communication skills there are numerous communication coaches that can help you in this all important area. The one I turn to most often is Leadership Coach, Joe Yazbeck of Prestige Leadership Advisors.[11]

Joe offers this advice, "After 30 plus years coaching professionals and leaders in public speaking, I have come to determine that the most essential ingredient necessary to creating an effective and impactful presentation is the most simple and rewarding to achieve. That ingredient is an authentic self. A natural, expressive, extroverted, and interested person appearing, for any reason, no matter the size of audience, is the surest way to attract an audience and hit your mark, regardless of your content.

"I have never seen a synthetic, contrived personality make a successful speech or presentation. I always coach in the direction of sculpturing before me; through all the scenarios I coach my client through, the authentic, real individual fully there and expressing. I want my speakers shining like diamonds. It is a wonderful creative process of self-realization and unleashed, unrestrained freedom of expression.

"That is stage presence! That is real charisma! That is exactly who the person really is appearing before you!"

The other coaches I have found to be well worth paying attention to are: Ali Brown of Ali International, LLC[12] and Felicia Slattery M. A. of Communication Transformation.[13] I assure you, both of these ladies are tops on my list. The key is to find one and learn from them. You'll be glad you did.

---

11 Prestige Leadership Advisors, http://www.prestigeleader.com
12 Ali International LLC, http://alibrown.com/
13 Communication Transformation, http://www.communicationtransformation.com/

Design

MARKETING MECHANICS

We have discussed many marketing ideas in the past, but little have we touched on design. This is just as important to your marketing efforts. Therefore, that is what we will delve into in this month's feature article, "Designing Your Marketing Message".

Marketing design is a seldom breached topic. As a designer, though, it is one aspect of design that we must thoroughly embrace. Most designs are not art for the sake of art. Instead, we focus on the art of design for marketing's sake. *Color* and *placement, white space* and *filled*, all have a bearing on how a design must be accomplished.

All that said, how can you as a business owner, remove yourself and your preferences from your marketing design in order to get your message across to your audience? The first thing you must do is to accept the fact that you are not necessarily your audience. Like you, they too have likes and needs, things that attract them and things that repulse them. It could very well be that your choices vs. theirs are somewhat similar as well as totally opposed to each other. Now that you have divested yourself of that gargantuan weight, let's look at who you ARE trying to attract.

> **Your aim is to provide only enough information to entice them to contact you.**

You must identify your target audience so that you can design your marketing pieces around their likes, needs and desires. Yes, this is as relevant to your design as what you say—or don't say.

Color analysts and designers will confirm that everyone loves blue and it is a color bought by consumers more than any other color. Red is an attention getter and is the reason for its use, as such, in advertising. Then you have the age groups—the younger the less complex color range you should use. Men vs. women? Yes, there are subtle color differences there as well.

As mentioned above, what you say—or don't say is a relevant aspect in design. Divest yourself of the long detailed text. Harness the power of simplicity. Weed out the unnecessary. Your aim is to provide only enough information to entice them to contact you. Thus, your end result will be clean and spaced not too tight and jumbled. Remember, as I always say, white space is your friend.

There are many more design theories that a professional uses when laying out your marketing pieces. Nevertheless, these few ideas alone will help you get started.

ENGAGING HOME PAGE DESIGN

Is your home page web design brilliant and engaging or dull and boring? "You can't judge a book by its cover," is a very true statement indeed. Nevertheless, we often do just that. While cover design is an important issue if you want to have good book sales numbers, have you ever considered how this translates to your website's home page? Your home page is as important—if not more—than a book cover should be to you. Since your visitors take but a few seconds to deem your site worthy for further investigation, this is where you should focus your efforts to provide a glance of the business that will capture their attention.

To begin, **get to know your target market**. After all, they are who you are building your site for. Start by asking yourself a few basic questions. Questions like: What are their desires? What are their color preferences? What is their income level? What is their level of education? If you don't know the answer to these questions by all means, create a survey and ask them.

Once you have a good handle on your target market, it will enable you to provide them with the information they seek in an appealing and easily navigated manner. I say easily navigated manner because this information will tell you if you need big and chucky, sleek and sophisticated, or cartoonish and colorful buttons and backgrounds.

Sometimes you may want to break out of the norm and present your brand in a whole new light. As an example that I was pointed to in one of my marketing newsletters, Luhsetea, a tea company, broke out of the norm to capture your attention in their use of a cartoonish, colorful dark blue and red design rather than the standard brown and green template.

When deciding where to place your **navigation** there are three basic placement options: *top, left, or right*. Each option has its own merit, so be sure you consider your visitor first before making this crucial decision. Top placement is becoming the norm. Visitors used to look to the left side for navigation information as a rule, but with today's instant gratification society web designers and business owners alike are opting for the top placement more often than not. As for right-side navigation, the reasoning behind this is simple. Most people are right handed and therefore it is easier to click on the right side of the page rather than to have to scroll all the way to the left.

Regardless of where you place your navigation, please *consider the color blind individual*; don't use blue on blue or other hard to differentiate combinations. One site I found helpful in this area is snook.ca's colour contrast check. You may find it helpful as well.[14]

Another consideration is the evolving **responsive web design**. In today's mobile connected society people are viewing your web site on multiple platforms. While responsive web design is still in its infancy, it is certainly a contender for your consideration when it comes to design.

Responsive web design isn't just about the reflow of content, the W3C is working hard to give you the option of resize and reflow for pictures and text sizes as well. One thing you should be aware of is that all browsers, cross platform, have adopted a standard default font size of 16 px. So, if you want smaller or larger text something other than normal must be specified in your design. And, if you want it to be responsive you can no longer use specific pixel dimensions, it's time to start using percentages, which translates to the use of em or rem measurements. Stay tuned as this is a developing technology and certain to take hold in the next generation of web design. But for now, at least consider making your site 'Adaptive'.

One parting thought: While you must design for your market you also must offer information, *above the fold*, that will capture their attention. A big fat "Welcome" is really, not what they are looking for, so as much as you want to welcome them, don't. Remember, you only have a few precious moments to intrigue them to looking further. Why waste even a second?

What they want to know is whether you have the *knowledge, service, talent, or product* that they seek. So, spend time writing your copy in a customer friendly, consumer centered style.

It can be both difficult and fun to design a user friendly, attractive website that will engage your visitor. Take the time to learn about your target market and create a truly unique and well-thought out experience. You'll be ever-so glad you did.

---

14   Snook Color Contrast Checker http://snook.ca/technical/colour_contrast/colour.html

COLOR PSYCHOLOGY: HOW TO USE IT TO YOUR ADVANTAGE

Small business owners often lack knowledge in the area of color psychology. Not only do they fail to employ the benefits it can provide in their marketing effort, but they often don't even know color affects their audience at all. So, to bring you up to speed on this important aspect of design for your marketing pieces I will share some of the hidden secrets of color and how you can benefit from implementing color psychology in your marketing materials.

The first mistake most small business owners make is designing their own marketing pieces. Their websites, logos, ads and stationary all reflect their color preferences with no regard to their audiences' perceived preference or cultural background. While you may have a penchant for one color your target audience may be repelled by it. Yes, colors have characteristics that when used properly will enhance your message and even help express it in a subtle but very real and effective manner.

When you hire a professional who has been trained in design, you are hiring someone who has had the proper training in this area. They know how to employ color to attract your audience and convey the message you intend. Without this knowledge you can do more damage than good. So, what are some of the basic colors and when and how should they be used? Let's look at just a few.

Black

Black is a color that expresses power, sophistication, prestige, security, emotion. It is often used by attorneys and other professionals for this very reason. However, overuse of black can be a problem for your reader. While black text on white is easy on the eye, the reverse is not so. It is also seen as a macabre color and is why it takes the forefront in funerals. Keep this in mind when you chose to focus on this color.

White

This color denotes purity, innocence, cleanliness, efficiency. Use this color as a design element, perhaps by adding white spaces to depict openness and allow of easy understanding of relationships or lack of relationships between your design elements.

Purple

Traditionally purple has been and is a color that depicts royalty, wisdom, dignity, status, creativity, luxury, and mystery. As far back as biblical times purple has been thought of as a color of wealth. Just a small amount of purple can go a long way to expressing this hidden message.

Green

Not surprisingly, green is characterized as the color that most adeptly conveys nature, natural energy, life, growth, environment, fertility, wealth, and, of course, go. Businesses that use green in their marketing and brand include lawn care, environmental organizations, and financial institutions.

Yellow

Yellow is the color of hope, life, optimism, cheerfulness, energy, happiness, caution and cowardice. The subtle hues and tones of yellow can mean different things to different peoples and cultures. While a bright yellow may be perfect for an uplifting feeling it should never be used as a textual element. Yellow is just too hard on the eye, so use it sparingly. A more golden yellow will indicate wealth and so is often used in relation to money.

Blue

Trust, security, responsibility, efficiency, calm, friendly, and intelligence describes blue's characteristics. This color is the color most often used in branding as it is the favorite across all age, gender, and cultural backgrounds. Again, the hue and tint of this color can denote different messages. As an example, dark blue sends a message of security while a light blue leans more heavily towards a feeling of friendliness and calm.

Red

The color of red signifies excitement, energy, urgency, love, passion, anger, violence, aggression, and strength. This powerful color quickly catches the eye of the beholder. That is why the red tie is called the power tie in business circles.

This is just the proverbial tip of the iceberg of color psychology. Employing the right color for your project can only enhance your marketing efforts. Choose wisely and with purpose. Consciously and consistently using color psychology can lead to increased sales and a stronger brand identity.

If you haven't a clue where to begin, try asking your customers for input on your design before putting it to use. Listen to what they tell you and benefit from their input. They are, after all, your target market and thus their words deserve your attention.

22 DESIGN TIPS FOR THE NON-DESIGNER

My name is Ginger Marks and I am here to assist you with tips on design for your business needs. With nearing 40 years in the business I am sure I will be able to provide a thought or two that will help you along your way.

Design Tips #1

This tip is a reminder to keep it clean and simple. White space is not just there to be filled up. Be sure to allow enough room for your visitor to breathe. If you have a lot of information to provide put in on a second or third page rather than on the same page. Remember this one rule if you remember no other.

Design Tips #2

Making your page fit in any screen resolutions is a must. People will view you page in different kind of screen resolutions. According to WC3, most set their screen resolutions at 1024x768 or higher.[15] That's the reason why you'll see white space on the right of your screen when you're viewing a web page with a resolution or higher. Many commercial sites solve the problem by putting a table on the left and set the width at 800 pixel. Doing this, their page will perfectly fit on most screens.

Here is another choice. Position your site in the middle of the screen. If there are people who have smaller viewports viewing your page, it will fit perfectly. However, when the group that has a larger screen views your page there will be space on both the left and right sides.

When setting your page width to 100% your page will looks differently on different machines. If your page is text based, it would be considered less harmful; but if your page needs a fixed composition, don't try this.

As a rule of thumb, when working with graphic lines, you should be careful to constrain its width so that it doesn't exceed 800 pixels. The reason for this is so that your visitor doesn't have to scroll horizontally to view your content on their smaller devices.

Design Tips #3

I am going to divulge one of my favorite sources. Pay attention here, this one is worth its weight in gold. Bookmark, subscribe, and get your hands and heart around Chuck Green's Ideabooks. Ideabook.com is on HOW magazine's Top 10 Web Sites list.

---

15   WC3 Screen resolutions http://www.w3schools.com/browsers/browsers_display.asp Last accessed May 30, 2013

It is a superb resource for the designer, copywriter, illustrator, photographer, design student, and anyone else interested in the disciplines of design and marketing. The comprehensive archive of free TUTORIALS offers insights on design, page layout, the use of color, illustration, photography, typography, print and web design, and the business of design.

Now you can't say I never gave you any really valuable tips. Enjoy!

Design Tips #4

Understanding should be your goal when designing. Whether you are designing a flyer or a website put yourself in the receiver's place. Make them feel like they are right there with you. Keep it self-intuitive. Confidently show them in a way that they come away saying, "I can do that!" or "I just can't live without that!" The end result is they understand, and like what you are offering or saying.

Design Tips #5

This design tip will help you set your site apart from the competition. When designing your background, add texture. A simple texture will give your site a feel instead of just sitting there. Texture is anything that gives a distinctive appearance or feel to the surface of a design or object.

Not every site has to be beautiful, but yours can be, with just a little customization.

Design Tips #6

When it comes to selecting your images you need to be sure you have the rights to use the images. There are basically three types of rights each with their own limitations. They are Free license, Public Domain is part of this group; Non-Free license, Publicity photos of people and events are in this group; and Depreciated, images that are not verifiable for copyright license.

Further, there are multiple levels of copyrights available, from single use purchase to time-limit usage. Be sure you aren't just copying and using images and illustrations that you find on the web. Even if the image is listed as copyright free that may not mean that you can use it for anything except personal use.

You need to decide what is more important to you, time or money. If you have a lot of free time to devote to searching for just the right image then go for it. However if you are a busy entrepreneur like me you may decide to invest in copyright licenses for your images or create your own.

Happy hunting.

Design Tips #7

This design tip is to 'Make it personal'. Add at least one element to your site to give your visitor the feeling that you are 'real'. A good way to do this is with quotes, audio, and/or video. Perhaps just a professional photo put up with a short message from you.

Design Tips #8

This tip is not for the faint at heart. You remember that roll-over effect? When working with large spreadsheets try creating a roll-over highlight effect for the rows so that it is easier for your visitor to follow along with you. If you need help working this one out give me a shout.

Design Tips #9

This tip takes our environment into consideration. Save a tree by creating mini-brochures instead of full size. You can still get your message across within the space, but miniaturizing your content will allow you to create two or three where only one was possible before. Not only will this save a tree but it will save you hard earned money as well.

If you need help in this area just ask. I will be happy to oblige.

Design Tips #10

I am glad you enjoyed that last little tip. Here's another one for your idea bank.

With all the color combinations available to you, do you find yourself not knowing what colors go well together and what don't? Check out this color schemer before you make your decision http://www. ColorCombos.com.

How about giving a monochromatic color scheme a look. Just work with tints and shades of the same color. It can make for an interesting and powerful look.

Design Tips #11

This design tip is pretty simple. Be sure you design a clear and simple navigation system. Look at it from your visitor's perspective. Keep it consistently in the same position on EVERY page of your site. Title your buttons/text clearly, so that the visitor will know where they want to go instead of what you think is a cool title. And most importantly make your logo link to your homepage. You might be surprised how many visitors click that before even attempting to find your "HOME" button or nav link.

Design Tips #12

Postcard Marketing can be an effective tool when used properly. To be most affective you need to send your postcard to your dormant client list. Those that have raised their hand or have purchased a while back most likely will not trash your marketing piece as soon as they see it. I would love to tell you that it can be effective tool for a cold list but that is generally not the case.

Be sure your cover image is reflective of your business. Something catchy or branded to your business works best. As with any other piece, be sure your message is clearly stated. What is your offer and how can they take advantage of it?

Then track your results! This is the area that is most often neglected. One way to know how effective your marketing piece is, is to specify the contact method or utilize a special code number that they will need to use.

Design Tips #13

.gif, .jpg, .tiff, .png, what's the difference? Why should you care?

There is a complex answer that only a rocket scientist could understand, but to make it as simple as I can to explain, the answer is best found in their benefits and deficiencies.

A gif image is used primarily for the web. It can be a single image or rotating. What do I mean? Those cute little smiley faces above the message box on a web site wink and blink and even send you kisses. Those are all gif images. The quality of a gif image is usually pretty low.

A jpg image is used primarily for photographs. Once placed on the web they begin to degrade and therefore require higher resolution for stability when used for print. Thus the invention of the tiff and png choices.

Tiff and png files are the higher end of gif and jpgs. A tiff file is the partner of jpg and the png is the partner of gif images.

When using images for the web you will want to use the smallest possible files therefore you will find the gif or png files most beneficial. However, with print tif files are far superior to jpg.

One other benefit of gif and png files is the ability to create transparent images.

I hope that you find this brief explanation sufficient. If you want more detail, I recommend you do a Google search or send me over a query and I will be happy to point you in the right direction.

Design Tips #14

When deciding on a color to use on the web you should keep in mind that there are only 216 to choose from that all computer monitors recognize. Vary off of these with the full 256 and you run the risk of your website not looking exactly the way you intended.

You see, the problem lies in the fact that different platforms use different color palettes. Both Macs and PCs have 256 colors in their system palettes, but only 216 of them are the same colors.

You can find the Web Safe Color chart here: http://html-color-codes.com if you want to know what the choices are that are available to you for safe web color design.

So next time you specify colors for background, text, or graphic images, make sure you're using these 216 browser-safe colors if you want to achieve cross-browser uniformity in your site design.

Design Tips #15

What is all the hoopla about CSS? CSS stands for Cascading Style Sheet. Before the CSS standards for web design, every page and every line of code in every page had to be hand tweaked for design. Now you can create one style sheet that is globally read by your entire website. It is now simple to change, when you want to, the way your site looks.

Let's say you want just a little darker green, go to your style sheet and find the element you want to darken and simply change the color coding to reflect the choice. ONE TIME and wallah you are done!

So DO use them rather than not.

If you need help figuring out just how to code a CSS sheet you will find more information here: http://www.w3schools.com/css/css_reference.asp

Design Tips #16

Resolution. If you are wondering why your images don't look so hot on the web or why they are so grainy when you print a web image most likely the problem stems from the resolution of your image.

What is resolution? Well it is the number of dots in an image. When you take a low number resolution image, 72 DPI (dots per inch) and expand the size what you are doing is pulling the dots apart. Therefore, the image becomes grainy. You can usually go down in size but not up and you absolutely must not go down and then back up!

The reason I mention 72 DPI is that is the standard resolution for web images, whereas for print the proper resolution needs to be 200 or better yet 300 DPI minimum.

So the next time you are working with images make sure they are the right resolution for your project.

Design Tips #17

I found this tip in my inbox this morning. It was just so perfect and well-presented that I am sharing it in its entirety, author intact. I know we all need to make use of this one!

Turn Your Fax Cover Sheets into Sales Tools by Janet Attard

The heading and text on most fax cover sheets takes up only about half of the available space on a page. The rest of the cover page is usually nothing but white space.

Don't waste all that unused space! Make your cover sheets do double duty by including promotional material for your products or services.

For instance, if you run a secretarial service, instead of just including your name and logo on a fax cover sheet, you could list your company's services in a column down the left side of the paper. Put the body of the fax in a box on the right side of the paper.

The new design could help remind recipients that you offer desktop publishing and PowerPoint preparation in addition to creating web pages. It would also be a good example of your typesetting and design capabilities.

If you sell products, redesign your cover sheets so you can include ads for products you want to feature. Your ad will ride free every time you send an outgoing fax to your existing customers, suppliers or others with whom you do business.

Design Tips #18

Sound vs. Mute

The most important aspect to consider when offering audio on your website is your visitor. When you take into consideration their tastes may vary from yours you should find yourself leaning towards not using sound bites. However if you still want to add that little extra rather than annoying your potential customers offer them the play bar and have it not start up when they arrive but rather only if they chose to hit the play button.

This little bit of extra code can save you potential income. Instead of using the background code try using embed and set the auto start to "false".

Another option is to offer a secondary choice of musical type. As an example, one might use jazz for one and country for the secondary.

One more step you should consider is the browsers that don't adhere to today's coding standards. Those that don't support the embed tag can be enabled to listen by inserting a click here link to the background source file.

Put all of this together and the code should look something like this:

<embed src="bgsound.mid" hidden="true" autostart="false" loop="1">
<noembed>Your browser doesn't support EMBED, but you can still listen to the background sound of this page by<a href="bgsound.mid"> clicking here.</a></noembed>

Design Tips #19

Do you use PowerPoint for your presentations? If so I have a site to recommend to you. They offer free backgrounds as well as paid ones. I highly recommend them and assure you their quality is well worth the time invested to sign-up for the free account.

http://www.indezine.com/powerpoint/templates/freetemplates.html

This is one of my very private sites so please don't distribute the link liberally.

Design Tips #20

When designing PowerPoint Presentations to solidify your credibility never use clip art. Stick with high quality photographs that represent the emotion your point is making.

Design Tips #21

Working with transparent gif images. To ensure your image doesn't have an ugly glow around it use a simple trick. When rendering your transparent gif image for the web be sure to use a blended edge in the same color or very close to your background. This will enable a smooth transition between the image and the background.

Now go put this one to work for you and if you have any questions, please email me and I will answer you promptly.

Design Tips #22

Whether you are designing a layout for an ad or a website, consider your visitor. How do you want their eyes to flow over your content? The natural flow of the human eyeball varies depending on what country your visitor is from or even whether they are right or left handed. So get to know your market first, and then lay your design out according to their flow.

New technology is in beta testing that tracks the users mouse, but it isn't confirmed that the mouse moves reflect the eyeball at this point in time. For those of you who are techno-geeks here's the info: The service is free and can be launched from the Feng-GUI site (http://www.feng-gui.com/), or remotely via a Firefox extension (http://www.feng-gui.com/tools.htm).

5 KEY ELEMENTS OF BUSINESS IMAGE DESIGN

What is a business image? It is the unspoken representation of your business. It defines how others perceive what you do and who you are. Simply said, it is your business identity. The business that has no business image in place actually has a poor business image. Therefore it is important they you create an image today if you haven't already done so.

When you consider what you want your business image to evolve into, think about the way you would want to be perceived. Would you personally go out in public without being properly groomed? I doubt it. The same holds true with your business. Things like, lack of stationary and re-used packaging illustrate to your customers that you are cheap or don't consider them valuable. While you may think that being fugal, pinching a penny here will cut your bottom line, they may conceive this seemingly insignificant act to mean that you may not be in business the next time they need your services.

What are the critical components of a professional business image? There are several pieces to be considered. While the whole may be different for each individual business owner, there are five key elements that make up a solid business image that must be addressed. Can you guess what those five would be?

Let's put our puzzle together.

1. Business Name & Tagline

Your business name is vital to you. It is one piece that cannot be ignored or taken lightly. Because you will carry this name with you for many years to come great care should be taken in the selection. It is not unheard of to change your business name, however each time you do you risk losing customers. So think carefully, get input from trusted friends and decided on the name that best fits your product or service.

While your business name should easily reveal who you are your tagline should reveal what you do. Keep it simple. A long and complicated tagline is easily forgotten or confused. Take a cue from the corporate giants, short and sweet, direct and to the point, make for memorable taglines. See if you know these taglines. Most of these I am sure you will recognize.

Taglines

It's the Real Thing

You're In Good Hands

Bring Out the Best

Fly the Friendly Skies

The Ultimate Driving Machine

And my personal favorite: We Make YOU Look GOOD!

Here are the answers, how'd you do?

It's the Real Thing—Coke

You're In Good Hands—Allstate

Bring Out the Best—Hellmann's

Fly the Friendly Skies—United

The Ultimate Driving Machine—BMW

We Make YOU Look GOOD!—DocUmeant Publishing & Designs

Be sure your tagline contains two important elements, that of emotional and functional words. It needs to quickly describe what you do. If you want to open a pet store, don't simply name it The Pet Store, that's a little stale. Try something memorable like, Paula's Pet Emporium or Perfectly Petaculous. One note on personalizing your business name, if there is even a slight chance that you may want to sell your business in the future, leave off the personalization. I am sure given the choice, as a buyer, you would prefer not to buy the business just to turn around and have to change the name and lose those loyal clients.

2. Logo

Selection of your logo is of paramount importance. The three things to remember in designing your logo are that it is easily recognizable, matches the look and feel of what you wish to portray and the colors enhance the image.

When deciding on your logo do a bit of soul searching and research before you begin the process; it is a very good place to start. Find out what is out there already, don't imitate, be unique and creative. Use the competition as a starting point to give you some ideas, DON'T copy!

The colors you choose should be carried throughout all of your business materials. If you use red and green or blue and white—stay with them when designing your website and stationary.

Speaking of stationary, let's move on to the importance of well-designed business materials.

3. Stationary

Stationary items that should be considered are letterhead, envelopes, business card, and forms. Your local office supply store has a number of business forms available for your use at a reasonable cost. Nevertheless, what do your customers think or perceive when they receive them? Does it show permanence, longevity and commitment? Spending just a little more time and money to create forms and stationary that are uniform can greatly affect your business' perceived value.

4. Marketing materials

Marketing materials should always carry your business identity. These items may be as small as a pen with only the name and address of the business. Items in this category should include brochure(s), flyers, coupon, gift certificates, card and postcards, t-shirts, hats, and other giveaway items. Pens are often the giveaway item of choice; people tend to hold on to them, and if lost or shared the new owner has your information. We call this "shelf-life" or your product's "life cycle."

5. Storefront/Website

As mentioned earlier, your image gives your business a uniform look and feel when all of the elements retain a 'oneness'. Your storefront/website is no exception. Whether online or offline this is your main source of customer interaction. Solidify your presence and demonstrate your credibility and reliability quickly. Let them know within the first few minutes what you do and how well you do it by presenting your unique business identity in the forefront of your business location. (What is typically called 'above the fold'.)

Take a step back from your business; look at it through your customer's eyes. If need be poll your customers to get a clearer vision. Once you have decided the image you want to represent you, use it throughout your entire business. Be it fun and whimsical or clean and professional, your image is an unspoken representation of your business, becoming its identity. As such, it will speak for you more clearly than words. When you have a complete business identity it ensures your customer will easily recognize who you are, what you do, and demonstrate your competence.

I challenge you to define or review your current business image. Ask for customer feedback and then solidify your place in the market. With all your pieces carrying your single message you will further exclaim your permanence.

CREATING PRESENTATIONS THAT WORK

Next month my husband, Philip, will be doing a presentation on Artificial Intelligence at the Rutgers's meeting. It has been interesting to watch it develop. As a designer and author of *Presentational Skills for the Next Generation*, I have, several times, mentioned to him that instead of using pictures in a folder, he should make them into slides with PowerPoint. Quietly, he took half my advice and created a garish colored background and put all his speaking notes on them. When he proudly turned to me and said, "What do you think?" I was at a loss for words.

After a brief pause, for contemplation as to how to answer, I told him that he should probably add some interest to the background. As I continued to gently nudge him in the direction of PowerPoint, he finally realized that it might be a good idea. "And hey," he proudly exclaimed, "you could design the slides and I could say, designed by DocUmeant Designs."

With my current workload, that wasn't quite what I had in mind. But I agreed, since I would be in attendance and people would probably think I had made the presentation slides anyway. Dutifully, so as not to offend him, I designed the slides with an attractive background, and put every bit of text on his text heavy slides.

While working on the slides I mentioned to him that he needed to add pictures to bring out the points, but his scientific mind wouldn't wrap around that idea. So, I quietly add a couple small images to just three slides. When I was done, I told him he should go over it and continue to edit the slides and rearrange them as needed. As he went along, he asked me if it would be okay to add example notes at the bottom of a few slides, so he wouldn't forget to bring out those points and perhaps even spur the audience to ask about them. Egads! His already text heavy slides were going to topple over the projector!

This is when I had to tell him that perhaps he should cut down the points to just a word or two and talk through them, rather than putting all the text on the slides. Perhaps even to use pictures to spur your words, I said, rather than all that text. After a brief rejection of that idea, he understood and embraced the idea. He finally got it!

Have you suffered through your fair share of boring, text heavy slide presentations? I hope you will learn, through this experience, how to make your presentations interesting and powerful rather than boring and dull. If you need help, I would be happy to help you too design your next PowerPoint slide set. Contact me and let me know at ginger.marks@documeantdesigns.com.

CUSTOMER SIGN-UP FORMS, DOES YOURS DO THE JOB?

C ustomer sign-ups is what being in business on the Internet is all about. Building your customer base is a long and tedious process. However, if your form isn't well designed you may be losing valuable opportunities.

Let's first look at what a sign-up form is and what it is not. A sign-up form is meant to collect names and emails of those who are interested in your product or service. They may or may not become your client or customer, but they have raised their hand and said I have an interest.

What it is not is a way to bombard your customers with marketing messages. Offer them free information, and upgrade options later. Your job is to take them from interested to customer. This can be done only by building a relationship with them. They need to trust you before they will take that next step.

Now let's look at your sign-up form. Is it easy to spot? Is the relevant information front and center? Are you asking for way too much input? Is it too subtle or over-designed? All these are factors that could be detrimental to your business sign-ups.

The actual design of your form should be simple and request only the name and email address. Any other information you want to collect should be obtained at a later date. Yes, a comments box could be included, but maybe your confirmation email can offer that opportunity. That's your call.

Make sure your form is placed in the top third of your webpage—above the fold. Right or left? Who's to say? This is debatable. More importantly is the color scheme and design. The theme should match your site. If your site is fun and funky, so too should your form be. If it is corporate, then a clean and polished looking will do the trick. You get the picture?

Colors should be accent colors to your site. To get an idea of what those are look to a color wheel. There are numerous ones available and some even go into excruciating detail. Lightly highlight the fields you require to make them easy to spot. If you have a sectional sign-up form, why not consider some nice iconography to accent those sections. These additions make it easy for the registering visitor to know at a glance the information you need. Keep it logical and clean. Drop shadows are not necessary and neither are gradients. Keep it simple and uniform but not dull.

Now let's turn to the fonts. Headlines should be that, headlines. Make them a size or two larger than your descriptive text or bold them to save space. When defining headlines vs. body text the norm is sans serif headlines and serif text or vice versa. Instructions should be clear, easily readable and understandable without having to hunt for them.

Talking about saving space, if this is an issue for you, why not put the form labels in the form field. This saves space by eliminating the form labels while ensuring the right information is replaced in the correct field without any confusion.

FREE REPORTS & WHITEPAPERS

Our email newsletter will keep you informed about new staffing industry reports, whitepapers, news & events:

Email Address

First Name

Sign me up!

What about the buttons? Should you have a reset button, or just submit? The answer is simple, what do you want them to do? I would guess you want them to submit. Therefore, use one button that clearly states your intended purpose, "Submit". There's no need for special wording. Tell them what you want them to do in the language they are used to seeing. Remember, confusion breeds loss. Keep things clear and easy to understand. However, words like 'Sign me up now', 'Get my report' and a few others may be relevant to your situation. Just be crystal clear with your instructions.

If you have a lot of information you need to provide to explain your offer, why not put the form on one side and the text on the other. This helps keep the information logically in one place rather than the top to bottom approach.

And lastly, remember, the information you need to collect will dictate the form fields and the design of your form. Keep it logical, clean, and easy to read and you'll have a workable form that functions as you intended. Oh and don't forget to test! We wouldn't want you to miss a sign-up because your form didn't work.

HOW TO CREATE EFFECTIVE CALL TO ACTION GRAPHICS

Your Call To Action (CTA) is the, number one, most important part of your marketing campaign. Whether online or off, it is the link from information to sale for your potential customer. This is why what you choose to represent your CTA should be well thought.

We are all used to the Click Here CTA. Nevertheless, you would probably agree that due to its overuse this text CTA has lost its impact. So how do you do to create an effective CTA? Follow these simple rules to increase your sales in your next marketing piece or website design or update.

Uniformity—Keep all your CTAs uniform. Your visitor will easily recognize your CTA if you use it each time you wish them to do something. We are creatures of habit and require similarity to easily recognize things.

Size—Whether you choose to use text or graphics make your CTA big enough to be seen from a distance. Whether your audience is young or old, size alone can have a definite impact on your turn-over rate. Too small and it may not be seen; too big and it will be ignored. However, even when your content can't be read at a distance, your CTA should continue to be clearly seen and understood. Again, keep it uniform in size as well as design.

Wording—Besides consistency in design, consistency in wording is an important element in CTA design. When considering the words to use, as I mentioned before, use something other than the overused Click Here. Be sure to start your CTA with an ACTIVE VERB: get, learn, see, find, modify, add, submit, etc. Consider including a benefit or result in the text of your CTA, if possible: Get your free subscription, Learn more, etc. Use fonts that are easy to read. Fonts such as Arial and Verdana are the best choices, while Times New Roman or fancy, flowery text are among the worst.

Placement—Due to the importance of your CTA you should always place your CTA in a highly visible place on your page. If you don't know where your visitor's eye falls on your page this will be more difficult for you to choose. There are many studies that indicate where the "eye path" of the Internet user falls. Considering this one element can make logical sense when you wish to increase your Sales Conversion Rate (SCR). Make your CTA the logical conclusion to your page's content.

Design—As with your website, your CTA design should remain consistent to your site's content. It is a good idea to use clean and professional design in your business elements. Save the outlandish and garish for your blog or personal sites. A clean, professional appearance coveys both credibility and longevity.

To further enhance your SCR make your CTA button stand out with the use of the Web 2.0 3-D effects that are now available.

Roll-over Effects—If your visitor has made it to your CTA button with their mouse they have already indicated an interest. A mouse-over effect could be a good way to reinforce their action and may increase their chance of taking the desired action or not.

No matter what CTA design you choose, track your results. The key to effective marketing is knowing what works. When you want to know how affective your efforts are, monitoring and assessing their effectiveness will give you the necessary edge to keep your marketing efforts on track. Never stop testing and gathering user input.

For more information or assistance with your CTA button design contact me at ginger.marks@doc-umeantdesigns.com.

RESPONSIVE WEB DESIGN: TIMES ARE CHANGING

Staying on top of the ever changing technology can be a monumental task these days. For business owners and authors alike this means the Internet landscape itself is constantly evolving. From new book marketing channels to your home on the web itself, there is always a new ap or technology to be considered. How best to evolve your website is the question at hand, or even should you.

It seems like just a little while ago a business owner need only have a web presence. Fixed width was the norm, centered pretty much a given. Then, up popped the flexible width websites which allowed all different sizes of desktops to view the content based on their screen width. This however, was merely the birthing pains of a new era in web design. Laptops, iPads, and iPhones are now in the hands of an ever growing population. According to Jeff Bullas,

- "Use of desktop computers is down for 35% iPad owners since they bought the device
- Use of laptops is also down since they bought an iPad at 39%
- 87% of owners are using it every day of the week
- 26% for half an hour to an hour per day
- 32% for 1-2 hours per day
- 24% for more than 2 hours a day."[16]

Just as we are scrambling to learn Adaptive Web Design to cope with the ever growing digital devices available the WC3[17] has decided to begin the implementation of new standards in design which they have dubbed *Responsive Web Design*.

No longer can the business owner keep up with this ever changing environment. It is time to let go and let the webmasters tackle this complex landscape. However, for those of you die hard do-it-yourselfers here's the tip of the iceberg of Responsive Web Design. Keep in mind though, that as long as your website if 'flexible' your website should be able to be viewed on most devices.

With *Adaptive design* code is written for each device, but with *Responsive design* one size truly fits all. To begin with we no longer express size in specific increments, such as pixels per inch, inches, or the like. Everything is sized as compared to a fixed standard. What are those standards? The most often used is the 'em'—the height of an 'm'. Each device from the iPhone's 320 pixel screen all the way up to your

---

16   http://www.jeffbullas.com/2011/04/04/29-statistics-reveal-how-the-apples-ipad-is-changing-our-lives/
17   http://www.w3.org/standards/webdesign/

desktop's 1480—and growing—pixel display need to show all of your website's content without the user noticing any adjustments or side-scrolling.

While you may have a multiple column website on your desktop, those columns, if left to only re-size on your iPhone will become so tiny that they can't be easily read. So, what responsive design enables is 'content re-flow'. This merely means that your columns that are side-by-side on your desktop will slide under each other on your smaller devices, as in your iPhone or iPad. And since your font too is specified in percentages rather than pixels it fits better in the host device too.

As for font sizes you may not be aware, but the standard font size for all browsers is 16 pixels (px). Therefore if you want your font size to be smaller than that, which most of us do, for example you will need to express your body font size as 62.5% to achieve a 10 px font and then when you want a larger 12 px font you would tell your font to increase to 1.2 em and for 16 px 1.6 em. Now that makes the math much simpler wouldn't you say? But, the caveat here is in deep parent/child relationship. However, I won't get into this discussion here.

Now, let's touch on the image resizing issues. The good news is that we have now clearer, crisper, high resolution displays, which allow us to bump up our dpi (dot per inch) from the web standard of 72 to a whopping 96! Even still, this won't help us in responsive image resizing and rendering across devices. Sure you can simply specify your image display as percentages, but that can leave you with muddy images on larger screens and anomalies on smaller ones.

The world of web design is fully aware of the impending image problem. There is actually a whole group dedicated to solving these challenges. In time they may come up with a solution that will be viable on all platforms. But for now, your web designer can recommend the best work-around for your website's images.

As you can see, things are changing fast, but don't fret. When you can afford to invest in a make-over of your Internet presence that is soon enough to invest in the new Responsive Web Design.

Article Series

BACK TO BASICS, PART 1

Are you experiencing the success that you envisioned when you first conceived your company? Are you happy with the productivity that your corporation is experiencing? If your answer to these questions is "No" then perhaps it is time you took a step back and looked at your organization from an objective point of view.

Take a cue from sports team coaches. Get back to the basics. So, what are the basics of business? Construction of your business plan is the most basic of the basics. The very first thing you should do it sit down with your business plan and look at what it says. Are you still on track or do you need to rethink and update it? If you don't have a plan written down I strongly urge you to sit down and compose your ideas and put them in writing.

Your business plan should be written as if you were explaining how you are going to sell your product or service to potential backers. Explain not only what it is you have to offer but how you are going to go about getting your product from design to consumer. How you are going to promote as well as package will be important points to consider. When viewed in this way you will find preparing or fine tuning your plan is a simple straight forward process.

Reuter's: The online consumer takes a mere three seconds to evaluate whether your organization is worth considering for their needs or not.

Now that you have your business plan in hand and are again ready to tackle the world let's look at some other basics that need to be addressed. If you have decided that your company requires or would be enhanced by offering an online connection don't try to do it by yourself. A recent Reuter's article stated that the online consumer takes a mere three seconds to evaluate whether your organization is worth considering for their needs or not. What that tells me is that even though you think you may be able to produce an online presence with little or no training that there is extremely more to it than you think.

A talented web designer will create a professional site and can help direct you to a web hosting company that won't be constantly down for repairs. The wrong server could be more costly than having an unprofessional business presentation on the web. Consider hiring a professional designer to compose your web presence, you will find it will make a world of difference to your bottom-line.

Most online business owners know the value of Search Engine Optimization (SEO) and the importance of having their web pages Search Engine Optimized. To ensure you don't miss this extremely important step you should seek out a talented professional that specializes in this field. With the assistance of a skilled SEO technician you can be sure your website has the keywords and phrases, links and titles arrange to provide you the Search Engine placement that you need to attract attention.

SEO is not just about placement of those keywords and phrases it is about analyzing the competition to find out how your company's website can compete with top ranking sites. You should consider hiring an SEO company to apply these techniques while constructing your site. Maintaining the SEO on your site will help ensure your company stays in the game.

Now that you have these basic tools in order it's time to look at how to go about spreading the word about your company. We will tackle this subject next time in Part 2 "The Nuts and Bolts of Business Building".

BACK TO BASICS, PART 2: THE NUTS & BOLTS OF BUSINESS BUILDING

In my last article we tackled the all-important issue of business planning. Now that you have developed your business plan and have the necessary financing to get your company off the ground it is time to look at how you are going to build your business.

How you treat your interested patrons and the integrity that you outwardly assert can greatly affect the continued growth of your organization. If you are contented with a constant turnover of clientele then incessantly pursue the almighty dollar over anything else. It is only when you value your integrity more than financial gain that you prove your worth to your customers and yourself.

What you will find when you are honest with people is that they respect your honesty. And it is when they witness that natural quality in a business owner and staff that you can begin to successfully build repeat business. Not only will your consumer come back time and again but they will be more apt to recommend your services to their friends and families. We all already know that word of mouth can be the best or worst form of advertising that you will ever receive depending on the way you treat your customers.

Likewise when you treat your consumer with disrespect, no matter how trivial or 'right' you might genuinely believe you are, just one discontented individual can economically ravage your business growth. People are more likely to inform perfect strangers about how you mistreated them. Once that individual tells one person the word spreads quickly throughout the business community and you may find not only your reputation tarnished but your business growth stunted as well.

Take a moment and reflect back to a time when someone you dealt with in business treated you unjustly. Did you just go home and sulk? Did you limit the discourse to your immediate family and close friends or did you tell anybody and everybody who would listen just how unfairly you were treated? Did you also say something like, 'I wouldn't recommend you go there!'? This type of defensive response is not unusual, in any dispute. No one given the opportunity to highly recommend a business or service would ever even take into consideration recommending one that we were not completely satisfied with through our own experience.

So how do you gain your customer's respect? Listen to them fully. When they speak listen to what they are saying. They will tell you precisely what their need is. You essentially grasp they are interested to some degree because they are there to begin with. Now, all you have to do is find out what specifically they are anxiously seeking. It is when you are prepared to go that extra mile for them that your customer becomes aware of your genuine respect for them. One way you can show your readiness to sufficiently assist them is when you don't have what they require or essentially need but offer to briefly explore the possibility of acquiring it for them or initially recommend another reliable source for them to look.

Success IS more than the dollars and cents. True success can only be found when you grasp that fact. When you successfully balance personal integrity and financial gains you can make money and be fulfilled in your business endeavors. To do this, memorize the three keys: effectively listen, generously give, and always show respect.

It is when you recognize that making a living and making a difference in other's lives can be the most satisfying part of your business practice that you will successfully attain true fulfillment and amazing prosperity. Open your mind and your heart to the absolute truth that business success and integrity can work hand in hand.

Join me next time as we tackle Part 3 of Back to Basics as we turn our attention to the all-important topic of marketing. Until next time begin to apply these three key principles; listen, give, and respect!

BACK TO BASICS, PART 3: MARKETING BASICS I

Now that you have these basic tools in order it's time to look at how to go about spreading the word about your business. To guarantee traffic, you have to do some marketing. Online, you can spread the word in a variety of ways:

☐ Submit to Search Engines (SE)
☐ Pay for Search-Engine placement
☐ Exchange links with other sites
☐ Press Release strategy
☐ Advertise
☐ Use promotions
☐ Networking
☐ Use email signature

So let's look at each of these in order.

Submit to Search Engines means just that. You have to let them know you are there. Once you have announced your presence by filling out the necessary forms you might consider purchasing a search-engine placement agreement.

When you can submit to search engines for free why would you ever want to **pay for Search Engine placement**? The answer is simple. Some SEs allow you to rank higher in their listing if you submit payment. What this means is that your listing will appear higher in the listings when a potential customer performs a search using your keywords & phrases. Let's say you submit to a SE without payment. They simply add you to the bottom of the list and move you up according to your relevance. This may result in your listing showing up on the 100th search result page. However if you submit with payment you may see your listing much earlier, maybe even on the second or third results page.

Think about your own habits. How many search results does it usually take you before you either find what you are looking for or simply give up and go on? I usually don't get as far as 20 pages deep. So, consider carefully the benefit of paying for SE placement for your business.

If you want to take full advantage of SE placement you may find it easier to hire a company that specializes in this area to assist you. These companies stay on top of the best way to virtually announce your presence and what search engines are looking for similarly to a SEO company. You may find these fees a bit of a stretch to start with but they are well worth the investment.

Link exchange; this is a confusing topic for most of us. We hear link exchange and we think of the link heavy site (link farm) where no one ever bothers to read all those banners let alone click any of them. This is not what I suggest you get involved in. Yes, there are reasons to go that route but what will drive traffic to your site is a link exchange with a company that draws the same clientele that you are looking to market to.

Let's consider a business that services air conditioners. OK, you are service technician what better way to expand your business than to 'link' to an air conditioner retailer. How about a small retail store like Lowes or Home Depot? They often work with outside specialist. So you contact the retailer and tell them that you are interested in promoting their store in exchange for them allowing you to put your business card in their 'window'. Of course, this is a win-win for both of the businesses and so an agreement is made. Now let's say the business removes your business card from their sales desk. What happens then?

You see what you are doing is giving away a bit of your ranking each time you offer to link to another site. Unless it is a reciprocal link it can affect your SEO ranking. So, what you need to do is to check back often to make sure the link is still in place and if it is not, remove it from yours as well. Conversely, if you can get another site to link to you without having to reciprocate that one link will incrementally increase your ranking. Search engines consider your site an authority site when they see these types of links and therefore give your site priority over reciprocally linked sites.

BACK TO BASICS, PART 4: MARKETING BASICS II

As a quick review thus far we have discussed:

- ☐ Submit to Search Engines (SE)
- ☐ Pay for Search-Engine placement
- ☐ Exchange links with other sites

Let's resume our discussion with **Press Release Strategy**.

If ever there were two words in the English language that make your heart start beating faster they are PRESS RELEASE. Does the thought of having to write a press release send shivers up your spine? Chances are you haven't the foggiest notion of what a press release really is or how to put one together. If you have been putting off using this very effective and inexpensive tool to market your product or service you have truly been missing the boat.

I am going to begin by explaining just what a press release is and is not. Many of us are under the misconceived notion that a press release is a big hairy monster that will never be tamed. We tend to think of them in this way simply because we have no clue as to how to begin writing one.

A press release is just that, a press release. What do I mean by that? A press release simply announces to the media that your business is involved with the community. It is an **announcement**. Its main purpose is to inform the media that there is a newsworthy event that you or your business is involved in at the moment. Some forms of media you might consider submitting to are newspapers, radio, television, magazines, etc. If your story is of interest, you may just end up being interviewed or in the very least they could run your press release in their publication. What it is NOT is an AD!

Press releases are **not** meant to advertise your business blatantly. You can be sure that when a reporter is looking for a story they are not looking for an advertisement for your business. They receive these overly long, overt advertisements under the guise of press release daily. They have one quick, effective way of dealing with this type of submission. FILE 99! No, they won't get back with you and let you know what you did wrong and why they aren't using your submission they simply throw it in the round file next to their desk.

So how do you keep your press release from ending up in the press release graveyard? First keep it informative, second keep it short, and third include your contact information.

Informative, your press release should be developed around a current newsworthy event. This can be a way your business is providing a service for the community or an event that your business is sponsoring. Let's take a look at what types of services and events that can be used to promote your business in a press release. There is a plethora of possible scenarios you could use. To name a few and to get your creative juices flowing consider these, bringing the blood mobile to your place of business to allow your employees and the public to join in a blood drive, donating a product or service to a charity, sponsoring an event such as a cancer awareness walk, volunteering your time to assist at a local shelter or clinic, or what about that noteworthy accomplishment or award. When using this last idea be sure that your focus remains on the community benefit that your award or accomplishment affords and not a bragging ceremony.

Keep your press release informative, short, and include your contact information.

Now that you have a newsworthy event in mind for your press release topic you need to put it together. I know that this is where you take out that blank white sheet and sit and stare at it for the next hour. What and how do you actually write it? *Keep it short yet pertinent.*

Let's use the example of sponsoring a charity event. Begin by creating **a catchy title.** As with any advertising piece you want to get the reporter to read further. The first couple of words are critical in accomplishing that feat. We are going to use Local Food Drive for Hurricane Katrina Victims. Notice we have not only used a charity event but a hot news topic as well. You will want to include a subtitle to further clarify. Using my business as an example I might write: DocUmeant to sponsor relief effort. Now you have the idea, the heading and the subheading.

Before you even write your heading be sure you place your name and contact information at the very apex of the release. You will want to clarify the date instructions at this point as well. Inform them whether it is "For Immediate Release";" For Release Before [list the date here]" or "For Release After [date]". My example event is going to be held on June 3, 2006 so I want to notify the public of this even prior to its occurrence. The date I will use will be a week prior to the event. You may want to release it sooner or later depending on your event. Too long and the public will forget it and too short and it will affect your turnout. Therefore I highly recommend that you *send your release out no later than ten days prior to the event.*

Now for the content; when writing a press release, say who, what, where, when, why and how in the first paragraph, if you can. Then give your summary story. Don't give them all the information as the purpose is to peak their interest enough that they will contact you for a possible interview; however give them enough information that if they don't they will still be able to publish your item.

Once you have finished writing your press release be sure to *signify the end of your press release*. This is done with the use of a few simple characters. Place ### at the end of your release.

Now you are ready to send it out and take advantage of this inexpensive yet useful tool. Be sure you hire a distribution company that uses Newswire[18] or you can expect mediocre results at best. That wasn't all that scary now was it?

Next month we will conclude this series on Marketing Basics with a brief overview of the last four very important marketing strategies, *Advertising, promotions, networking and the use of email signatures.*

---

18   Reuters Newswires, http://evo.staging.thomsonreuters.com/newswires

BACK TO BASICS, PART 5: MARKETING BASICS III

This month we will complete our study of Marketing Basics.

Thus far we have discussed:

- ☐ Submit to Search Engines (SE)
- ☐ Pay for Search-Engine placement
- ☐ Exchange links with other sites
- ☐ Press release strategy

We will conclude our discussion by briefly touching on the benefits of our last four marketing solutions:

- ☐ Advertisements
- ☐ Promotions
- ☐ Networking
- ☐ Email signature

As we already know advertising can be a costly venture. The key to effective advertising can be found in the creation of a memorable ad. When your ad copy is bland and unimaginative it is easily overlooked or forgotten. What you want to do is first create ad copy that will spark an action. If you need assistance in developing a catchy ad there are many capable ad copy writers that can assist you in this area. As a writer myself I stay in touch with other writers that have developed a successful reputation in this field of expertise. You may want to search out an established ad copy writer or contact me for a referral. Once you have developed your memorable ad you will want to investigate the best placement for your ad.

Consider carefully your market area. If your market is automobile related for example you will want to place your ad in online and offline areas that focus on males or perhaps dealer publications and sites. Look not only for the general market but get specific. Are you trying to capture a young audience or an older more established group? If you were selling Yachts would you advertise in the local high school paper or yearbook or would you look more toward placing you ad in a boating community paper or magazine. Effective advertising is not only what but where.

Now let us look at the use of **promotions**. As we discussed with press release strategy promotions can be very effectively used to give you reason to write a press release. Promotions in and of themselves allow you the opportunity to bring your business into focus within the community. You can create your own promotion or simply become involved in a community event. When considering how to spend your time and money on a community event as a promotional tool you must first weigh and balance the benefit against the cost. If you feel it is a worthy opportunity you may want to not only donate your services but align your business with the event or promotion by becoming a sponsor. In sponsoring an event you will gain not only name recognition but you will be recognized as a leader in the community as well.

Recognizing the benefit of **networking** whether online or off will allow you additionally to build your name recognition. Whether you choose to join in your local networking organization such as the local chamber or civic group or online in a networking forum or group the key to successful networking can be summed up in one word, **relationships**.

If you really want to be a successful networker you must recognize that success comes with involvement. Become an active participant. Offer to assist in areas that you see a need or volunteer when you are able. If you simply sign-up and never attend or in the case of online networking never post to the board how will others know you are even a member?

This brings us to the final point which is the invaluable use of an **email signature**. With each and every posting on a message board or email response you should consider attaching a tagline and your business URL, unless the URL attachment is frowned upon. Your email signature can then be used as a subtle way of establishing your presence and informing the community of your business offering.

Let me give you an example with my own signature. First you will list your name, in my case it is Ginger Marks if you have a title such as mine, Publisher & Designer then that is established directly after your name. Then under that you will want to come up with a catchy tagline that tells your audience what you have to offer them. When on my favorite networking community, Ryze, I used "Isn't It Time Your Ryze Page Reflected YOU!?" Now with this tagline I have established myself as a web page designer as well as the above title of Publisher without having to directly list myself as such in my title. This further allows me to avoid the long list of titles that could develop by listing all of my titles after my name. Lastly if you are allowed, you will want to provide your business email address. I highly recommend that you include the full URL when listing your business website. This allows the link to often be clickable for ease of use by those wishing to contact you. In certain instances listing only a partial URL will negate this benefit to the reader.

This then concludes our discussion of marketing and business building basics. I hope you found this series beneficial and will begin to put into practice some of the valuable tools and information that has been presented here. If I can offer one last bit of advice it would be to **establish yourself as an expert in your field** by presenting yourself as one. When you hint that you are an expert ears open that would otherwise be closed to you. Consider marketing your business and yourself with the use of eBooks and articles as well.

GET INTO THEM, PART 1

Everyday new businesses start and fail. Some hang in there by-a-thread, while others grow and flourish. Today's economic conditions may have some bearing on your business, so to blame it for your business lags or failures if far too easy. No matter what the economy's condition, people still have wants and needs. Those of us who realize that fact early are apt to weather the economic storm. Bottom line, your product or service is still in demand. You just need to find the right audience and focus on them.

The first step to accomplishing this is to realize that "it's not all about YOU!—it's about THEM!" It's about their wants and needs, their likes and dislikes. Until you realize and embrace that fact you will never see the growth you so earnestly seek.

"Get into them!" In order to do that, you must first identify just 'who is them'. This group is known as your 'specific', 'targeted', 'niche" market. I know you've heard that term before. There's a very good reason for that. When you know 'who' you're marketing to you will be enabled to give them the information they need to buy. You have to show and tell them why it's important for them to make that transition between looking and buying. If you don't know who 'they' are, and what they want or need, how can you ever expect them to understand how you can help them?

Once you know who your target market encompasses, your next step is to learn all you can about them, their wants and needs. Armed with this information and the knowledge of your product or service, you will easily be able to find their need and which 'feature' of your offering is most beneficial to them. Remember, people don't buy features, they buy benefits.

Now, look at the 'features' you have to offer and consider carefully how they will benefit your potential customer. Your customers are looking for one or more basic benefits, and if you can meet their need, you can be sure they will buy.

What are those basic needs? These five basic needs are categorized as:

1. Physiological
2. Safety
3. Belongingness
4. Social esteem and
5. Self-actualization

and equate in selling to:

1. Need
2. Greed
3. Fear
4. Pleasure
5. Vanity
6. Impulse
7. Fatigue

Taking the time to figure out how what you have to offer can impact your customer in one of these ways. When you take that one important step you will readily know how to share your offering in a way that will cause them to not only listen but to eventually buy.

GET INTO THEM, PART 2

Customers want to be treated as partners. They want salespeople or organizations to involve them in the transaction, to recognize their intelligence, while informing them about the product or service. Never talk down to them.

Buyer Motivations

1. Cost
2. Quality
3. Prestige
4. Credibility
5. Convenience
6. Time Saving
7. Money Savings
8. Innovation
9. Ease of Use
10. Opportunity to be a trendsetter
11. Reliability

Identifying the Seven Buyer Motivations

Until you know what your prospective clients want or need, you're in no position to sell them anything. All you can do is present the product and describe its features. When you know what the client is looking for, however, then you can pitch the product to their wants or needs. So, what motivates people to buy stuff?

- **Need/Problem:** Customers may already know that they have a need or problem, but many others are clueless. Until your customer recognizes the problem and realizes that viable solutions are available, they see no need for what you're selling. Early in the process, raise your customer's awareness of the problem. Only then are you prepared to lead your customer through the process of analyzing available solutions.

- **Greed:** Numerous products and services are designed to help people make more money. If you're in corporate sales, that's pretty much all you sell because businesses are in the business of making money. If what you're selling can make people more productive or can boost revenue or cut expenses, then you can sell your product by playing to your customer's desire to make money.

- **Fear:** Fear sells. Some claim that fear sells better than sex, and they might be right. Just think of all the advertising invested in marketing products that protect us from real or perceived threats. Fear sells everything from home alarm systems to bottled water!

- **Pleasure:** If you're selling in a feel-good industry, such as vacation travel, hobbies, or home décor, marketing to your customers' pleasures is paramount. But even in industries in which pleasure isn't the central focus, you can often sell luxury-class items by focusing on the pleasure they're likely to provide.

- **Vanity:** People not only want to feel good, they want to look good, and they want other people to think they look good, too. If you're in the beauty business, from hair care products to plastic surgery, your marketing and selling strategies need to target the customers' desire to look good.

- **Impulse:** People often buy stuff because everyone else is buying it. (Just check out all the ribbon stickers on the backs of cars!) You don't need to be a great salesperson to take advantage of a hot trend because people often purchase these items impulsively. Success depends more on distributing the product and placing it in high-profile locations.

- **Fatigue:** Pushy salespeople can be very successful simply by wearing the customer down, but avoid taking this approach. It may work for a door-to-door salesperson who wanders from town to town, but when you're trying to build a reputation that secures future business, bully tactics are counterproductive.

Sure, you're selling a product or service, but your customer buys to solve a problem or meet a need. Early on, focus more on your customer and on identifying problems or needs.

PRESENTATIONAL SKILLS, PART 1: MANAGING YOUR FEAR

Is the fear of being in front of a crowd hampering your true potential? Are you a bundle of nerves at the very thought of public speaking? Do you recognize the benefit your business would receive by stepping up and publicly offering a bit of education or advice on your specific area of expertise?

Whether you are presenting personally or on the Internet, in a chat room that is text based, or a fully functional Audio/Video (A/V) chat room, it takes the same or similar training to accomplish your goal. Do you even know what your goal is? Have you considered the 'why' of what you have to share? But I digress; this is a topic best left to another time and place. For now let us focus on the subject at hand.

It might surprise you to learn that most public speakers experience some sort of stage-fright no matter how frequently they have *performed*. Take me for example. I have been in front of formal groups, off and on, since I was four years old. Let's not say specifically how old I am now, but suffice it to say I have more than fifty years of experience. In that time I have presented various subjects, and in different modes, from speech to singing & even a bit of acting. I still get butterflies.

Managing your fear is simply a matter of being properly prepared and focused on the task at hand. When the butterflies hit, take deep breaths, not so many that you make yourself dizzy though, and concentrate on the fact that YOU are the expert. Your audience is there to receive what you have to share. They want, no they need, you to ultimately succeed. They are silently rooting for you, not against you. This is particularly the situation if they have paid a fee to gain entry to hear your presentation.

> **Your audience is there to receive what you have to share. They want you to ultimately succeed.**

If you are genuinely ready and have properly prepared for your presentation you may find these suggestions are sufficient. Like me, once you get going your fear may just get lost in the rhythm of your offering.

Something physical you can do, if you still have the jitters after accepting these facts and being fully prepared, is to look just above the audiences' head. Pick an object, like a clock on a back wall or one individual in the group, or if you are able to, look at your audience, and give your presentation to it or them. Be mindful here, not to be overly obvious, by not looking around the room just a bit.

One thing you never want to do is fidget. Things like constantly wiping your hands on your clothes, twirling your hair or even the simple act of shifting your weight back and forth from one foot to the other can portray to your audience a sense of inadequacy. This in turn can render your entire presentation invalid.

Also, hiding your hands behind your back, or in your pockets, is a silent signal to your listeners that you have something to hide. Keep those hands either at your sides, when not in use, or cupped in the famous triangle position. I am certain you have seen speakers with their hands in this position numerous times before. Simply touch both thumbs and each corresponding finger together while holding your hands just under your chest in a relaxed stance.

These are but a few suggestions to help you along the path to discovering your true potential as a public orator.

To learn more about these and other tools that will enable you to capture your audience and leave them definitely desiring more, pick up your copy of *Presentational Skills for the Next Generation*. Available in both print and digital form through Amazon.com (http://www.amazon.com/dp/0978883144/) or by Email directly to me at ginger.marks@documeantdesigns.com.

PRESENTATIONAL SKILLS, PART 2: HOW TO CAPTURE YOUR AUDIENCE

Develop Solid Presentational Skills

Whether you are presenting a speech or just offering advice your goal should be to provide just enough information to your audience to get them to take action. That action could be anything from signing up for your newsletter, buying a product or service, or even becoming a referral source for your business.

The first thing you need to do is decide what that "action goal" will be for you. If you have an informational product then you will need to decide if you want your audience to purchase your product or divulge their private contact information by signing up for your newsletter. The latter can be the most difficult goal to accomplish. People are leery of giving out their information, and for good reason. With all of the spam out there your first challenge is to convince them that what you have to offer is of value. Once that objection is countered you still have to overcome their fear that you will become just one more "spammer" that they have to weed out of their daily lives. If on the other hand you have a physical product like candles or t-shirts your end goal would be to make a sale.

Once your objective is decided you need to consider what type of presentation will best suit your purpose. I'll use candles as an example. This type of product is best presented in person. You might want to do in home demonstrations or you might consider a slightly bigger audience at a small clubhouse or church recreation building. Allowing your audience to *feel*, *touch* and *smell* your products can do a lot for the number of sales you enjoy. Informational products lend equally well to the large group setting and the one-on-one. Either way your goal is to get your product into the hands of the consumer.

Choose your tools well. The props you use should enhance the information you are presenting without taking away from what you have to share. If you are uncomfortable in handling your props they will become distracting instead of a helpful addition. Practice not only what you are going to share but how to handle the props so that you don't look and feel awkward.

Will you be using A/V (audio/video) equipment? If so be certain that you either know how to use it or have someone there to assist you that does. The last thing you need is to prepare and practice only to find out you don't know how to use the projector that is being provided. Think of it this way, if the projector light burnt out would you know where to find a bulb or how to change it? How would the lack of the projector affect your presentation? Would you be able to go on without it? If not then you should definitely have a tech person there, just in case.

The art of presenting is not difficult to master. Practice, prepare, and present your information in a confident tone. When you are prepared and know your subject well you will have the confidence that you need to muster in order to prove yourself worthy of your audience's attention.

One last tidbit; no matter what your objective, you should consider each opportunity a chance to build a referral base. Oftentimes we simply forget to ask for the referral. This inaction leaves "money on the table" so to speak.

If you would like to learn more about how to put together, prepare, and present an effective presentation that will cause your audience to take action I highly recommend you pick up your copy of *Presentational Skills for the Next Generation*. It is available through amazon.com (http://www.amazon.com/dp/0978883144/) in both print and digital form and is currently in its Third Edition.

PRESENTATIONAL SKILLS, PART 3: EFFECTIVE PRESENTATION DESIGN

What is the most important thing to know when designing a slide presentation? How do you layout your presentation so that it doesn't become boring or overdone? Why should you care? These are all questions that I will attempt to answer briefly here.

Presentational design is the most commonly design work improperly done. What is being done wrong can totally annihilate any chance that your presentation will be effective. Rather it can become distracting not only to what you are speaking about but what is presented on the slide as well.

When designing a presentation for business, remember the rule, "less is more". You should be sure to only list one thought per slide, thus ensuring that it is legible to the person sitting the farthest away. This can be easily accomplished if you make the text large enough, but also the background not overly distractive. When utilizing a template look for something faint in color or perhaps a gradient. Don't be misled by a busy graphical background. These can interfere with the visibility from a distance.

If you are speaking in an intimate setting you can use one of your more attractive slide templates. However stick with the one thought per slide rule as you still want your audience to perceive you as the expert and not be overly distracted by the slides themselves.

If you want to tie together several points on one slide, one way to guarantee that the point you wish to make is what is being focused on, is to fade out the points that you are not speaking about on the slide you are showing. For instance, if you had three points to cover you should create three slides, one for each point. The first slide would have the first point dark, the second slide would have the first point lightened and the second point dark, and finally the third slide would have the first two points listed in a lighter text color with only the third point in the darker color font. This will allow the audience to relate to all three points while still focusing on what you are speaking about rather than trying to figure out which is the point of focus.

Now let's talk a bit about white space. White space is important in the planning of your slides as well. What is white space? It is the area of the slide that is left blank so that the background shows through. When planning the slide layout be sure not to fill your slide so full of information that it loses its effectiveness. Busy or cluttered slides are hard to read. Your audience will again be more focused on reading your slide than listening to what you are saying. Remember, use only key points on the slide; the rest should be stated by you. Don't use the slides as a crutch whereby you list all your points on them. Your desire is for the audience to listen to you and the slide presentation to simply augment what you are saying, not the other way around.

Your presentation is a tool you create to help explain a thought or a point of view. If you remember that it is merely a tool to help you look more professional and to make your audience better understand and grasp your key points you will do much better in putting it together.

These are just a few suggestions for creating a presentation that will effectively take you from novice to professional.

Designing your presentation is but one aspect of effective presentation. Now that the digital revolution is in full swing presentations are being given both in person and via webcams in the fully functional audio/video environment. Being prepared for the technical difficulties that may arise in that unique platform takes proper planning. Find out more about this subject in my book *Presentational Skills for the Next Generation*. It is available in both print and digital form from amazon.com at (http://www. amazon.com/dp/0978883144/). In it you will discover ways to prepare yourself and suggestions for your winning delivery too.

HOW TO PROMOTE YOUR BUSINESS, PART 1: BUSINESS BUILDING TIPS

Build it and they will come! Right? Well maybe and maybe not. You put all your time and effort into structuring a business that you just knew would fly all on its own. You sunk every penny you had in the bank and maybe even got your family to 'invest' too. But things just aren't working out how you thought they would. Has your dream has become a nightmare, or at least not quite what you imagined? Now is the time to look your business over and decide where to go from here.

I am going to share some valuable tips that I have used to develop my own businesses over the last thirty plus years. I hope you will learn and utilize at least one of them.

If you are really serious about building your business then you will want to pay close attention to what I am about to tell you. *It's all about them.* Now, you are probably saying to yourself, I know that. But do you really? Do you focus your actions on how your product or service can benefit others or merely attempting to make the sale?

In business as in life when you focus on others, with the right mindset, you will succeed. A successful marketing campaign focuses on your clients and customers wants and needs. Stop and consider your own buying habits. Your shopping tends to be for things you need, but when you get to the store is it filled with only the necessities or are their lots of not so necessary items too? Well of course there are the 'toys', and then there is the candy aisle; and what about the video section or the jewelry? What do you think there are more of in the store, want items or need items? I will go out on a limb and say it probably is 80% wants. Even in a grocery store you will find convenience items in every aisle. Sure they have bread, milk, flour, butter, sugar, etc. But they also have frozen pizza, chips, and candy. Need I say more?

So how should this realization affect you and the way you market your business? Let's take your advertising as an example. When you are putting together your ad campaign are you focusing on what your product will do for your customer or what your product does? What it will do for the customer is called a benefit; what your product does is termed a feature. The way to attract your customer is to focus on the benefits, not the features. This is one tip that I hope you will always remember. Put it to work for you today and watch your business grow beyond your wildest imagination.

So how do you get the word out? Well, you could spend hundreds of dollars on an advertising budget. What about the Yellow Pages in your local phone area? Absolutely! If you can afford to put even a small ad in your local directory do! You will find that it solidifies your commitment and offers credibility as well as letting your local community know you are in business. Other directories you might consider are the smaller Business and Religious directories. Look around your local retail shops. Usually you will run across one or two. Pick a copy up and see if it is a good fit before you invest in it yourself.

You could do a marketing blitz mailing, such as a coupon directory or postcard advertisement, or you might even attempt to put together an email campaign. Another more economical but time consuming venture could be to get involved in networking groups, both online and off. There are several available choices. In your local area there are sure to be small business networking groups as well as your local Chamber of Commerce. Online the choices are even more varied. Start out with a quick search for 'network group' and you will have plenty to choose from.

Another practical way to boost your sales is by doing presentations. Yes, I did say presentations. I know that the thought of public speaking scares the pants off of many a small business entrepreneur. However, the benefit of presentational speaking is obvious. First, you are seen by your audience as successful and, even better, as an expert in your field. Second, people want to associate with and purchase from successful people.

If you have a fear of public speaking or if you simply don't know how to go about creating and delivering a presentation I highly recommend you pick up your own copy of my book *Presentational Skills for the Next Generation*. In it you will find out not only how to put a presentation together but how to deliver a closing that will leave your audience wanting more. You can order it in both print and PDF forms through Amazon.com or contact me directly. (http://www.amazon.com/dp/0978883144/)

Presentations can be given both online and in person. They can be as brief as the thirty second one liner or as in depth as you want it to be. Whatever your level of speaking experience, when asked what you do, you should be able to explain your business in a short yet intriguing manner. Master your *thirty second spot* if you haven't already done so. That is the one advertising method you will use every day of your life.

I hope you have discovered at least one idea to help you develop a more successful and profitable business. If you would like additional information on building your business feel free to contact me at DocUmeantDesigns.com and I will be happy to help you develop your true marketing and business potential.

HOW TO PROMOTE YOUR BUSINESS, PART 2: TELESEMINARS AND AUDIO/VIDEO CONFERENCES

Are they a good fit for your business? Anyone who has a business and has toyed with the idea of sharing their product or service in a large group setting eventually comes to the topic of public speaking. With the advent of the Audio/Video (A/V) capabilities presentations are now being given from the comfort or our homes and offices. If you are considering how to take advantage of this marketing trend for your business but don't but don't know where to start an expeditious search on your favorite search engine could be the quickest way to begin.

Text chat rooms are fine for some businesses and come at a nominal fee, but if you have the financial resources to rent an online A/V chat room or teleconference service your marketing dollars could end up bringing a two-fold benefit. Perhaps it is time you considered offering online A/V presentations or teleseminars.

A/V chats and teleseminars are fast becoming the hot new marketing trend. A well thought out promotion can be organized in a short time and with very little effort. If you have a customer base that you have developed from offering an ezine or newsletter you can create a simple email to let them know when, where, and how to access your presentation. If not, I recommend you begin to compile your list today.

Once you know who your target market is you next need to decide on a topic that will interest them enough to set aside time from their hectic schedule to attend. You might want to offer them an incentive to join you such as a product sample or information source. As an example, when I began my ezine, you may remember, I offered you a Resource & US State Abbreviation List. Also, presentation notes or audio copy of your presentation given after the fact can increase your credibility as well as your customer base.

Don't feel like you have to provide this service free. Your customers know that there are fees involved with hosting a teleconference, just like there are for hosting any conference. Figure out a reasonable fee that will cover your expenses and confirm the value of the information you will be providing. You might even surpass your expectations and earn a profit from your teleconference.

Recently I read a testimonial from Barbara Thompson, the author of a weight loss book. She states, *"I sponsored my first teleseminar called 'It's All About Food' and 114 people signed up at $19.95 each. That's $2,274.20 in revenue. I recorded it, so I have a brand new product that will go into my shopping cart. I couldn't have done it without you!"* There you have two good reasons for considering adding teleseminars to your list of marketing plans.

Deciding on the conference host can be the most important decision you will make when planning your teleconference. Be sure to select one that fits your intended audience number. Don't over extend yourself here; limit your available 'seats'. This will do two things for your marketing efforts, first it will keep you within budget and most importantly it will give your target market an incentive to register early, to say nothing of the perceived value it will garner.

Also, be careful that you hire a company that offers several choices of available services. You will need to decide if your presentation and your pocketbook can afford the use of a moderated A/V chat room or teleconference line or an un-moderated one. Don't skimp on quality; free is not always cost-effective. When selecting your provider a poor quality connection can do more harm than good. One company, e-Teleconferencing charges $75.00 for a one hour conference with 100 lines.[19] This includes recorded mp3 file. They also have lower end services that run about $35 for 10 lines. An un-moderated A/V chat room can be secured for the modest fee of $15 per hour from some companies. This environment offers the additional advantage of video which can add tremendously to even a modest presentation. Check around, do your research; there are plenty of companies to choose from.

If you are unsure how to put together a presentation that will demonstrate your product or service in a way that will prove valuable to both you and your audience, you may want to pick up your copy *of Presentational Skills for the Next Generation*, available now at amazon.com (http://www.amazon.com/dp/0978883144/).

---

19   e-Teleconferencing http://www.e-teleconferencing.com

COMMIT TO DO!

How many times have you made an attempt to do something only to fail? Have you ever attempted to start a project, quit smoking, or lose weight, only to wind up either worse off than when you originally began or with a half-completed project?

What about that business you swore you would promote this year? That book you were going to write? Did you get it done? After numerous attempts at initiating an activity do you conclude you just can't adequately motivate yourself to accomplish the task? Do you allow 'things' to get in your way?

Perhaps the challenge is not that you haven't formally set your ultimate goal, but rather that you have decisively committed to failure. Think back, did you say I am going to 'try'? The word try in itself is the beginning of the end. 'Try' is simply not as motivating as 'DO'!

Webster's definition of try is 1a: to examine or investigate judicially b: (1) to conduct the trial of (2) to participate as counsel in the judicial examination of 2a: to put to test or trial *try one's luck*-- often used without (3) to make an attempt at—It is clear that even Mr. Webster fundamentally realized that to try was a pledge ONLY to try.

When you *try* to accomplish something you often fail simply because you have released yourself from the guilt of failure; you never said you were going to do, just that you would try. Therefore, when you do fail you can say "been there, done that" without feeling like you failed. However, the reality is; you did fail!

I have found that when I commit to DO, things get done! That one simple word purposely produces a mindset for success! I recall when I began my business, 30+ years ago, I simply decided to DO! I didn't say, I am going to TRY, I said I AM GOING TO…! No option for potential failure there.

Another effective illustration I recall is when I decided to stop smoking. I had TRIED several times before, but the day I said 'I QUIT!' that is the day I REALLY did quit!

How do you purposely produce decisive success? Yes, do start with a clearly defined goal in mind. Yes, do successfully create a plan, write it down, and make it a reality. But most importantly decide ultimately to succeed! Commit to DO! To be truly successful and to remain committed to your ultimate goal, 'Commit to DO' today!

COMMIT TO EXCELLENCE!

The potential for success lies within you. Granted you must be brave, committed, and flexible; you also must remain clearly focused on your goal. Whether that goal is to build a small customer base or you intend to capture a large market share, your commitment to excellence in relation to your customers and your product or service can be the key ingredient to your success.

Remaining compassionate while staying on track can be a bit of a trick. While at times a valued customer may have special needs and you might want to go that extra mile for them, you must clearly distinguish when and where to draw the line. Yes, be flexible but don't get taken advantage of. Give them anything you can while remaining true to yourself.

If a customer needs to be a little late for an appointment or requires an extension on the pay-by date and you can accommodate them, do so with reservation. Help them to recognize there is a limit to your understanding and generosity. Don't just blindly let them slide into a bad habit.

Sometimes the hardest thing to do is "fire" a customer or client. You may consider that impertinent, or even unrealistic, however if a customer or client is overly demanding, constantly late, or in any manner inconsiderate, you don't have to continue to service them. They may ultimately wind up costing you more than they are worth.

Recently, I read about a young woman who had built a thriving company. She permitted her biggest client to constantly stretch their pay-by date and when her client suddenly filed bankruptcy she was faced with down-sizing her business. The end result of the loss of this business client forced her to impose a pay-cut on her employees and herself. Thankfully, her company survived; could yours? Let us recognize the lesson revealed by her setback. Don't be afraid to say "No" when you are uncomfortable with a situation.

To be truly successful in business today, competitiveness, compassion and clarity of vision are entrepreneurial musts.

COMMIT TO WIN!

In today's fast paced competitive world we tend to rush from one point to the next. Learning to 'multitask' is beneficial for your assistant, but can be deadly to the successes you are endeavoring to achieve. When you look at successful people you know or have learned about you immediately recognize that they are genuinely, singly focused on their objective. Coming to the realization that you need to steadfastly focus on your ultimate goal is only the beginning.

So what is the next step? Picture yourself with the prize! No matter how silly or how trivial you may think it is, the simple act of creating a visual image of yourself having successfully achieved your objective and looking at it every day can purposely effect an observable sense of success. If your ambition is to be the top sales rep for your company or become the champion of the Indy 500, make it a fact in your mind; accept no excuses.

Now that you have that winning posture displayed on your bathroom mirror, on the partition of your cubicle, or somewhere you will notice it often throughout the day; are you prepared to truly commit to win?

To be successful you must persistently remain focused on your goal. Easy for me to say but hard for you to do, you might sincerely believe. Do you think that you're not special enough to literally make your dream a reality? Even the slightest doubt can steel your prize away. Often in life we are thrown off track by this obstacle or that challenge. It is when you allow 'things' to get in your way that you lose your central focus. Take your example from the hurdler, jump over it and keep going.

Think, eat and sleep success! Commit to win! As you set about making your dream a reality you will come across naysayers that will try to steal your vision. Turn and run; don't look back!

If you are in sales you've probably heard of the 'Law of Averages'. What is being referred to here is the 'Law of Large Numbers'. This law states that everything will ultimately 'average out' or 'what goes around, comes around'. Therefore, if you are steadfastly endeavoring to be the number one salesperson, don't be thwarted by those that say 'no'. Look at each and every 'no' as one less that you need to get in order to achieve a 'yes'. After each and every 'no' look up at the sky, snap your fingers and cry 'NEXT!'

Now, discipline and skill will be the tools you need to acquire. *Even the most successful person you know initially began their journey with exactly the same chance of success as you have now.* They, likely, sought out a mentor, someone who could adequately supply them with effective training and hone their skills until they too could achieve their goal. Do you really want a coach that will embrace you and tell you how wonderful you are or one that hones your ability and fervently incites you to be the best you can be? Embrace your failures; learn from your mistakes and steadfastly determine to accept nothing but victory.

These are all essential steps to achieve ultimate success. Omitting or 'short-cutting' just one of them can significantly hamper your success journey. Whether you are a ballroom dancer or business owner, training for the Olympics or learning a profession, the one that walks away with the 'gold' is the one that is decisively committed to win. I challenge you to formally establish your goal, envision yourself as having successfully achieved it and commit to win!

HOW TO WRITE AN EBOOK, PART 1

S o you wish to write an eBook. You have heard the buzz ~ eBooks are *'where it's at!'* You may have even read one or two. Are they worth the effort? Where do you start? What do you need to get them published? Can you *actually* **sell** them? The answers to these questions will be the topic of the ensuing series I have entitled **"How to Write an ebook"**.

How many of us can recall when the very first e-book was made available to the public? Seems like only yesterday when we toted an armload of books and planners everywhere we went. Today all one requires is a cell phone!

E-books are not only beneficial to the discerning reader but also to the literary composer as well. It is both for the writer and the discriminating reader that I offer these suggestions to effectively introduce you to eBook composing.

Initially there are some things you should sufficiently comprehend. What is an eBook and why would you even want to write one? How do you start? What can be used and what can't? All these questions and more will be discussed in this series. Follow along as we begin our discourse.

What is an eBook?

The "e" in eBook stands for *electronic*. Simply put an eBook is a book that has been digitally rendered. How that is done depends on what you specifically desire to provide. There are numerous choices of software available and some have features that you will defiantly need while others are very simple and basic compilers. Besides these choices you should decide if you absolutely need a true eBook created for the handheld device or a PDF form.

ePub eBooks and PDF eBooks are very different in their creation and as such each software program has its individual nuances that you will need to comprehend.

What is the difference in eBook compilers?

Let's look at some of these differences. The **Palm eBook Studio**™ is a genuine eBook compiler allowing for titles, covers, authoring details and publishing information that would normally be found in the first few pages of a printed book. On the other hand PDF compilers simply transfer whatever content your document has into a medium that will preserve your document's format.

The Palm eBook compiler allows images to be incorporated as long as they fit certain size restrictions: 8-bit PNG file, no larger than 64K and 148 px tall by 158 px wide, whereas with a PDF eBook if you can place the image in your original document it will remain in your converted book. PDFs also offer the advantage of the capability to include audio and video files. You should be aware that the free PDF compilers such as **CutePDF**™ may not offer these features.

Yet another component that you may find worth the investment is the ability to create a Table of Contents. This feature allows you to not only create and automatically update your table of contents but to include jump links between the table and the pages they make reference to. You may be able to find inexpensive PDF programs such as **PDFill**™ that may prove a satisfactory alternative to the limited free versions and the cost prohibitive **Adobe Acrobat Professional**™ software.

My software of choice is the full Adobe Acrobat Professional for PDF eBook rendering and Palm eBook Studio for true eBook authoring. I chose to invest in these products as a business tool because of the frequency of use. These systems afford me the opportunity to efficiently provide quality service to my business clients which they have come to reasonably expect.

However, if you are just beginning this phase of business development you may find these products far more expensive and difficult to use. On the other hand if you crave the freedom to design a masterpiece with your eBook you may very well decide, like I have, that the expense and the learning curve are worth the investment.

Next time we'll begin with an investigation on why you might want to create an eBook. We will look at some of the compelling reasons to invest your time, energy and money in developing eBooks and how to begin the design process.

Addendum: Kindle and Smashwords have taken over the ebook industry. For information on the use of and when you should opt for these formats give me a call and I'll be happy to help explain their strengths and weaknesses.

HOW TO WRITE AN EBOOK, PART 2

N ow that we have some of the basic differences let's look at **who** and **why**. We will look at some of the compelling reasons to invest your time, energy and money in developing eBooks and how to begin the design process.

EBooks can be useful to the individual or business person if you desire to:

1. Promote a product or service
2. Drive traffic to your website
3. Create or build on an existing customer database
4. Inform/educate
5. Tell a story

To be an eBook author you don't have to be an *experienced writer*; however a *skilled editor* should assist or at least review your work before you publish it. If you can't afford to hire an editor then you might ask a *friend* or *family member* to assist you. Another idea for new authors is to hire a *ghostwriter*. Never publish a work *of any kind* without first having another pair of eyes look it over. We have a tendency to miss our own mistakes.

If you wish to promote a product or service you could benefit from the distribution whether free or for purchase eBook offerings. Info products can be huge moneymakers.

Let's look at an example here. We'll use the skin care industry as an example. There are two very different types of individuals who could benefit from the use of eBooks.

1. Product driven/Business driven
2. Information/Service driven

Both could benefit by sharing application tips and tricks or scientific information that a potential customer could benefit from. When you offer information that your potential customer finds useful you quickly gain the status of expert in your industry or field.

To help you make use of the benefits of eBook authoring I recommend you consider taking advantage of this marketing tool by requesting your buyer information via a sign-up form or email request form. This allows you to rapidly assemble your client base from interested browsers. We'll talk about this unique way of building your customer database shortly.

Perhaps your goal is to simply drive traffic to your website. EBooks might be a good tool for you to consider. They should be topic specific to your key industry. If you had a successful beauty salon you might consider topics as diverse as health and nutrition, exercise or simply skin care and health. You could discuss the latest hair and fashion trends. Sprinkle throughout and in closing you could make reference to your company webpage for more information. **Be sure to include a link to your website for ease of access.** What you wouldn't want to write would be topics unrelated to your product or service. For example, our successful beauty salon owner wouldn't gain anything by offering an eBook on the topic of auto repair.

A visitor who has come to your site is more apt to secure your product or service if they are well informed. This is why eBooks are an exceptional tool to reasonably furnish relevant information to your prospective client or consumer.

There are three basic types of information you should take into consideration.

1. Helpful/educational
2. Newsworthy/recent event
3. Entertaining/telling a story

As you can clearly observe there is a broad range of worthwhile possibilities.

Another very distinct reason to compose your eBook is to offer your customer an incentive to disclose their contact information. Blogs, eBooks, newsletters and such can be just that tool. It is at this point that you should make your visitor aware that they will receive a free subscription to your newsletter or product sales information. Capturing their data is as simple as composing a form that calls for their subscriber information prior to providing the link or email that will provide them access to your end product, these are called **Opt-In Forms**. However, you might consider what is known as **Double Opt-In Form**, the simple reason, to ensure the individual requesting your product is fully informed that you will be transmitting supplemental information at a future date or time.

> **A visitor who has come to your site is more apt to secure your product or service if they are well informed.**

A Double Opt-In Form requires you to confirm your request by email. Once they subscribe you should send them a thank you email. This is where you will welcome them and include the instructions for download.

Finally, let's look at the advantage eBooks have over printed publications when it comes to simple story telling. These types of eBooks are simply an alternative to a full printed publication. *They can be used to create a passive income stream.* While printed books are costly to produce and require maintaining an inventory, packing and shipping, the eBook requires no inventory and can be downloaded in a flash. That's what makes eBooks so appealing to both the author and the end user.

As with the printed version if you intend on selling your book through a reseller except for Amazon you will eventually need to secure what is known as an ISBN. This stands for International Standard Book Number and is a unique number assigned to each distinct form and revised version of book you sell. Publishers use this number to assist in cataloging books. The agency providing these numbers encourages and promotes the importance of the ISBN for proper bibliographic listing in Books in Print, Forthcoming Books, and other directories.

The concept of eBook authoring is a widely accepted means of transferring information. In today's fast paced environment and considering our desire for ease of access, eBooks are the prefect tool to get the job done.

Join me in the subsequent edition as we delve into 'How' to get from concept to delivery. "Putting it all together."

HOW TO WRITE AN EBOOK, PART 3

So far we have discussed the **what, who**, and **why** of eBook writing. In this discussion we will attempt to explain the **how**. As before, for the sake of brevity I will constrain this discussion to the PDF rendering. For those of you who are seeking information on the other software available contact me directly at publisher@documeantpublishing.com.

In our previous discussion I mentioned a few PDF programs that are available including Adobe Acrobat™ and CuteFTP™. Your software of choice will determine your finished product. Each software has its own pros and cons as well as limitations.

To assist in renderings for both my own writings and those of my clients there is only one software that enables me to create the quality product my clients have come to expect. That software is Adobe Acrobat Professional™. When deciding which software best fits your needs you should consider its *cost* and its *capabilities*.

We will assume at this point that you have written your manuscript or compiled your articles. Your next step is to **decide on your layout**. Things you will need to consider should include the **cover image** you will use and whether or not you will need a **table of contents**, and if so whether you will link the entries to the text being referenced.

Additionally, you should **choose a color theme** so that your finished product compliments the look your document suggests. For example, if you are writing a children's story your colors and graphics could lend to the bolder, brighter schemes with clip art for images. On the other hand if your writings are for instructional business or scientific purposes you may want to stick with the more conservative shades and true photographic images. In serious business literature and even more so in the technical and scientific publications you will find they contain mostly charts and graphs with a few photos.

Another thing to remember is the use of Power Boxes (or callouts). These colorful elements highlight important information while giving your completed book a little pizzazz.

After all is said and done you will want to remember to include elements that most all books contain. These are the *copyright clause, publishing data, dedication and acknowledgements* and last but not least your bio. All publications of considerable length, except for novels, should have a good index.

Your author bio can be placed either at the beginning or end of your publication. Be sure to keep it short and sweet. Usually one or two short paragraphs and no more than five or six sentences are more than enough. I prefer to see one paragraph with only three to four sentences in the bio. Further I personally prefer to see it located after the main content with your concluding thoughts following that and containing your contact information and links to your website(s).

Finally, I would like to give you an idea of the proper sequence for your compiled eBook. This is the order and elements you should include in your eBook. However, if you plan to offer a 'sneak peak' you may consider front matter better placed as back matter. This allows your sneak peak to include the meat of your publication.

I.   Cover image

II.   Title page

III.   Copyright page

IV.   Dedication

V.   Acknowledgments

VI.   Table of Contents (if included)

VII.   Main Content

VIII.   Author bio (may be included after copyright page)

IX.   Concluding remarks with contact information and URL(s)

X.   Index (if needed)

The first page should be a cover page image. It should list the title and author along with that image only. Your second page should be the title page. Put your title and by line as well.

Now in order of placement on your copyright page:

1. Copyright page

    a. Copyright © date and your name

    b. Copyright clause ~ clearly written. Something like All rights reserved.

    c. Acknowledgements list ~ list all the people/companies supplying their products or services. For example when I create eBooks for my clients I list myself in bold type as **Ginger Mark, DocUmeant** under that **Copy edits, book page layout and design**. For eye appeal I skip a line here and then follow that with the **URL**. You should have your artists listed here as well.

    d. ISBN# ~ If you are planning on retailing your work the next line will be your ISBN#, under which you will list, in order, *Manufactured in country, the edition number and date*. Ex. First edition, 2006. If you were given a **Library of Congress Catalog Card Number** you would insert it before the ISBN with the number following the full title for the number.

Now, on to the next page. Here you will present your **Dedication**. Remember the rule less is more. After your dedication is where you should write your **Acknowledgements**. Thank each and every person who enabled you to finish this project including your editor and family members. If you have a quote you wish to include or a word of advice that will go on the following page.

At this point all of your preliminary information should be in the proper order. Your story begins here. If your work is inclusive of a table of contents you should list it first. I like to include jump links to chapter headers; however your software may not allow that option.

Following your story you should place your photo (if you like) and **author bio**. As I mentioned before keep it short and sweet. You may include links here if you like or save those for the final page in the concluding comments.

Your manuscript should be ready to begin the conversion to PDF format at this point. Follow the instruction in your complier and create a cover image to attach to the file for advertising purposes.

A 3-D cover will give your eBook a polished, professional image and in the range of ten to fifteen dollars it is money well spent. I prefer to create a 3-D image for my clients but a flat image file will suffice.

That's it! Your eBook is now ready for distribution. Congratulations!

I hope you found this series helpful and will take the necessary actions to make the most of this valuable tool.

BALANCE VS. DRIVE: WHAT I WANT VS. WHAT I CAN DO, PART 1

This is an age-old challenge. Whether it's your personal life or business that is affected the challenge remains the same. How do you discover the perfect balance? When do you say, "Stop the bubble machine!"?

Like me, you may be highly motivated to succeed. The challenge is to know when to take on a new project or take a brief respite. Once I get my hands on a project I feel compelled to do my best as expediently as possible. This can be a good thing, but more often, it is like an addiction. The problem lies in the fact that I want to complete the task 'yesterday'. This is what is defined as **Drive**. There are times, during the day, that 'normal' folk take breaks. These times allow for re-energizing and refreshing. I can't begin to count how often I have missed a meal or networking event simply because I felt the stress of getting a project completed even before it was due.

Can you relate? If so, then like me you may be suffering from the lack of balance in your business and personal life. Has your family or marriage suffered because of your determination? If so, perhaps you will find some of the techniques I have used will help you too.

The first step is to accept the fact that you have an uncontrollable urge to over-achieve. Once you accept that fact, you are well on your way to achieving evenness in your life.

In the subsequent article I will uncover several ways to help you achieve the sense of balance you seek.

BALANCE VS. DRIVE: WHAT I WANT VS. WHAT I CAN DO, PART 2

J ust after writing the beginnings of this article, I was IM'd this message, "this is not like me to want to give up, but how do you re-group and focus without loss?"

This woman was dealing with what she knew she should be doing and what she needs to do for her health. This is a very good example of the need to find balance. Obviously her "drive button" was stuck in the 'On' position. My reply for her situation was, "You have to remember that if you don't take care of you, everyone and everything around you will suffer."

She replied, "Funny, it felt like I needed permission to do what I felt was needed."

Let's start there. When you don't have balance in your life, things tend to feel out of control. To gain back control sometimes you just have to stop, close your eyes, and refocus your energy.

So, how do you take back control of the over-achiever in your life? You must first realize and accept the fact that you are a doer. You don't let life get in your way. You prefer to take responsibility and control your destiny rather than watch life evolve around you. However, self-control is necessary to combat your over-active drive mechanism.

Once you acknowledge your personality trait to push yourself beyond the norm, you will find it easier to catch yourself when you begin to let your life pass you by while you focus, single-mindedly, on your business, to the detriment of your health and relationships.

One way of dealing with this character trait is to schedule time off. Rather than saying you will have lunch if and when you get hungry, schedule it. Then stick to it!

OK, I hear you, "but I only have five more minutes to go and then this project will be done and when I get back from lunch I can begin the next project."

Let me ask you this, how many times has five minutes turned into ten and ten into twenty, etc? Stick to your commitment to yourself and your family. Take your breaks when it is time, not when your projects dictate.

This has been the hardest thing for me to do, but I guarantee you that your life and your family will be happier with this one small change.

Diet is often linked to imbalance in many areas of our lives. This can also be a key in maintaining your life balance. Check with your dietitian to see if your diet needs correction.

A positive outlook is another area that can affect your drive. If you are seeing only the lack of completion and not the small victories you may continue to push yourself to get things done in one sitting, where two or three could deliver better results.

When you take a break from your work, whether for a meal or just a bit of fresh air, you refresh and rejuvenate yourself. This will enable you to be more productive and rest your mind for clearer thought when you take up the task again.

Start slow, practice self-control. As you gain experience you will find it easier to recognize trouble spots and find the balance that you desire to achieve.

7 DEADLY SINS OF GOAL SETTING, PART 1

The New Year is nearly upon us. It is time once more to visit the issue of goal setting. What are you planning to accomplish next year that you haven't previously? Do you see yourself as the top salesperson at your company? Do you desire to successfully increase your customer base; promote your business or maybe you simply want to save and plan for a vacation in some exotic locale?

We all have the best intentions when it comes to getting things done. However, for most of us there just aren't enough hours in the day. At times you may have wondered at the end of the week where all that precious time went. Believe me, you are not alone.

Goal setting, whether for mundane daily tasks or a billion dollar operation is an activity familiar to everyone. The larger our operating domain, the more important it is that we "get it right".

So just what can you do to effectively guarantee you achieve your goals? How do you successfully complete your tasks efficiently and effectively? I will attempt to effectively respond to these questions by helping you avoid some of the pitfalls of goal setting.

1. **Failure to create a plan**—Does that sound a bit strange? Actually 2 out of 3 people who have trouble in this area merely haven't taken the time to consider the actions necessary to achieve their goals.

2. **Lack of or poor organization**—Step back and look at the big picture. Think about what you wish to accomplish and how to complete the task within the time frame you have allocated. Consider all the aspects that will come into play. Draw on your resources whether they are materials or a human that will effectively guarantee your objectives are accomplished.

3. **Fear of the loss of control**—This one is a big problem for many of us. How often have you had the thought, if I could just have someone else do this simple task . . . only to discount that thought because you don't believe it would be completed as effectively and efficiently as you could do it yourself.

If you expect your business to grow beyond what you are able to accomplish yourself you have to be prepared to share responsibilities. Other qualified individuals or companies can assist you when the timing is right to take your business to the next level. You have to learn to balance increased production with increased overhead.

These are just the first few snares to avoid when initiating your goal planning. Successful goal planning is an integral part of business development. In Part II we will discuss the last four pitfalls of goal planning, how to overcome and succeed.

7 DEADLY SINS OF GOAL SETTING, PART 2

In the first part of our series we discussed the lack of planning, organization and the fear of loss of control. In Part II I am going to continue this discussion. Let's jump right in.

4. **Failure to designate tasks**—This goes right along the same line as fear of the loss of control. When you finally do yield the reigns long enough to understand the necessity of allocating the menial tasks, you will have initiated the first steps of developing the team you will need to attain your goal.

   Before you over commit yourself or limit your growth consider who can effectively assist you. Perhaps you need to hire a new employee but you don't want the headaches of the overhead. Consider the possibility of utilizing a placement agency that will handle all the financial and legal aspects of employee management. Maybe your need is for a subcontractor who will help you organize your workspace allowing you the freedom to become more productive. Perhaps you want to accomplish a task that you are just not trained to do. If that is the case, find someone that has the skill to assist you and ask them for their input or cooperation.

5. **Failure to prioritize**—Once your goal has been decided upon one of the most important thing to accomplish is the development of a task list. Prioritize your tasks; write them down. Once you complete the first task it will equip you to initiate the next which in turn will enable you to remain focused on your goal. It is when we attempt to do everything all at once that we often become overwhelmed with the project at hand and lose focus. This is the precursor of failure.

6. **Failure to implement**—Take action! The fact of the matter is if you don't implement your plan your plan is worthless! How many times have you sat down and figured out what you need to do, how you are going to do it, and what tools you'll need to accomplish the task only to fail at implementation?

Goal setting has two components, *planning* and *implementation*. The more realistic the planning the better the results of the implementation will be. Every year business professionals and managers set aside (or press their employees to allocate) time to design their business plan for the year ahead. Then once that task is completed they return to the same old habits of the previous year without even a hint of the required action to achieve their goals.

If your plan doesn't incorporate effective measures to ensure its implementation then it will likely fail. We are all familiar with the partially crossed off "to-do" list at the end of the day—how about a trillion dollar real life example?

In 1980 President Reagan promised to balance the budget by 1984. In reality the plan was never implemented. He never proposed a balanced budget in his eight years in office or curbed Congress's ballooning spending programs. In 1985 the Gramm–Rudman–Hollings plan promised a balanced budget in 1991—it was never implemented. In 1990 Congress enacted a program to balance the budget by 1993—it was not implemented. In 1995 another plan—never implemented.

The lesson here is that the plan must match expectations with reality and include measures to ensure execution in the face of obstacles and opposition.

7. **Failure to establish a reward system**—For most people it's all about the reward. Think about it. How many game shows are there? How often are incentives given in sales meetings? It's all about discovering what keeps you focused on the task at hand. When you have rewards to eagerly anticipate you increase the chance of accomplishing the task.

Think of a reward that is realistic for the goal you want to attain. Don't limit yourself to just the end reward; consider also small rewards for accomplishments along the way. You may decide a night out, or a trip to a masseur is just what you need. Make it realistic and rewarding enough to keep you on track and go for it!

Create a plan, organize and prioritize, implement, designate, and follow-through. Accomplish your goal(s) one step at a time and reward yourself for a job well done.

DISCOVER HOW TO ENTERTAIN ON A BUDGET, PART 1

To most people these two words, entertain and budget, are miles apart. But they don't have to be. Whether you are a young adult who wants to impress your friends, a new business owner looking to impress your clients, or a mom or dad who simply wants to take a break from the office to entertain a few friends you will find these tips useful.

No matter whom you are or what your background, we all enjoy getting together with family and/or friends. However, when money is tight you don't have to opt out of host or hostessing if you utilize some sensible alternatives.

Your first task should be to decide the theme for your event. This will help you to create your guest list as well as help you see what pre-party elements you can bypass and what areas you will want to make extra special.

If you are planning your wedding festivities you will want to focus on the comfort and enjoyment of your guests. For this type of event you could save a ton of cash that could be used for a more practical purchase like your honeymoon or your first home purchase by simply narrowing your guest list. After all is said and done only you and your immediate family and very best friend will remember your party. Most of your guests will remember the wedding. So have a larger wedding if you must, but limit the wedding party to save major dollars.

For most of us we simply want to entertain a few friends. Be sure to supply a comfortable amount of room for your guests. If yours is a dinner party you will want to ensure you have enough chairs for your entire guest list. If it is a cocktail party you can and should opt for *milling* room rather than so many chairs.

Another consideration is where you have your event. This can also either be costly or not. Here is a list of some inexpensive alternatives.

1. Your own home or backyard
2. Your local church Fellowship Hall
3. A local residential clubhouse
4. A local business or entertainment complex, i.e. skating rink, bowling alley

5. Park or picnic area
6. The beach or lakeside
7. Your family or friend's home

The latter suggestion I offer with the thought of further spreading the expense by hosting a Progressive Dinner. These types of parties can be most memorable and fun.

Just what is a Progressive Dinner? Simply put, each course of a meal is prepared and presented by a different diner. My recommendation here is to plan carefully the route to minimize driving distance.

The next issue you need to decide is whether to give out invitations or not. Although a phone call is often less costly than a printed invitation you may want to consider sending them to at least some of your invitees. The more formal your event the more likely this should be done. Some ideas to consider that can help cut down on the expense here are:

1. Computer generated invitations
    a. Printed
    b. Emailed
    c. Online greeting cards
        i. Send Out Cards
        ii. Online digital greeting cards
        iii. Evite.com invitations
2. Hand crafted cards
    a. Quilled
    b. Stamped
    c. Embossed, or otherwise embellished
    d. Calligraphy

Hand crafting your invitations can be fun and will provide a unique invitation that may be cherished by the recipient for many years to come. You can even have a group of close friends or family members assist you with your invitation design and creation. Think about the laughs and memories you will be making at the same time.

DISCOVER HOW TO ENTERTAIN ON A BUDGET, PART 2

Now that your venue is selected and your invitations are done next you will need to plan the menu. This is one area that can be easily controlled. If you want to really impress your guests but don't want to go over your budget I suggest you splurge on the dessert. This is the final thing your guests will consume and will therefore be the most remembered. If you are having a cocktail party you can do this with the hors d'oeuvres. Depending on your budget you can offer:

1. Homemade
2. Store bought
3. Catered
4. Shipped

Homemade can be time consuming and tedious. Store bought convenience items from your frozen food section will be far less so, but your deli or bakery may supply a fresher choice. Catered food, on the other hand, while expensive for an entire meal can be a nice alternative for those who want just one special course.

Mail order is fairly new as a viable alternative. You can mail order anything from steak and fruit to dessert. A dessert from a special bakery you have fallen in love with is always a good idea as long as you don't go overboard and over budget. Be sure to place your order so that it will arrive in a timely manner and still be fresh for your event.

While considering what you will serve also think about how you will serve it. While paper plates may be convenient for clean-up and a wise selection for your picnic be sure to invest in a plate that is strong enough to stand up to the task. For reliability you will find the coated paper products and Chinette° plates perform the best. However, if your party is indoors real plates and glasses add a hint of sophistication to your event.

A word of advice on beverages, "go light". Alcohol, beside the effect it has on people, can be one of the most expensive items you provide. To avoid this expense you might consider offering non-alcoholic alternatives or mixers and suggest your guests bring their own liquor. Another idea is to limit over indulgence by carefully calculating the number of servings per guest that you can afford and stay within your budget.

One last comment, if presentation is important for your event the use of linens, both on the tables and for guests, will add a touch of class and beauty to your event. This seemingly insignificant flair will absolutely be noticed and appreciated.

Resources

ARTICLE SUBMISSION SITES

Article Garden

Associated Content

Ezine Articles

Free Article Submission Organization

Go Articles

ISnare

Reuters Newswires, http://evo.staging.thomsonreuters.com/newswires

SelfGrowth

Auto Responder Services

AWeber, http://aweber.com

Constant Contact, http://cjaffiliate.roving.com/?AID=10296666&PID=2121146

Your Mailing List Provider, http://www.YMLP.com

Bookkeeping Services

FreshBooks, http://www.freshbooks.com/

Infusionsoft, http://www.infusionsoft.com/

VerticleResponce®, http://www.verticalresponse.com/

Communication Coaches

Prestige Leadership Advisors, http://www.prestigeleader.com

Ali International LLC, http://alibrown.com/

Communication Transformation, http://www.communicationtransformation.com/

Conference Sites

e-Teleconferencing, http://www.e-teleconferencing.com

Dictionary Sites

Your Dictionary, http://www.yourdictionary.com/library/misspelled.html

Articles & Books

Attard, Janet. "Turn Your Fax Cover Sheets into Sales Tools." Business Know How Oct 2007. http://www.businessknowhow.com/businessideas/marketing/turn_your_fax_cover_sheets_into_sales_tools.php

Books by Ginger Marks, http://www.GingerMarksBooks.com

Bullas, Jeff. "Statistics Reveal How the Apple's iPad Is Changing Our Lives". Jeff Bullas Apr 2011. http://www.jeffbullas.com/2011/04/04/29-statistics-reveal-how-the-apples-ipad-is-changing-our-lives/

Carroll, Jane. *Bertha Size Your Life!*, http://www.berthasize.com

"City Councilwomen Seek Fresh Air and New Ideas". Nevada Today, 2009. http://www.unr.edu/nevada-today/news/2009/city-councilwomen-seek-fresh-air-and-new-ideas

Edelman, Russ, *Nice Guys Can Get the Corner Office*, http://www.amazon.com/dp/1400158370

Friedman, Karen. "Craft Verbal 'Keepers' Trim the Fat." PRNews Nov 2010: 2. http://www.prnewsonline.com/topics/media-relations/2010/11/08/how-to-craft-verbal-keepers-and-trim-the-messaging-fat/

Green, Chuck. *Ideabooks,* http://www.Ideabook.com

Marks, Ginger. *Presentational Skills for the Next Generation*, http://www.amazon.com/dp/0978883144/

Marks, Ginger. *Weird & Wacky Holiday Marketing Guide*, http://www.HolidayMarketingGuide.com

Michaels, Denise. *Testosterone-Free Marketing*, http://www.marketingforher.com

Parker, Roger C. *Looking Good in Print*, http://www.amazon.com/dp/193309706X

Slattery, Felicia. *Cash In On Speaking,* http://feliciaslattery.com/blog/

Tabares, JoJo. *Say What You Mean When You Are In Business*, http://artofeloquence.com/

Watson, Don. *Death Sentences*, 2005 May. http://www.amazon.com/dp/1592401406

White, Rebekah. *My Time Cannot Always Be Your Time*, http://healyourselftalk.com/my_time

SHOPPING
Art
Amanda Tomasoa: http://www.saatchionline.com/amandatomasoanz

Lisa's Art & Horses: http://www.lisasart.com

Foods
Sage Hill Farms: http://www.sagehillfarmsandvintagestore.com/

Annie's Accent Bakery: http://anniesaccentsbakery.vstore.ca

Watkins: http://www.watkinsonline.com/ddemell

Home & Garden
Custom Card Covers: http://www.documeant.net/cards.html

Gourmet Candles: http://www.burningwithlove.scent-team.com

Pampered Chef: http://www.pamperedchef.com/

Holiday Cards: http://www.kimemerson.com

Roses & Teacups: http://roses-and-teacups.com

Send Out Cards, https://www.sendoutcards.com/sandymorgan/

Packaging

Cello-in-a-box: http://www.celloinabox.com

Creative Gift Wrapping: http://www.creativegiftwrapping.com/ConsultantProgram.html

Fashion & Jewlery

Chic Boutique: http://www.chloeschicboutique.com

Young Living: http://www.youngliving.org/fdurham

Premier Designs: http://www.premierdesigns.com/

Books

Cash in on Speaking: http://www.communicationtransformation.com/cashinonspeakingebook.html

Heritage Makers: www.createalegacy.org

Marlin the Christmas Elf: http://www.lulu.com/content/537509

Jesus Gandhi Oma Mae Adams: http://www.amazon.com/gp/product/1894936604/

Presentational Skills for the Next Generation: http://www.amazon.com/dp/0978883144

Whatever! A Baby Boomer's Journey Into Middle Age, http://www.therawreviewers.com/artman/publish/Whatever.shtml

Toys & Games

Discovery Toys: http://www.discoverytoyslink.com/esuite/home/playtoteach

Bright Minds: http://www.brightminds.us

Bible Toys: http://www.blessedtoys.com

Stuff A Friend: http://www.stuffafriend.biz/members/eulademv/

MARKETING

EMSI: Contact me for a formal introduction at publisher@documeantpublishing.com

Mommy's Neighborhood: http://www.mommyneighborhood.com

Marketing Salad: http://www.marketingsalad.com

Trailer to the Stars: Contact me for a formal introduction at publisher@documeantpublishing.com

Weird & Wacky Holiday Marketing Guide (annual): http://www.holidaymarketingguide.com

WEB DESIGN

Color Blender, http://www.colorblender.com/

Color Combos, http://www.ColorCombos.com.

Feng-GUI site, (http://www.feng-gui.com/)

Feng-GUI Firefox extension, (http://www.feng-gui.com/tools.htm)

InMotionHosting,https://secure1.inmotionhosting.com/cgi-bin/gby/clickthru.cgi?id=gmarks&page=7

Snook Color Contrast Checker, http://snook.ca/technical/colour_contrast/colour.html

WC3 Standards in Web Design, http://www.w3.org/standards/webdesign/

Web Safe Color Chart, http://html-color-codes.com

MISCELLANEOUS

BizFilings, http://www.bizfilings.com/

Family Preparedness Guide, www.opm.gov/emergency/PDF/NationalFamilyGuide.pdf

In Design, PowerPoint templates, http://www.indezine.com/powerpoint/templates/freetemplates.html

Send Out Cards, https://www.sendoutcards.com/sandymorgan/

Skype an Author, http://skypeanauthor.wetpaint.com/

WhiteSmoke, http://www.WhiteSmoke.com

Wikipedia, http://www.wikipedia.org/

ABOUT THE AUTHOR

GINGER MARKS was born in the midst of a world in turmoil. The events surrounding her birth in 1955 were monumental in both social and political movements. The civil rights movement was in full swing, and the first ever nuclear-powered submarine was launched off the coast of Connecticut. The game of Scrabble debuted and Bill Haley and his Comets had teenagers jumping from their seats to dance to the song, Rock Around the Clock.

Born into a family gifted with musical, speaking, and writing, as well as art, it was of no surprise when Ginger picked up the pen and wrote her first poem at the tender age of eleven. So in late 2000, it was no surprise to her mother, an established author and speaker, when she began writing articles that espoused the virtues of business ownership, after founding and operating a successful surgical clinic for over twenty years.

Within five years, Ginger completed her first business book, *Presentational Skills for the Next Generation*. Soon after which, she established her publishing company, DocUmeant Publishing. She is an award winning publisher and internationally known designer. Ginger is the CEO and Founder of CALOMAR, LLC which is the parent company to three successful businesses, DocUmeant.net (writing), DocUmeant Designs, and DocUmeant Publishing. In 2013 she was named by Covington Who's Who as Entrepreneur of the Year and her design firm is among the Highest Rated firms at DesignFirms.org which lists over 20,000 designers, developers & marketing professionals.

During her entrepreneurial career she has owned and operated a surgical clinic, a bar-b-que restaurant, and held several sales positions including that as a License Financial Advisor. This experience is what enables her to speak on various aspects of business ownership.

Currently she resides in Clearwater, Florida with her husband Philip who works beside her as her copy editor.

Register for Ginger's monthly ezine, Words of Wisdom and receive Ten Truths of Business Ownership© (http://www.documeant.net/#bonus) and your F*R*E*E* **Special Report** - How to Create Long Sale Copy Web Pages.

Index

www.ingramcontent.com/pod-product-compliance
Lightning Source LLC
Chambersburg PA
CBHW062037090426
42740CB00016B/2939